Freud, Lacan, Zizek and Education

All areas of education policy and practice are driven by unconscious investments in igno-rance, or idealised images of transformation of the individual, society and economy. The promise of fulfilment and associated threats of disappointment or destruction tend to domi-nate conscious accounts of education. Other more vulnerable or unspeakable aspects of our engagements with education are covered over when we account for learning, and justify teaching as professionals, policy makers and researchers; but they leak out in slips, lapses, emphasis, paradox and contradiction.

Freud's account of resistance and repetition; Lacan's theorisation of the role of language and desire; and Zizek's elaboration of these ideas in a theory of ideology and enjoyment – all provide tools for exploring the vulnerable, uncomfortable and often surprising *other* side of education: the hidden, unconscious and unspoken desires that we invest in educational institutions and practices. This collection offers glimpses of this other side of education produced in empirical studies using a variety of methodological approaches: practice-based theoretical speculation, policy analysis, ethnography, interviews and free associative meth-ods, as well as ideological critique of the field of critical educational practice and research. The book foregrounds political and unconscious aspects of investments in the fields of edu-cation and educational research.

The chapters in this book were originally published as articles in Taylor and Francis journals.

Claudia Lapping is a Reader in Psychosocial Studies and Education at the Institute of Education, University College London, UK. She is interested in the use of psychoanalysis in empirical research methodology, in unconscious processes in educational institutions, practices, and in the production and re-contextualisation of legitimised knowledge. She is the author of *Psychoanalysis in Social Research* (2011) and the co-editor of *Knowing and Not Knowing: Thinking Psychosocially about Learning and Resistance to Learning* (with Tamara Bibby, 2016).

Education and Social Theory

Series Editor: Stephen J. Ball, Institute of Education, University College London, UK

Social theory can help us to make sense of many aspects of contemporary education by providing analytic concepts and insights. Social theories are tools of analysis and interpretation for educational researchers that enable us to make sense of the processes, effects and outcomes of educational experiences and institutions.

Drawing together selections from the best work previously published in Taylor and Francis journals to create powerful and effective collections, this series highlights and explores the social theories critical to educational writers, researchers and scholars. Each book focuses a different key writer or field of theory, with the overarching aim of providing an overview of the social theories important to education research, but also of showing how these theories can be applied in a practical manner in the current education landscape.

Books in the Series:

Foucault and Education
Edited by Stephen J. Ball

Marxisms and Education
Edited by Noah De Lissovoy

Actor Network Theory and Education
Edited by Tara Fenwick and Richard Edwards

Feminist Posthumanisms, New Materialisms and Education
Edited by Jessica Ringrose, Katie Warfield and Shiva Zarabadi

Freud, Lacan, Zizek and Education
Exploring Unconscious Investments in Policy and Practice
Edited by Claudia Lapping

The Education Assemblage
Edited by Greg Thompson

Bourdieu and Education
Edited by Diane Reay

Freud, Lacan, Zizek and Education

Exploring Unconscious Investments in Policy and Practice

Edited by
Claudia Lapping

LONDON AND NEW YORK

First published 2019
by Routledge
2 Park Square, Milton Park, Abingdon, Oxon, OX14 4RN, UK

and by Routledge
52 Vanderbilt Avenue, New York, NY 10017

First issued in paperback 2020

Routledge is an imprint of the Taylor & Francis Group, an informa business

British Library Cataloguing-in-Publication Data
A catalogue record for this book is available from the British Library

ISBN 13: 978-0-367-58614-0 (pbk)
ISBN 13: 978-0-8153-6281-4 (hbk)

Typeset in Times New Roman
by codeMantra

Publisher's Note
The publisher accepts responsibility for any inconsistencies that may have arisen during the conversion of this book from journal articles to book chapters, namely the possible inclusion of journal terminology.

Disclaimer
Every effort has been made to contact copyright holders for their permission to reprint material in this book. The publishers would be grateful to hear from any copyright holder who is not here acknowledged and will undertake to rectify any errors or omissions in future editions of this book.

Contents

CONTENTS

Citation Information

The chapters in this book were originally published in a variety of Taylor and Francis journals. When citing this material, please use the original page numbering for each article, as follows:

Chapter 1

Before, after, in and beyond teacher education
H. James Garrett
Teachers and Teaching, volume 19, issue 6 (December 2013) pp. 647–659

Chapter 2

Interrupting the frame: reflective practice in the classroom and the consulting room
Julie Walsh
Pedagogy, Culture & Society, volume 22, issue 1 (March 2014) pp. 9–19

Chapter 3

The significance of 'participation' as an educational ideal in education for sustainable development and health education in schools
Jonas Andreasen Lysgaard and Venka Simovska
Environmental Education Research, volume 22, issue 5 (July 2016) pp. 613–630

Chapter 4

Learning to fail and learning from failure – ideology at work in a mathematics classroom
Hauke Straehler-Pohl and Alexandre Pais
Pedagogy, Culture & Society, volume 22, issue 1 (March 2014) pp. 79–96

Chapter 5

An ideology critique of global citizenship education
Alexandre Pais and Marta Costa
Critical Studies in Education, DOI: http://dx.doi.org/10.1080/17508487.2017.1318772 (April 2017) pp. 1–16

Chapter 6

Recognising desire: a psychosocial approach to understanding education policy implementation and effect
Alex Moore
Oxford Review of Education, volume 32, issue 4 (September 2006) pp. 487–503

Chapter 7

Psychical contexts of subjectivity and performative practices of remuneration: teaching assistants' narratives of work
Claudia Lapping and Jason Glynos
Journal of Education Policy, volume 33, issue 1 (January 2018) pp. 23–42

Chapter 8

Talkin' 'bout a revolution: the social, political, and fantasmatic logics of education policy
Matthew Clarke
Journal of Education Policy, volume 27, issue 2 (March 2012) pp. 173–191

Chapter 9

The sublime objects of education policy: quality, equity and ideology
Matthew Clarke
Discourse: Studies in the Cultural Politics of Education, volume 35, issue 4 (October 2014) pp. 584–598

Chapter 10

The explosion of real time and the structural conditions of temporality in a society of control: durations and urgencies of academic research
Claudia Lapping
Discourse: Studies in the Cultural Politics of Education, volume 38, issue 6 (December 2017) pp. 906–922

For any permission-related enquiries please visit:
http://www.tandfonline.com/page/help/permissions

Notes on Contributors

Matthew Clarke is Professor of Education at York St John University, UK. His research in educational policy is internationally recognised as contributing to a new interdisciplinary field that brings together political and psychoanalytic theory to provide novel and significant critical insights into global policy issues in education and teacher education. His most recent book is *Teacher education and the political: The power of negative thinking* (2017).

Marta Costa is a Tutor in Education Studies at Manchester Metropolitan University, UK. She holds an MA in Education Studies and has worked with children and young people in a variety of settings (children centres, secondary school and college) and roles.

H. James Garrett is Associate Professor and Graduate Coordinator in the Department of Educational Theory and Practice at the University of Georgia, Athens, USA. His research focuses on the ways in which learning and learning to teach, while rewarding and exciting, are also home to difficulty and burdensome complexity. He is interested in exploring issues related to those difficulties by using psychoanalytic theory.

Jason Glynos is a Reader in the Department of Government at the University of Essex, Colchester, UK. His research interests include political philosophy, Lacanian and post-Marxist discourse theory and the philosophy and methodology of social science. He is the author of *Logics of Critical Explanation in Social and Political Theory* (2007) and the editor of *Traversing the Fantasy* (2005) and *Lacan & Science* (2002).

Claudia Lapping is a Reader in Psychosocial Studies and Education at the Institute of Education, University College London, UK. She is interested in the use of psychoanalysis in empirical research methodology, in unconscious processes in educational institutions, practices, and in the production and re-contextualisation of legitimised knowledge. She is the author of *Psychoanalysis in Social Research* (2011) and the co-editor of *Knowing and Not Knowing: Thinking Psychosocially about Learning and Resistance to Learning* (with Tamara Bibby, 2016).

Jonas Andreasen Lysgaard is Associate Professor in the Danish School of Education at Aarhus University, Denmark. He is the author of *Learning from Bad Practice in Environmental and Sustainability Education* (2018). His work focuses on education for sustainable development, environmental education and educational pedagogy.

Alex Moore is Professor of Education at the Institute of Education, University College London, UK. He is the author of *Schooling, Society and Curriculum* (2006) and *The Good Teacher: Dominant Discourses in Teaching and Teacher Education* (2004).

Alexandre Pais is a Reader in the Faculty of Education at Manchester Metropolitan University, UK. He is the author of *The Disorder of Mathematics Education: Challenging the Sociopolitical Dimensions of Research* (with Straehler-Pohl, 2016). His particular research focus is in mathematics education.

Venka Simovska is Professor of School Development, Learning and Wellbeing in the Danish School of Education at Aarhus University, Denmark. Her interdisciplinary research combines social science, psychology, educational science and health-promotion sciences. She is the Coordinator of the Schools for Health Research Group, an international network involving scholars from 28 European countries.

Hauke Straehler-Pohl is a Researcher in Primary Education at the Freie Universität Berlin, Germany. His research interests focus on the sociology, politics and philosophy of education, with a particular emphasis on mathematics education. He is interested in the social pathologies that impede schools from creating the conditions for a 'good life' for all.

Julie Walsh is based in the Institute of Advanced Study and the Department of Sociology at the University of Warwick, Coventry, UK. She is a qualified psychoanalyst (UKCP accredited), and her current research project is entitled 'Test-Cases in Shameful Sociability'. She is the author of *Narcissism and its Discontents* (2014) and the editor of *Shame and Modern Writing* (2017) and *Narcissism, Melancholia and the Subject of Community* (2017).

Introduction: the death drive and education

Claudia Lapping

Psychoanalysis and, more specifically, the Freudian/Lacanian tradition within psychoanalysis, unravels our questions and our attempts to tame 'education' as a bounded, knowable entity. A psychoanalytic approach foregrounds the resonances of particular kinds of clues – slips, lapses, emphases, wording, inflection, juxtaposition – so that unexpected connections, blockages and aporia are opened up, overflowing the limits of what we might usually recognise as 'policy', 'teacher', 'student' or 'learning'. So, rather than beginning by specifying issues or problems in education that psychoanalysis might help us to understand or solve, I am beginning with a reading of a text that might help us to formulate new questions that we might address towards something that we may or may not recognise as 'education'.

I begin, then, with an exegesis of four extracts from 'Beyond the Pleasure Principle' (1920), the essay where Freud, famously, reflects on developments in psychoanalytic practice, based on the experience of the clinic, and their implications for our understanding of human subjectivity. It is also where he introduces the idea of the death drive: a theorisation of the human condition as structured, not by a drive towards pleasure but by a deadening repression. This concept, articulated and re-articulated in the work of Freud, Lacan and Žižek, illustrates the way in which psychoanalytic approaches have the potential to produce a radical re-encounter with educational processes. The four extracts I'm going to look at can be related to four stages in Freud's conceptual elaboration of the death drive. They also, though, represent Freud's methodological compulsion: the curiosity with which he listens to empirical clues, even when they challenge his own previous theories, and the passion with which he follows speculative lines of enquiry, even when confronted with darkly disturbing results. As a reader, I am confounded by a sense of his writing as a compulsive narrative of his thinking, and by his refusal to turn away from the initial, already troubling, traces of the implications of his own speculations.

Freud's text is incredible in innumerable ways. My exposition here is inevitably reductive, aiming to set out the architecture of his argument in order to suggest how different elements might have implications for thinking and research about education today. The extracts I'm going to look at offer a starting point for thinking about the way his argument knits together four sets of ideas: trauma, repetition and memory; repression and transference; his theorisation of the compulsion to repeat; and the way this leads him to a re-conceptualisation of the drives, the impulses or the systems that organise the psychical level of human subjectivity, and to the concept of the death drive. Following this account, I briefly indicate some of the ways Freud's concept has been re-articulated by Lacan and Žižek, and then attempt to explain why

1

I think it is relevant to the papers in this collection. Each of the chapters in the book, I think, offers a glimpse at the ways in which aspects of teacher professional identity, progressive curricula, pedagogic relations, and education policy, are not what we thought they might be. Further than that, I think that many, perhaps even all, of these papers can be understood to in some way hint at something like a death drive at work in the field of education.

Conceptualising the death drive: four stages in 'Beyond the Pleasure Principle'

Trauma, repetition and memory

In the first stage of Freud's argument in 'Beyond the Pleasure Principle' he sets out an empirical basis for raising doubts about the primacy of pleasure in the psychical structuring of human subjectivity. This involves drawing together what is known from work with patients suffering from a variety of traumas. Early in the essay he talks about the significance of the dreams of patients suffering from trauma following peace-time accidents; he mentions his earlier work, in the very initial stages of development of the psychoanalytic method, with patients known as hysterical neurotics; and he refers to observations that have been made of symptoms in patients suffering from war trauma. He describes the way observations across this work have identified certain kinds of symptoms that can be understood as repetitions of the traumatic event:

> The study of dreams may be considered the most trustworthy method of investigating deep mental processes. Now dreams occurring in traumatic neuroses have the characteristic of repeatedly bringing the patient back into the situation of his accident, a situation from which he wakes up in another fright. This astonishes people far too little. They think the fact that the traumatic experience is constantly forcing itself upon the patient even in his sleep is a proof of the strength of that experience: the patient is, as one might say, fixated to his trauma. Fixations to the experience which started the illness have long been familiar to us in hysteria. Breuer and Freud declared in 1893 that 'hysterics suffer mainly from reminiscences'. In the war neuroses, too, observers like Ferenczi and Simmel have been able to explain certain motor symptoms by fixation to the moment at which the trauma occurred.
>
> (Freud 1920: 282)

Here Freud asks us to consider the relationship between trauma, repetition and memory, or a strange form of memory through repetition. To understand this, I think it is worth wondering about his forceful assertion of the need to be astonished by these fixations or repetitions. His suggestion that patients' repetition of their trauma 'astonishes people far too little' might be a reference to the inconsistency of this phenomenon with own earlier theorisation of dreams as wish fulfilment (Freud 1900). Alternatively, he might be referring to his conceptualisation of afterwardsness or deferred action, which suggests the experience of trauma is related to pre-existing wounds in the psyche (Laplanche and Pontalis 1973: 111–3; c.f. Garrett in this collection), rather than dependent on the strength of the immediate experience that initiates the symptoms. In line with this, quite apart from the curiosity of the phenomenon in itself, Freud suggests it is not possible to understand the strange re-occurrence of traumatic experience in dreams, or in other symptoms, as something explicable solely by reference to the strength of the experience itself. Another explanation must be sought; and it is possible, or likely, that this explanation will challenge the initial conception of the human psyche as pleasure seeking.

Repression and transference

This understanding of the potential significance of repetition for conceptualising the human condition, Freud explains, has been further informed by his more recent psychoanalytic work with patients. The clinical aim, at this point, is to address the symptom by revealing its unconscious meaning, its relation to repressed memories and desires and thus dissolving its function in the patient's psychic life. In early psychoanalytic practice it was thought that this aim might be brought about if the physician was able to interpret this meaning and explain it to the patient, and thus provoke the patient's own memory and understanding. However, Freud explains, this approach was not successful:

> But it became ever clearer that the aim which had been set up – the aim that what was unconscious should become conscious [by means of interpretation by the analyst] – is not completely attainable by that method. The patient cannot remember the whole of what is repressed in him, and what he cannot remember may be precisely the essential part of it. Thus he acquires no sense of conviction of the correctness of the construction that has been communicated to him. He is obliged to *repeat* the repressed material as a contemporary experience instead of, as the physician would prefer to see, *remembering* it as something belonging to the past. These reproductions [...] are invariably acted out in the sphere of the transference, of the patient's relation to the physician [...] The ratio between what is remembered and what is reproduced varies from case to case. The physician cannot as a rule spare his patient this phase of the treatment. He must get him to re-experience some portion of his forgotten life, but must see to it on the other hand, that the patient retains some degree of aloofness, which will enable him, in spite of everything, to recognise that what appears to be reality is in fact only a reflection of a forgotten past.
> (Freud 1920: 288–9)

The thing that is important here, in relation to the previous extract, is the way the traumatic event or repressed material is not remembered, but repeated, and, importantly, that it can be repeated within the clinical relationship. Freud thus suggests that the repetition happens in the transference, in the relationship with the analyst, and that this acting out in the very strange scenario of the clinic can bring about a shift in the relation to the symptom. There are several other points worth noting; firstly, the difficulty or impossibility of the patient remembering 'precisely the essential part' of their experience. This 'essential part' is the aspect of the traumatic event that compels the repetitious behaviour: the thing that can't be known and must instead be repeated. Secondly, Freud says that it is important that 'the patient retains some degree of aloofness', though it is not clear exactly what is meant by this (c.f. Walsh in this collection). Carried out with 'some degree of aloofness', Freud proposes, the repetition, in the clinical situation, will enable some kind of a shift to take place. So, in this section Freud moves from discussion of the way traumatic experiences are repeated to reflect on what he has learnt about that repetition through his clinical work, about the complexity of the relationship between repression and memory and about the transference as a site for bringing about shift or change in the repetition.

The compulsion to repeat

However, this learning from clinical observation has implications that go further than clinical work with patients: they extend to our understanding of the psychical structure of the human subject, and the psychical limit of the human condition. The observation of patients' repetitions of unpleasurable or traumatic experiences, manifest in apparently unwanted behaviours or relationships, puts into question the assumption that our psyches are primarily structured by a drive for pleasure. The further move Freud makes in theorising this leads him to formulate the idea of a 'compulsion to repeat', and to speculate on the relation of this compulsion to the pleasure principle:

> But how is the compulsion to repeat – the manifestation of the power of the repressed – related to the pleasure principle? It is clear that the greater part of what is re-experienced under the compulsion to repeat must cause the ego unpleasure, since it brings to light activities of repressed instinctual impulses. That, however, is unpleasure of a kind we have already considered and does not contradict the pleasure principle: unpleasure for one system and simultaneous satisfaction for another. But we come to a new and remarkable fact, namely that the compulsion to repeat also recalls from the past experiences which include no possibility of pleasure, and which can never, even long ago, have brought satisfaction even to instinctual impulses which have since been repressed.
>
> (Freud 1920: 291)

Freud refers again to the repetition of unpleasurable experiences and makes a distinction between the repeated repression of instincts, restricting instinctual pleasure to achieve the pleasure of living a legitimate social life; and the repetition of experiences of pure unpleasure. This is the thing that Freud finds remarkable and in need of explanation. Why would we continuously repeat experiences that have no pleasure associated with them whatsoever? Freud suggests that these repetitions, which appear to have no justification and to be beyond an individual's control, might be understood as driven by an unconscious compulsion to repeat. He elaborates this function as 'a manifestation of the power of the repressed', linking the compulsion to the forgotten, repressed element of traumatic experience.

The death instincts

What, then, are the further implications that follow from the idea of the compulsion to repeat? The final and very radical concept that Freud comes to at the end of 'Beyond the Pleasure Principle' is the idea of the death instincts, or the death drive. Following from his discussion of the compulsion to repeat, he turns to biology and botany, and the study of germ cells in the reproduction of living organisms, in order to think through the possibility of a drive that doesn't seem to be directed towards pleasure or creativity. He pauses, before coming to the end of his speculations, to reflect on the distinction between the 'ego instincts', the instincts that repeat unpleasurable experiences, and the sexual instincts:

> The upshot of our enquiry so far has been the drawing of a sharp distinction between the 'ego-instincts' and the sexual instincts, and the view that the former exercise pressure towards death and the latter towards a prolongation of life. But this conclusion is bound to be unsatisfactory in many respects even to ourselves. Moreover, it is actually

only of the former group of instincts that we can predicate a conservative, or rather retrograde, character corresponding to a compulsion to repeat. For on our hypothesis the ego-instincts arise from the coming to life of inanimate matter and seek to restore the inanimate state; whereas as regards the sexual instincts, though it is true that they reproduce primitive states of the organism, what they are clearly aiming at by every possible means is the coalescence of two germ-cells which are differentiated in a particular way. If this union is not effected, the germ-cell dies [...] It is only on this condition that the sexual function can prolong the cell's life and lend it the appearance of immortality. But what is the important event in the development of living substance which is being repeated in sexual reproduction [...]?

(Freud 1920: 316)

Here, as I have suggested, Freud is trying to see whether he can extend his understanding of repetition and the compulsion to repeat to sexual reproduction, the sexual function. Is the sexual function also an example of the compulsion to repeat? Or can we make a clear distinction between sexual reproduction and the death drive? In what way, he asks, might it be possible to understand sex as a repetition of a previous event, a drive to restore a previous inanimate condition, a point of stasis? He does not know:

[...] We cannot say; and we should consequently feel relieved if the whole structure of our argument turned out to be mistaken. The opposition between the ego or death instincts and the sexual or life instincts would then cease to hold and the compulsion to repeat would no longer possess the importance we have ascribed to it.

(Freud 1920: 316)

It seems, perhaps, that Freud is wanting to draw back from the implications of his previous speculations. He's been speculating about the possibility that perhaps the human psyche, rather than being structured by a drive towards life and towards progress, is structured by a drive to repeat, and to repeat unpleasurable and destructive experiences; and he seems genuinely hesitant and uncertain at this point in his exploration.

In the final sections of the essay, Freud looks to a range of different biological, botanical and philosophical works to explore the possibility of maintaining the distinction between life and mortality, or between instincts towards creation and those towards death. He also turns to earlier developments in psychoanalysis, and notes observations that the libido is often directed, not externally, but at the ego itself (324), that instincts towards a stagnant self-preservation, for example, can be understood as libidinal (325), as well as the presence of a sadistic component in the sexual instinct (327); and thus begins to collapse the distinction between the sexual function as a force towards life and the ego instincts as a force towards death.

Although still qualifying his speculations as a starting point for further investigation rather than a finalised theory, Freud eventually concludes that 'The pleasure principle seems actually to serve the death instincts' (338). This suggests, perhaps, the way the multiple deathly aspects of life and pleasure that he has identified are structured by the more transcendental power of the death drive, the force constituted in the repression of knowledge of trauma, the excess that cannot be symbolised. Both Lacan and Žižek reiterate that it is impossible to see life and death instincts as separate or opposed systems. Lacan talks about 'a myth of the dyad' (1953/2002: 261), and Žižek cites Deleuze's elaboration of the way the two are essentially intertwined: 'Eros and

Thanatos are distinguished in that Eros must be repeated, can only be lived through repetition, whereas Thanatos (as transcendental principle) is that which gives repetition to Eros, that which submits Eros to repetition' (Deleuze, cited in Žižek 2011: 305).

Lacan and Žižek: the site of pleasure and the site of the death drive

Freud's account of the death drive does not fix the concept but rather, as he suggested, opens up a new field of enquiry. For both Lacan and Žižek, the conceptualisation of the death drive is crucial because it points towards the centrality of unconscious automatism in the human condition: 'a blind automatism of repetition beyond pleasure seeking' (Žižek 1989: 4). Both Lacan and Žižek have reworked the death drive in a variety of ways. Lacan's re-articulations of the concept can be mapped to the stages in his theorisation of the relation between the subject, language and the unspeakable excess of the 'Real'. Žižek more explicitly turns the concept of the death drive towards the workings of ideology in the political field. Their work maintains key elements of Freud's initial idea, while also suggesting new conceptual, methodological and political openings.

Žižek's account of three periods in Lacan's conceptualisation of the death drive (1989: 131–3) provides a helpful indication of some potential interpretive trajectories. He distinguishes these periods in Lacan's thought according to what they constitute as the field of pleasure, and what they constitute as beyond pleasure, the site of the power of the repressed. In the first period, pleasure is in the field of objects; and it is the symbol that represents the object that contains the death drive. The symbol or word is thus the site of the powerful excess of meaning that is repressed in the naming of the object. Lacan says: 'the symbol first manifests itself as the killing of the thing': so, the named object is left to endless repetition, an apparently harmonic but lifeless unity, thus avoiding confrontation with the forgotten trauma contained within the symbol or name (Lacan 1953/2002: 262; see also Evans 1996). In the second period the death drive is situated in the symbolic order: language understood as a differential system that temporarily attributes value to otherwise meaningless signifiers. Pleasure, meanwhile, is situated in the (imaginary) experience of meaning. Žižek says: 'When the human being is caught in the signifier's network, this network has a mortifying effect on him; he becomes part of a strange automatic order' (1989: 132; see also Garrett in this collection). In this period there is an emphasis on the pleasurable but deathly repetition of meanings attributed by the network of signifiers, and on the repressed trauma of the subject's encounter with the meaninglessness of our existence. Finally, in the third period, the death drive is positioned beyond language, in the Real, and the symbolic order itself is identified with the pleasure principle (132). In this period Lacan defines the Real as 'the field of the Thing'. The 'Thing' here refers to an absolutely unknowable force that drives symbolisation (Evans 1996: 205). The Real, as the field of the Thing, is thus designated by Lacan as a site: 'onto which is projected something beyond, something at the point of origin of the signifying chain' (Lacan 1992: 214). What this suggests, I think, is that the trauma that cannot be assimilated, that is both the initiation and the unsayable aspect of the subject, is projected into the Real, which thus contains the force of the repressed, the death drive. Importantly, though, symbolic and Real are intertwined, and the trauma, Lacan says, 'is registered in the signifying chain and dependent on its existence' (212). So, while simultaneously beyond knowledge and meaning, it is from the site of the Real that 'doubt is cast on all that is in the place of being' (214).

The elaboration of these different ways of conceptualising the site of pleasure and of the death drive may seem slippery – but perhaps it might help to remember that the force of the death drive is itself unknowable, so is situated speculatively and undecidably in successive stages of Lacan's thinking, in the word, the symbolic network of signifiers, or beyond language in the Real. There are also significant continuities: while in his earlier theorisation Lacan talks about the relationship between the name and the possibility of memorialisation (1953/2002: 263), in his later discussion he describes the field of the Thing as a dimension where 'history presents itself as something memorable' (1992: 212). Both periods in Lacan's work thus stick closely to Freud's account of death drive as ghostly memorial site of forgotten trauma: 'a speechless curse' (Lacan 1953/2002: 263). The impossibility of fixing the site of the death drive is perhaps indicative of this phantom aspect, as Lacan specifies:

> I don't even say that at this point of speculation things still have a meaning. I simply want to say that the articulation of the death drive in Freud is neither true nor false. It is suspect; that's all I affirm. But it suffices for Freud that it was necessary, that it leads him to an unfathomable spot that is problematic, since it reveals the structure of the field. It points to the site that I designate alternatively as impassable or as the site of the Thing.
>
> (1992: 213)

Following Lacan, Žižek uses the concept of the death drive to foreground the blind automatism of repetition in the political field and the need to be faithful to the otherness of the Thing (1989; 2000; 2011). Both progressive and totalitarian politics, he argues, try to tame or limit the possibility of an encounter with trauma – offering visions of harmony and control in the relationship between humanity and nature (1989: 5; see also papers by Pais and Costa, Lysgaard and Simovska in this collection). Freud's conceptualisation of the death drive, in contrast, confronts us with the radical antagonism of the human condition and the impossibility of assimilation of trauma, its meaning and inevitability, into social and political life. The death drive, Žižek says,

> defines *la condition humaine* as such: there is no solution, no escape from it; the thing to do is not to "overcome", to "abolish" it, but to come to terms with it, to learn to recognise it in its terrifying dimension and then, on the basis of this fundamental recognition, to try to articulate a *modus vivendi* with it.
>
> (1989: 5)

Now, finally, we can come back to education, in a position to formulate questions about the role of repetition, the repression of trauma, the compulsion to repeat and the conceptualisation of a death drive in concrete processes of education:

- If we tend to become, in some way, perhaps unconsciously, fixated or stuck within traumatic events, is it possible to trace this kind of automatism or repetition within education policy, curricula or pedagogic relations?
- If, at an individual level, we cannot remember the most significant parts of repressed traumatic events, what are the implications for the way such events are recalled or repressed in education policy, curricula and practice?

- If human subjects and societies can be understood as always seeking to 'restore an earlier state of things' (Freud: 336), rather than seeking progress and the new, what is the potential for bringing about transformation through education?
- Freud's account of the *transference* suggests how repetition, carried out with 'some degree of aloofness', might potentially subvert that which it repeats. Can we bring this insight to bear on contemporary questions in the field of education?

Without necessarily directly referencing the death drive, each of the papers in the collection addresses at least one of these fundamental questions.

Freud, Lacan, Žižek and the death drive in education

The papers in the collection are roughly grouped to explore different aspects of educational processes: the experience of unfathomable repetitions in the classroom and the potential to shift these through the creation of transferential spaces (Garrett; Walsh); the complicity of both curriculum research and critical pedagogic practice in maintaining idealised images of education's transformative potential (Lysgaard and Simovska; Straehler-Pohl and Pais; Pais and Costa); unconscious relations between professional subjectivity and policy driven school practices of performativity and accountability (Moore; Lapping and Glynos); the way ideals of equity and universality in education policy act to cover over the antagonisms of the Real (Clarke; Clarke); and the political implications of the incongruent and fantasmatic temporalities of contemporary educational institutions (Lapping). Each paper draws attention to something opaque or unknowable, a repressed element or an unconscious desire, an unexpected force at work in educational processes.

The first two papers might be thought of as explorations of the pedagogic encounter as a site of transference. Both start from experiences of unknowable repetitions in the classroom that can block relationships and learning. H. James Garrett draws on a visit to a Holocaust museum with a group of student teachers to offer new insights into the way teachers carry past experience into their work in the classroom. His analysis draws attention to symbolic repetitions that shaped the group's engagement with the exhibit, and that made it difficult to articulate elements that didn't fit with their prior expectations of 'the holocaust'. He suggests that this very inarticulability is also a moment with the potential to create something new, and draws on one participant's reflective writing to suggest how the visit to the museum might have shifted her previously rigid sense of her own educational history. In the second paper, Julie Walsh reflects on a difficult tutorial with a student whose inability to speak in the lesson was opaque to her, as teacher, and also very probably to himself. In considering the possible ways she might have eased the situation, she suggests the role that texts or text fragments can play in the creating the necessary distance, Freud's 'degree of aloofness', for transferential repetitions to be transformed into new knowledge. Taken together these two pieces are suggestive of the potential for creating transferential spaces, where repetitious patterns might be rendered other, shifted or transformed. Following their suggestions, we might be inspired to experiment with such spaces in the contexts of education and research, as well as in clinical work.

Three papers in the collection draw on Žižek's conception of ideology as a defence against the inevitable trauma of the Real. They analyse contemporary educational ideals – 'participation' (Lysgaard and Simovska), 'global citizenship education'

(Pais and Costa) and 'mathematics for all' (Straehler-Pohl and Pais) – as fantasies that cover over the unassimilable complexity of the real conditions of education, politics and change. All three papers also deploy the Lacanian/Žižekian notion of 'interpassivity', the idea that frenetic activity in service of an ideal works to displace rather than to enact its supposed objectives. They observe how this concept offers insights into the workings of educational initiatives articulated within institutional systems that value the activity for purposes of accountability rather than politics. Lysgaard and Simovska explain: 'this position can be achieved by the subject (the individual teacher) through interposing another object, the ideal of participation, between him or herself and the hoped for change'. Of particular interest are the slightly different ways in which the papers interpret the possibility for a dynamic, lively politics to emerge in these hegemonic conditions of repetitious automatism. Lysgaard and Simovska are interested in the potential for the teacher's desire for political engagement to make a difference despite the deadening force of the symbolic context; while Pais and Costa foreground the risks of activity that unconsciously reproduces the conditions it aims to resist: 'the dangers of inhibiting a structural analysis and a possibility of a change beyond individual agency'. The ethnographic case study analysed by Straehler-Pohl and Pais provides a stark example of a teacher whose attempts fail, for whom 'The [...] fantasy of pursuing the superior aims of education enables her to repress the traumatic insight that all she is doing is actually working against these aims'. However, as Lysgaard and Simovska seem to suggest, the potential political productivity of a concrete intervention within a specified context, may not be decidable in advance.

A Freudian/Lacanian understanding of the relation between repressed desire and language is taken up in the papers by Alex Moore, and by Jason Glynos and myself. Structured by an initial, unknowable traumatic event, desire is the remnant of affective force that moves between the Real and language. Continuously moving, desire seeks signifiers that simultaneously express and cover over the unspeakable nature of its trauma. Repetition is enacted when desire is channelled through signifiers or signifying structures that are similar in their ability to carry out this dual purpose of articulation and disguise. Moore's paper explores teachers' responses to national- and school-level policy directives. In an analysis of his interviews with two teachers, both of whom found themselves in conflict with the increasing regulation of school curricula and assessment, Moore traces the way one participant is still able to find points of articulation of desire within his practice, and thus remains in his role; the other participant, no longer able to achieve this, leaves the profession. In a similar way, in our analysis of our Lacanian-inspired free associative interviews with teaching assistants, Jason and I trace the way particularly ambivalent or painful aspects of participants' positioning in relation to the performative culture of the workplace can be understood as transferential repetitions. These repetitions were manifest in signifiers and signifying structures – 'never ask', 'it's dodgy, but' – that individual participants' reiterated both in narratives of the workplace and in spontaneous associations to childhood events. These repetitious elements simultaneously constitute participants' professional subjectivities and the institutional field of the school. They suggest the significance of desire and trauma in the structuring of educational practice. While these studies indicate moments where desire is trapped in existing signifying circuits, they also raise questions about a politics of desire that might open up new signifying possibilities.

Matthew Clarke's two contributions to the collection explore the role of policy discourse in temporarily taming desire by offering a utopian vision of a harmonious education system contributing to economic prosperity. In 'Talkin' 'bout a revolution: the social, political and fantasmatic logic of education policy', Clarke draws on Lacanian-inspired political theory (Glynos 2008; Glynos and Howarth 2007) to examine the way one Australian policy, 'Quality Education', reiterates neoliberal logics of competition, atomisation and instrumentalisation; asserts a politics of consensus; and offers a fantasmatic promise of universal choice and participation. In 'The sublime objects of education policy', he explores the function of the signifiers 'equity' and 'quality' in the field of global education policy. His argument has two stages: first he maps the juxtaposition of these terms in a signifying chain that occludes antagonisms between incompatible ideas; then he demonstrates the elusive content or emptiness of the signifiers themselves. Precisely because of this emptiness, they are invested with excessive significance, or desire, that cannot be fulfilled. We might, tentatively, align this with Lacan's second theorisation of the death drive, where the repressed trauma is situated in the signifying chain, and pleasure is identified with the fantasy of meaningful existence. Or, to put this more forcefully, using Matthew Clarke's comment on a draft of this introduction:

> the notion of the death drive is utterly and fundamentally at odds with the overt (fantasmatic) ideology of education policy and practice, with its insistence on the positivity of educational experience, despite the fact that education can be read as a technology of violence in the lives of teachers and students.

In the final paper in the collection, I attempt to trace the way such invasions are enacted in the distinctive temporalities of contemporary higher education institutions. Drawing on Lacan's theorisation of the fantasmatic construction of temporality, in his paper on 'Logical Time', my analysis of interviews with academics suggests how their subjectivities are suspended between the contrasting linear temporalities of external regulation and disciplinary community, alongside the more narcissistic, self-referential temporality produced in the process of research. The invasions suggested in this analysis are traced in leakages of anxiety and destabilisations of subjectivity that appear in the hinges between these contrasting and incongruent temporalities. Such leakages might be understood as the registration of 'Real Time', traumatic in its unassimilable finitudes and infinitudes, within the symbolic field of the university.

Conclusion: '… a forgotten past'

Taken together these papers suggest, quite powerfully, the way the force of the repressed can be discerned in pedagogic relationships, curricula discourse, education policy and institutional practice. Since it is inevitable that the past shapes the present, we might use these insights to develop a sensitivity to the way such repetitions can be indicative of the force of the repressed; and also to the possibility of creating sites of transference in the fields of education and research, to support shifts in repetitious patterns.

While some quite significant aspects of the transference produced in clinical psychoanalytic relationships cannot be replicated in other settings, a creative exploration of the resonances between psychoanalytic, educational and research relationships can productively draw on an understanding of the transference to support the articulation of both educational and political desire. In exploring such possibilities, it is important to avoid closing down 'transference' to just one meaning or practice. Let us take, for example, Laplanche's distinction between the transference of experiences and feelings from childhood and the transference of 'the originary infantile situation' (1999: 229), the specific enigmatic relation between child and adult that initiates subjectivity. An exploration sensitised to this kind of distinction in the manifestation of transference might produce new theorisations of an originary transferential situation that is specific to the field of education, and of its meaning and effects for learning and politics. This might be a way of formulating a project for an ongoing politics of the field of education. To develop such a project, we should be open to the possibility of using textual practices of both reading and writing (c.f. Garrett; Walsh) and experiments with free association (c.f. Glynos and Lapping) to create spaces where repetitious patterns might be observed and engaged. We might also draw on an understanding of the transference and its relation to repression to inform participatory activist processes across diverse aspects of our practice. This might be a way of addressing both education and research as necessarily political fields that inevitably resonate at a structural level: the narcissistic pleasures of education and research in the service of the death drive of politics. Finally, it is important to note the impossibility of recovering the forgotten material that re-emerges as a force of repetition and stasis across the educational field. All we can do, in our ignorance, is to take note of its ghostly dimension and of our own implication within it, and to use this 'degree of aloofness' as a tentative space for a politics of educational desire.

References

Evans, D. (1996) An Introductory Dictionary of Lacanian Psychoanalysis, London, New York: Routledge

Freud, S. (1900/1958) Penguin Freud Library Volume 4: The Interpretation of Dreams, Penguin Books

Freud, S. (1920/1984) 'Beyond the Pleasure Principle', in On Metapsychology: The Theory of Psychoanalysis, The Pelican Freud Library Volume 11, Penguin Books, 275–338

Glynos, J. (2008) 'Ideological Fantasy at Work', Journal of Political Ideologies, 13/3, 275–296

Glynos, J. and Howarth, D. (2007) Logics of Critical Explanation in Social and Political Theory, London: Routledge

Lacan, J. (1953/2002) 'The Function and Field of Speech and Language in Psychoanalysis', in Ecrits: The First Complete Edition in English, Trans. B. Fink, New York, London: W. W. Norton & Company

Lacan, J. (1999) The Ethics of Psychoanalysis: The Seminar of Jacques Lacan Book VII, Trans. D. Potter, London, New York: Routledge

Laplanche, J. (1999) Essays on Otherness, London: Routledge

Laplanche, J. and Pontalis, J-B. (1973) The Language of Psychoanalysis, London: Karnac Books

Žižek, S. (1989) The Sublime Object of Ideology, London, New York: Verso

Žižek, S. (2000) 'Melancholy and the Act', Critical Inquiry, 26(4), 657–681

Žižek, S. (2010) Living in the End Times, London, New York: Verso

Before, after, in and beyond teacher education

H. James Garrett

The author uses a trip to a Holocaust museum to explain and illustrate psychoan-alytic concepts from Freud to Lacan in order to re-imagine persistent dilemmas in teacher education. The author suggests that psychoanalytic vocabularies provide an additional and productive lens to conceptualize productive possibilities in teacher education.

Introduction

Teacher education programs attempt to address, confront, revisit, and refine student teachers' pasts. The status of the past in teacher education is located in 'the apprenticeship of observation' (Lortie, 1975) as well as in the challenge of becoming conscious of one's own 'personal practical knowledge' (Clandenin, 1986, cf. Korthagen, 2004). However, despite the broad agreement in teacher education upon the notion that the teacher's past is significant, the complexities of subjectivity make it difficult to formulate interventions into the past that aid in the ability of student teachers to enact a creative pedagogy (Britzman, 2003a). Conceptual change is hard work. However, student teachers must come to an awareness of their past and the ways that their own narratives of schooling might impact the ways that they are experiencing their teacher education program and, perhaps even more importantly, how they are enacting the beginning phases of their teaching careers with diverse young learners.

Without recognition of these processes and this past, teachers run the risk of mis-taking thoughtful practice with a reproduction of their own experiences of/in schools. It seems as though teachers are expected to begin on the first day of their teaching practice having come to terms with their past in ways that allow them to successfully facilitate the academic achievement of their students. It is, as one of my most recent students put it, 'a mess.' While there is significant variation in approaches to teacher education (see, e.g. Wilson, Rozelle, & Mikeska, 2011), there is one thing upon which most teacher educators agree: it is exceedingly difficult to change future teachers' minds about what it means to theorize and practice the work of teaching. It is hard, in other words, to reconstitute or recast the past.

This paper places its focus on the status of the past in the pedagogy of teacher education and the degree to which that past is activated in the present. The theoreti-cal constructs utilized herein follow curriculum theorists such as Pinar (2004) who have problematized the ways in which the past effects the present. Other scholars whose work takes psychoanalytic theory into the spaces of formal schooling have considered issues of the past as being always brought to bear in teaching and learning, always playing out within the psychical dynamics of classroom life (e.g. Britzman, 2006; Matthews, 2007; Taubman, 2006). In utilizing psychoanalytic theoretical constructs, the past will pester and prod the teacher and the student, but most frequently, those interventions will stay outside of the conscious awareness of the parties. It will, however, manifest itself in resentments, jokes, frustrations, and all sorts of unpredictable events in the classroom. Some will feel like they belong there, others will not. The past is active and present.

I will be conceptualizing the past in terms of the ways in which psychoanalytic theory provides a way of interpreting classroom life that allows for a focus on the strange and estranging in teaching, learning, and learning to teach. In this paper, I used two psychoanalytic constructs (the Lacanian notion of the symbolic register and the Freudian concept of 'deferred knowledge,' or nachträglichkeit), in order to investigate two persistent phenomenon in teacher education: the status and influence of the personal/social past and the ways in which that that past can be rewritten. To introduce and illustrate the ideas, I will focus on an experience I had with research participants at a Holocaust museum. This 'other space' of the museum will serve as a pedagogical location that I will then use as an analog for the formal spaces of teacher education. Following these illustrations, I will turn my attention to how those terms might allow teacher educators to think a new about persistent problems in teacher education.

Theory and context

It is important to highlight that what I write here is rooted in the very position(s) I occupy and assume in relationship to theory, scholarship and education. So, briefly, I am a white male of means, an assistant professor of social studies education at a large research university in the American South who utilizes psychoanalytic research to think about the ways in which social studies/teacher education can locate creative potentialities within a sociopolitical framework that is largely anti-intellectual and pro-capital (Pinar, 2004; Zizek, 2007). I utilize psychoanalytic theory to implicate the ways that knowledge is mediated and experienced by teachers and students as being in many ways outside of conscious awareness but already embedded in and shaped by larger personal/social systems of meaning. The psychoanalytic vocabulary here – though hoping to be provocative and generative – is not provided with the intention of being a cure-all. What I offer is a vocabulary that I find helps the subject tolerate the difficulties of working in the twenty-first century.

Using psychoanalytic theory to investigate the landscape of pedagogical encounters is something that allows for an examination of the things that initially do not make sense, do not fit, frustrate confound or perplex (e.g. Bibby, 2010; Britzman, 2009; Pitt, 1998). What the practice of psychoanalysis does for patients, in the best of cases, is to allow for a creative accommodation of problematic aspects of the past. It does not, in this sense, attempt to solve problems as much as it does help individuals to understand those problems in a variety of ways so that various conceptualizations may be drawn upon at various times to accommodate and reduce the accompanying anxieties. As it relates to teacher education, psychoanalytic inquiries may not offer the sets of strategies that we often desire (Farley, 2013), but what it might do is help us think about the nature of that desire as a lesson in and of itself. It may help us to think about the persistent kinds of questions that occur as being themselves the location of hopeful and creative interventions in the thinking of the student, the student/teacher, and the teacher educator (Farley, 2009; Tarc, 2011). Thinking about teacher education psychoanalytically, then, means an acknowledgement of the problems of resistant students as well as idealistic ones (and that idealism is also a form of resistance), a recognition that all sorts of things get in the way of our best efforts as teachers, which the past is always on our breath, and that this past is open, ultimately, to being reworked and contextualized – even though such work is difficult.

Context of inquiry

This paper analyzes and interprets a set of data to illustrate, theorize, and highlight implications for teacher education. It is not an empirical piece but is based on an empirical research project and its results. The larger study that gave rise to this museum visit focused on the ways in which social studies preservice teachers made sense of, and made pedagogical, encounters with 'difficult knowledge' (Britzman, 1998; Garrett, 2010, 2011; Pitt & Britzman, 2003). The six participants, four female (Lynne, Patty, Grace and Eva) and two male (Ben and George) – all middle to upper middle class white students in a large university's teacher education program, were asked to join me at the museum. Before we entered, participants were asked to write about their thoughts in a journal. Participants and I then viewed the museum exhibitions, listened to the testimony of a Holocaust survivor who was speaking at the museum that day and then had an hour-long group discussion in one of the museum conference rooms. After the museum visit, I had participants provide me their journals and notes from the museum visit. Two weeks after the visit, I transcribed our discussion, and then sent them copies of the transcripts and their notes for further comments.

What became apparent as I read and re-read this particular data through a psychoanalytic lens was that many of the meanings generated in and around the Holocaust museum were populated by something that seemed beyond the individual as well as the topic of study. What was said was said 'in' the museum, but it was 'of' other places and times altogether. This particular paper is motivated by the degree to which that interpretation echoes within my work and thinking about teacher education: that what students say, how teachers react, what desires and fears are described in relation to teaching practice are all filled with something 'other.' That something other, I think, can be brought into a temporary focus by thinking with the Lacanian 'symbolic register' and the Freudian notion of 'deferred knowledge.'

Introductions and illustrations in the museum

The symbolic register

Jacques Lacan's contribution to psychoanalytic thinking is a re-reading of Freud's structural model of psychic life and a lending of a poststructural read to it. His articulation of the unconscious is conceived around three 'registers': the real, the imaginary, and the symbolic. Briefly (and over simply), the real is the one which cannot be accommodated into the thought structure or experience of an individual. It is, in many ways, representative of the prediscursive stimuli that a person may sense, but cannot perceive. Perceptions, then, are within the imaginary and once they approach and then are codified in language, they become part of the symbolic. The psyche, for Lacan, is located outside of the individual and is therefore subject to the sociopolitical discourses that circulate and dominate in any particular space. The symbolic register constrains, orients, and allows for certain kinds of sense making dependent upon one's location in it. Much like a constellation imbues collections of individual stars with a given meaning, and it is populated with signifiers and is given its structure and logic in the relationships between those signifiers. Because of the ways that signifiers like teacher, student, classroom, school, clock, and others work together to form meanings, they stitch together a fabric that, as Lacan posits through his theorization of the symbolic field, predetermine possible articulations of experience. The result is that our conscious thoughts are often not the equivalent of our experiences in the world, they are those experiences mediated, shaped, and, at least in part, determined by our location in the symbolic field. That signifier ('student' or 'teacher') provides a location in the symbolic field that subject will occupy and, as Lacan (2006):

> illustrates determines subjects' acts, destiny, refusals, blindnesses, success and fate, regardless of their innate gifts and instruction, and irregardless of their character or sex and that everything pertaining to the psychological pregiven follows willy-nilly the signifier's train, like weapons and baggage (p. 21).

To put the symbolic into familiar terms, I propose a simple (perhaps, oversimple) example. When I am subjectively located as a 'student' (a specific kind of subject position), I may want class to be over. I may pack my things. I may text a friend. I may read a newspaper on my computer. But I do not call class to an end. I do not even have access to a vocabulary that would call a class session to its end. Not only do I not have the authority to end class, the coordination of the symbolic field would likely influence my thinking to such a degree that I would not even think the thought of producing the utterance: 'class dismissed.' At that time, I literally am not in possession of those words. It would not even register as a possibility. As a student I do, think, and say particular things. As a teacher, though, I have access to, and am activated by a different situation in the symbolic. The texting, the packing up, and the open laptop computer would frustrate me. Those same actions that I just undertook as a student are, to put it in these terms, no longer available to me. I am, Lacan might say, being pulled through the symbolic chain. In the next section I will explain how those symbolic coordinations 'worked' in the context of the museum visit and, later, in terms of the given and possible in teacher education.

Using the symbolic to theorize the museum visit

One of the signifiers that research participants occupied outside of the Holocaust museum was one of 'museum visitor.' I invited students to write their thoughts in the area outside of the Holocaust museum before we entered. Here, I read those thoughts via Lacan as 'being spoken' by a particular location in the symbolic. For a first example, George (a white, upper middle class conservative male) wrote, 'I have an idea of what to expect. I get 'surprise emotional' when I experience things like this, and I do my best to hold it in.' Ben, who, like George, is a white, upper class male, included sentiments that are in some ways similar to George's in that he asks: 'Why do I immediately feel the need to turn the music down or off? (written about his drive to the memorial) I fear not being able to 'measure up' to the memory. The Holocaust is intimidating, and so this place is as well.' Grace, a white middle class female wrote: 'I expect to view a lot of the stories and exhibits through the lens of my own mother's death, a death that was not as atrocious, but which taught me nonetheless about being separated prematurely from someone you love deeply.'

Of course, it could be argued that all people enter a space with expectations. I agree. However, the evidence of the symbolic coordination predetermining meanings is found in the excess of these written articulations. It is found in the uncanny, ironic, and cross-purposeful speech acts. When George writes that he has an idea of what to expect, and in the very next statement discusses his 'surprise' emotions, we are able to understand that because of the signifier 'Holocaust museum visitor' he is expecting certain experiences. The excess of his statement is that his surprise has already been structured for him. How can surprise work in advance?

Occupying the same position, Ben's need to turn down the music is spoken through the social meanings that the Holocaust has taken over time – that there is certain music that is appropriate to such engagement, and there is other music which is not. And when Grace writes about the ways she expects to experience the exhibits through the lens of the death of her mother, it may at first seem that the signifier she is occupying is one of grief, the lost daughter, the separated. But she also does acknowledge the broader themes of the Holocaust. She has learned what will happen in the experience. None of the participants had been to this Holocaust memorial and museum. Yet they knew what to expect. The story had already been written.

These examples orient us to the ways that in a Lacanian conception of social knowledge we are never fully in possession of the meanings we make in the world. To further exemplify that Lacanian notion, I turn now to the final part of our visit to the museum, where we all filed into an auditorium to hear the testimony of a Holocaust survivor; a Polish woman who had fled to Russia before the Nazis began their deportations, and who had moved to Costa Rica when she was a teenager and then to the USA as an adult. She did not have a number tattooed on her arm. She did not tell a horror story of bearing direct witness to murder, starvation, and disease. I noticed my participants embodying what I interpreted as boredom. As we discussed her testimony, participants were disappointed. Ben elaborated by saying:

> You hear Holocaust survivor and you are like someone who went through the camp, or something! And then you get there she was with the Russians and then she went to Costa Rica and it was, OK, this is something and she is definitely a survivor of the time period. But when you think about Holocaust survivor you think of something specific … this is not something that I thought it would be but that is fine.

Ben is able to acknowledge the autobiographical testimony as 'something' but is unable to articulate exactly what. He cannot access an appropriate word or descriptor. While he acknowledges that she was a 'definitely a survivor of the time period,' he denies her the subjectivity that is due a survivor of the Holocaust even though she most certainly is. Together, we discussed our reactions and thought about why it was that we experienced the fidgeting, the boredom, and the wish for something different.

I theorize this elaboration by claiming that Ben's location as 'listener to a Holocaust survivor' determines his reactions to the story. He is disappointed; other participants said they were 'bored' or 'fidgety.' Their bodies manifested discomfort. I expressed my surprise at the survivor's testimony as well. Our signifiers had spoken us, by our position in the symbolic field. Even though the articulation is spoken by the signifier (so to speak) in this case, we also meet for the first time a creative potentiality. Here, we are temporarily outside of the symbolic. It is an instance of Ben being confronted with the limits of the symbolic field, where there was something that escaped the ability to be articulated, and as I will discuss below, is a moment we ought to recognize, even cultivate, with student teachers. We were forced to think new thoughts that would help us to rewrite old events.

Summarily, the participants' position in the symbolic field shapes and gives meaning to our experience before we even get to be in the moment of experience. Our experiences, it might be said, 'posses' us – rather than the other way around. As we approach the limits of the structured understandings that are made more likely vis-à-vis a particular symbolic location, we are more likely to come to the limits of our understanding. I propose that those times when we brush up against those limits are the times when learning is most likely.

Deferred knowing (nachträglichkeit)

While we are, in essence, caught in already existing webs of meaning, this does not mean that meanings are once and for all. Meaning and truth are constantly being routed, written, and rewritten. Indeed, meanings are always being pulled along the same symbolic chains that while in one moment locate us in one place, in another moment restructure our ways of knowing. I feel differently about using profanity with friends than I do with family, for example. I 'know' differently in different places. The symbolic chains are, to put it rather crudely, slippery and well lubricated.

When old memories are drawn upon in new situations, the constellations into which those memories fit change, resulting in new meanings being made out of, or read onto, old events: the Freudian concept nachträglichkeit, or deferred action. The idea of deferral 'rules out the summary interpretation which reduces ... the subject's history to a linear determinism envisaging nothing but the action of the past on the present' (Laplanche & Pontalis, 1973, p. 112). Deferral is presented at the outset of the invention of psychoanalytic practice and as Freud explained 'the material present in the form of memory-traces [are] subjected from time to time to a re-arrangement in accordance with fresh circumstances – to a retranscription' (Freud, 1896, cf. Laplanche & Pontalis, 1973, p. 112; see also Britzman, 2000).

In this process of deferred knowledge, the experience, a memory, comes to take new meaning in our lives. The force of this process is not something about which the subject is generally aware. A new set of circumstances may unconsciously remind us of an old event, and the old event is edited and re-authorized in the present. Just as the symbolic field works to structure understandings, in acknowledging the ways of deferred actions 'we are always ... retroactively giving the elements their symbolic weight by including them in new textures' (Zizek, 1989, p. 59). If the symbolic chain represents the psychic force of the unconscious that structures our understandings in ways that premeditate meaning, then the dynamics of deferred action help us to understand that what begins as experience in one scene can take on new meaning in light of other circumstances. Once again, the social and historical events combine with the personal perceptions and experiences to make and remake what are spoken as our thoughts, opinions, and perceptions. In the museum, one of the participants' narrations of an exhibit exemplifies this process.

Using deferral to theorize the museum visit

The first exhibit in the Holocaust memorial and museum we visited was housed in a circular room and was comprised of two juxtaposed timelines. On the top half of the room was a timeline of Jewish diaspora history, including demarcations of anti-Semitic events throughout it as well as, of course, the accelerating worldwide anti-Semitism that culminated in the Holocaust. On the bottom half of the room was a timeline of 'traditional' historical events. For example, the invention of the light bulb and airplane was on there, as other events were easily recognizable from traditional world history courses. There is no other route into the museum exhibits, so every visitor must pass through this first room. Describing that exhibit, Grace discusses the ways in which knowledge is retroactively constituted.

> It makes you realize the ... not bias ... but the limited scope of what you learn, or what I learned, in my academic career. There is not really an awareness of ... what was may be the more important event besides the invention of the telephone. It made me feel like in schools we should we talking about the global perspective and the global human race instead of this focus on nationalism and what is going in your bubble.

Grace's personal history of schooling, her investment in the quality of her academic career, sets the stage for an experience of a shift in the account of that history. Here, we see the degree to which the historical narrative on display, with its juxtaposition of progress and/of genocidal policy, interacts with Grace's deeply held personal beliefs. Others, of course, might have interpreted this timeline in ways that sit in a different relation to the events. One might, for example, wonder how the rest of the world continued on their courses of action and allowed the progression of hatred and anti-Semitism to flourish. The personal histories, social knowledge, and pedagogical display interact and the accounts of that display are articulated as an artifact of such interaction.

For my purposes in this paper, I would like to focus on the way that knowledge is retroactively constructed in Grace's articulation. While on an initial read of her statement, she is articulating a newly arrived at decision about what she ought to do as part of her pedagogy, reading the quote as an example of deferred knowledge would have us consider the fact that she is reworking the entirety of her academic career. In the face of a new set of significations of history, what had – we might presume – been an adequate education in this moment becomes 'limited.'

Therefore, despite our time in the Holocaust memorial center being in many ways predetermined vis-à-vis the symbolic field and as it relates to what participants understand in relation to the Holocaust itself, the meanings that individuals make in light of those exhibits is radically uncertain due to the workings of 'afterwardsness.' What we are left with is a glance at learning that yields nothing to linear chronology or progress. Expectations and 'prior knowledge' about the Holocaust, not just the historical event but also the socio-emotional and economic circulation of its meaning, impinge on creative potentials, are internalized, and then erupt in a precodification of an experience before it has even happened. And then, as the time line coils back onto the psychoanalytic spool, those experiences become retroactively shaped as new events give shape to the past.

Summarily, what 'happens' in the museum in many ways has happened before the physical experience of being there and also comes to have different meanings in many moments after. 'New' knowledge is, in this sense, a reworking of old knowledge in that it returns as a difference (Felman, 1987). It is within this vein that Britzman works with the related term of 'after-education' to refer 'both to past mistakes and to the new work of constructing one's history of education after the experience of education' (Britzman, 2003b, p. 4). This might mean that what happens in a particular pedagogical situation might be best thought of as a provisional space of meaning making where students are writing and rewriting their experiences within the tensions of the symbolic and through the mediating influence of unconscious processes like deferred knowledge.

Making the museum experience an analog to teacher education

The museum visit, and my analysis of it, is analogous to the spaces of teacher education. The student teacher, just as the museum visitor, occupies a particular position within the symbolic. The student teacher, like the museum, indicates a position in which 'the subject is nothing other than what slides in a chain of signifiers, whether he knows which signifier he is the effect of or not' (Lacan, 1998, p. 50). Unconsciously, the student–teachers (and, of course, the teacher–educators. And, of course, the researcher) are being influenced by their location within various and competing symbolic coordinates. And, the experience of being in a teacher education classroom is likely to be re-authored as students come to have experiences in different subjective locations through the processes of deferred action.

Two persistent problems in teacher education frame my inquiry: the ways in which teacher education programs attempt to mediate the influence of the individual's past on their teaching present; and the persistent complaint about the 'theory' of the university and the 'practice' of the classroom. Each of these problems is complicated. I propose here that understanding these problems in terms of the symbolic field and deferred knowledge (illustrated above in the context of the museum visit) might help open productive possibilities for navigating them.

In teacher education, whether the goals of the particular programs are those of social justice, critical, antiracist, culturally relevant pedagogies or best practices, there is broad acknowledgement that prior (social and historical) positionings matter. Teacher education classes are populated with assignments that attempt to draw up, and draw upon, students' pasts through autobiographical writing and narrating histories of learning. Teacher education scholarship acknowledges the often-overriding influence of the 'apprenticeship of observation' (Lortie, 1975). These influences are codified within dominant modes of thinking, what a sociocultural theory might identify as Discourse, and what Lacan might call the symbolic.

Within psychoanalytic thinking, though, it is acknowledged that not only do the individuals' social conditions and history configure their orientation to the world, but that those orientations, the rules and codes, are lived within the relationship between self and world in ways that are most often outside of conscious awareness.

So it is not only that teacher candidates arrive with orientations and expectations, and it is not only that they prefer to hold onto those orientations and expectations, but it is also the case that the resistance to new modes of thinking are rooted in processes of which most are not immediately aware.

The difference between some other education theories and the Lacanian notion of the symbolic is that the former thinks of what students bring with them as being primarily located in the past while the latter would focus on interpreting this past as being structured and activated in the present. This makes for a potential space of intervention because of the possibility of focusing on different questions, for example, the degree to which student teachers articulate often similar stories about why they want to teach, what they want to teach for, and what purposes education might serve. We might, for example, ask our students why these stories sound so similar in helping to open the possibility for new thoughts and new relationships with their educational pasts. We might ask about what other stories they had told about their histories in schools and why those stories have been different in different contexts.

The process of deferred knowing means that we are always re-writing these pasts to suit particular purposes. The focus would be on which past, and what articulation of it, is utilized in any given particular moment and Lacan helps us wonder to what ends those articulations and activations are being used. When, for example, the participants are writing about the perceived need to turn down the music, upon what pasts are they drawing and why? As such, acknowledging this process though open-ended inquiry with our students may serve as a site of intervention in what passes for common sense understandings in formal education contexts.

Acknowledging the process of deferred knowledge in practice may allow the pedagogue access to different questions that could open up new possibilities for understanding. I, for example, could have asked the research participants questions like: Why do not you think this is a Holocaust survivor? Why do you think you were bored? What do you make of that boredom? What about your prior education seems to have failed in this moment? What would it mean for you if you thought about your education as not providing what you thought it had? These kinds of questions, I think, while not leading to a better teaching practice necessarily, do open hold open the possibility for new and changing meanings to be provisionally offered.

Further, understanding students' resistance to new ways of thinking about schools, society, and education in terms of the symbolic will not solve the problems of resistance that teacher educators face. But just as I might have asked about the interpretations of the museum, when students are resisting new ideas in their teacher education courses, one might ask about what version and what pasts they are relying to tell their stories. What other versions of the story of wanting to be a teacher might we tell?

Understanding the often unconscious influence of the symbolic may help to explain these problems in ways that do not place the blame on the student, or on the teacher educator. Our resistances to learning new things, just like George's 'surprise emotion,' are structured in advance through the symbolic. What we can do is examine the kinds of things (experiences, beliefs, historical accounts, and theoretical dispositions) that structure those reactions (see den Heyer & Conrad, 2011). The notion that the symbolic operates in all sociopolitical as well as personal contexts gives new life to the prominent acknowledgement of 'prior knowledge,' in that the symbolic activates different sets of prior knowledge at different times and for different

reasons; reasons as often as not existing and operating outside of conscious awareness. Further, in acknowledging the ways that knowledge and experience restructure
and narrate the past, students and teachers may feel encouraged to wonder about
what new meanings will come of the experiences that are happening within that
often dissatisfying place of the teacher education classroom. Because of the ways
that individuals will always be 'sliding' through different subject positions and locations in the symbolic, we might further be able to listen for traces and hints of how
students are making sense and articulating that sense to us in the classroom. This
makes a resource of student resistance where once there was a problem (see Garrett
& Segall, 2013).

These psychoanalytic concepts might also aid in understanding the problematic
noncongruence between what is encouraged in teacher education classes and what
happens in the field. There is an acknowledged shortage of the kind of powerful
teaching that we want to encourage, and it is difficult to match up student teachers
exclusively with practicing teachers in the field who are doing the kind of work we
find exemplary. This being the case, we know that the symbolic positions of university classroom and public school classroom are going to be speaking different subjects. The tensions that arise from this reality are worthwhile ones to be sure. The
psychoanalytic vocabulary offered here is an aid for those experiencing these tensions as another way – among several – of making sense of them. Instead of locating this particular problem in terms of 'theory' vs. 'practice,' as is frequently
expressed, we begin to think about what the different locations authorize in terms of
what kinds of vocabularies are on offer. If we do not address this issue in explicit
ways, we risk being spoken by what Lacan calls 'the master signifier' (the dominant
discourses) which would hold that what happens in the schoolroom is 'real' and that
what happens in the university teacher education classroom does not really count. It
is not the real Holocaust survivor.

It seemed that the participants already knew what to expect upon entering the
museum and then largely had their expectations confirmed. Any disconfirming evidence was tossed away as 'bad' knowledge. The Holocaust survivor should have
had a different story to tell. It was 'something,' remember, but it did not fit the signifier. Similarly, student teachers arrive in our classrooms not only with prior experience, but located in a symbolic position vis-à-vis those experiences that will
unwittingly shape their articulations of their time learning to teach. Where in the
museum participants were able to say that 'this is not a Holocaust survivor,' in a teacher education classroom we ought to understand that if we go outside of expectations then the immediate reaction might be to label the class, the readings, the
questions as 'bad' or 'something,' but definitely not the work that would help them
be 'real teachers.'

While at this point it might seem as though, we ought to assume a position of
defeat that would be a mistake. One might think about the workings of the symbolic
as a mechanism of inertia. It is not as though one cannot change the direction of a
moving object. One must understand, though, that such a change does not just happen without an understanding of that process. Here is where there are productive
and creative potentialities in the use of these psychoanalytic conceptions of the symbolic and of deferred knowledge. What this means in the context of teacher education is that one could imagine the disruption of the symbolic field being manifested
as frustration, excitement, anxiousness, or presentations of the difficulty to symbol-
ize what is felt by the subject. Those affective reactions indicate a pressure being

exacted upon the manner by which a subject can articulate their experiences. In the face of such experiences, we may ask: what other ways can you think of that people might react to this? What other reactions can we imagine having? What might these reactions indicate about our particular stances toward teaching and learning?

The symbolic can be, and often is, predetermining in our understanding the social world. However, once we understand that process, the effects of such an understanding can be rather liberating (Ruti, 2011) due to the ways in which it reveals choices where before there were simply taken for granted actions. The hope is that we might facilitate the recognition of old patterns of understanding and behavior, hold them up for scrutiny, and make decisions as to whether or not those old patterns are useful in the way we hope them to be. We can help students see the ways that they are activating particular versions of the past in order to highlight for them the ways that they retroactively make new meaning out of old events. The hope is that we might learn to make new mistakes and reduce our propensity to repeat the old ones.

Conclusions

The location of the past and its influence on the present are in constant motion. This conceptualization of the relationship between past and present has a significant impact on ways of thinking about pedagogy. The location of the past and the knowledge of that past provide the framework for this paper. The museum visit was not just about the museum. It was not only about the Holocaust. It was not only about a research project, or participants' families. It was also about the ways in which each of those fit into a larger fabric of meaning that make it more likely to make particular, though temporary meanings out some kinds of experience than others. Further, it is a way of knowing that is at once outside of conscious awareness and works 'in' the moments of experiences.

Not only does the individual past never rest in the plot on a time line, but the social past has peculiar location in pedagogy as well. The social past, or history, is on the very breath of the pedagogical utterance: racially coded, gendered, classed, sexualized, prohibiting ways of knowing and enabling others. The past does not rest quietly in the textbook. It is open to revision and repurposing. It does not always show up how and when we might it expect it to.

The symbolic field is the nexus point between individual and social, comprised of/in both. If we only think of the social as what occurs 'out there' or 'back then,' then we are not able to see the ways that the social past is, in a point of fact, lived in the present. We could think of 'history' in a similar way. Based upon any set of experiences, framed by a particular constellation of meaning and then interpreted within any given context, a student in a classroom is shaped by any number of these factors that comprise the symbolic field. Further, in light of an encounter that sufficiently displaces or offers new subjective positioning within that symbolic register, the knower will begin to 'know differently' that very same past which now structures a new understanding. That is the weight of deferred knowing. It may help us see the difficult encounters in spaces of teacher education in generative light.

If this is the case, then what kind of space is there for hope? If our actions and attitudes and expectations are all predetermined in relation to the social spaces we occupy, then what chance is there that any new ways of experiencing the world and orienting oneself will be developed or stumbled upon? It is right to worry about these processes. However, the symbolic field can be disrupted; deferred knowing is its evidence. Fortunately, for us, such a disruption of the symbolic field is part of a process of learning. And because learning fundamentally reorders the experience of the past through the process of deferral, perhaps a teacher's education can aid in producing such experiences where significant and directed reordering takes place.

References

Bibby, T. (2010). *Education – An impossible profession? Psychoanalytic explorations of learning and classrooms.* New York, NY: Routledge.

Britzman, D. P. (1998). *Lost subjects, contested objects: Toward a psychoanalytic inquiry of learning.* Albany, NY: SUNY Press.

Britzman, D. P. (2000). If the story cannot end: Deferred action, ambivalence, and difficult knowledge. In R. I. Simon, S. Rosenberg, & C. Eppert (Eds.), *Between hope and despair: The pedagogical encounter of historical remembrance* (pp. 27–58). Lanham, MD: Rowman & Littlefield.

Britzman, D. P. (2003a). *Practice makes practice: A critical study of learning to teach.* Albany: SUNY Press.

Britzman, D. P. (2003b). *After-education: Anna Freud, Melanie Klein, and psychoanalytic histories of learning.* New York, NY: SUNY Press.

Britzman, D. P. (2006). *Novel education: Psychoanalytic studies of learning and not learning.* New York, NY: Peter Lang.

Britzman, D. P. (2009). *The very thought of education: Psychoanalysis and the impossible professions.* Albany, NY: SUNY Press.

Clandenin, D. J. (1986). *Classroom practice: Teacher images in action.* London: Falmer Press.

den Heyer, K., & Conrad, D. (2011). Using Alain Badiou's ethic of truths to support and 'eventful' social justice teacher education program. *Journal of Curriculum Theorizing, 27,* 7–19.

Farley, L. (2009). Radical hope: Or, the problem of uncertainty in history education. *Curriculum Inquiry, 39,* 537– 554.

Felman, S. (1987). *Jacques Lacan and the adventures of insight: Psychoanalysis in contemporary culture.* Cambridge, MA: Harvard University Press.

Freud, S. (1896). Letter 52 (to W. Fleiss). In *Sigmund Freud: The origins of psychoanalysis.* New York, NY: Basic Books.

Garrett, H. J. (2010). *Difficult knowledge and social studies (teacher) education.* Ann Arbor: Proquest, LLC.

Garrett, H. J. (2011). The routing and rerouting of difficult knowledge: Social studies teachers encounter when the levees broke. *Theory and Research in Social Education, 39,* 320–347.

Garrett, H. J., & Segall, A. (2013). (Re)considerations of ignorance and resistance in teacher education. *Journal of Teacher Education, 64,* 294–304.

Korthagen, F. A. J. (2004). In search of the essence of a good teacher: Towards a more holistic approach in teacher education. *Teaching and Teacher Education, 20,* 77–97. doi:10.1016/j.tate.2003.10.002

Lacan, J. (1998). On feminine sexuality: The limits of love and knowledge 1972–1973. In B. Fink (trans.), J. A. Miller (Ed.), *Encore: The seminar of Jacques Lacan, book XX.* New York, NY: WW Norton.

Lacan, J. (2006). *Ecrits: The first complete edition in English.* New York, NY: Norton.

Laplanche, J., & Pontalis J. B. (1973). *The language of psychoanalysis.* London: Karnac.

Lortie, D. (1975). *Schoolteacher: A sociological study.* Chicago, IL: University of Chicago Press.

Matthews, S. (2007). Some notes on hate in teaching. *Psyhoanalysis, Culture & Society, 12*, 185–192. doi:10.1057/palgrave.pcs.2100125

Pinar, W. (2004). *What is curriculum theory?* Mahwah, NJ: Lawrence Erlbaum.

Pitt, A. J. (1998). Qualifying resistance: Some comments on methodological dilemmas. *International Journal of Qualitative Studies in Education, 11*, 535–553. doi:10.1080/095183998236449

Pitt, A. J., & Britzman, D. P. (2003). Speculations on qualities of difficult knowledge in teaching and learning: An experiment in psychoanalytic research. *International Journal of Qualitative Studies in Education, 16*, 755–776.

Ruti, M. (2011). Winnicott with Lacan: Living creatively in a postmodern world. *American Imago, 67*, 353–374.

Tarc, A. M. (2011). Disturbing reading: J.M. Coetzee's 'The problem of evil'. *Changing English, 18*, 57–66.

Taubman, P. M. (2006). I love them to death. In P. Salvio & G. M. Boldt (Eds.), *Love's return: Psychoanalytic essays on childhood, learning, and teaching* (pp. 19–32). New York, NY: Routledge.

Wilson, S. M., Rozelle, J. J., & Mikeska, J. N. (2011). Cacophony or embarrassment of riches: Building a system of support for quality teaching. *Journal of Teacher Education, 62*, 383–394.

Zizek, S. (1989). *The sublime object of ideology*. New York, NY: Verso.

Zizek, S. (2007). *In defense of lost causes*. New York, NY: Verso.

Interrupting the frame: reflective practice in the classroom and the consulting room

Julie Walsh

In this paper I consider some of the affinities between the teacher–student dynamic in academic supervision, and the therapist–patient dynamic in the therapeutic relation. Drawing on my own experiences, I identify several difficulties that pertain to these two settings. First, in the context of the classroom, I consider how the requirement to speak and the requirement to write call for different modes of engagement, and can provoke different types of anxiety. I explore the function of mediating texts as a way of engendering a critical distance from one's own speech acts. I then turn to Sigmund Freud's intriguing evocation of the quality of 'aloofness' as that which should colour the patient's engagement with the transference situation. I shall treat Freud's recommendation of aloofness as a mode of critical distance – and a type of impersonality – that can be put to work in the classroom as well as in the consulting room. Finally, I ask what happens when distance fails; when there seems to be no space for impersonal critique. One way of thinking about the failure of distance is through the lens of shame. Here I focus my thought on the contention that the scope for shaming is especially prominent in vocational settings that challenge and interrogate the subject's capacity to know.

Introduction

I am sitting opposite a young man of 19 years of age. It's just the two of us. We've not met before. Let's call him Matthew. We've been in the room together for over 10 minutes now and we've not got started. Matthew cannot meet my gaze. I offer another possibility of a beginning: Matthew shrugs his shoulders and blushes ferociously. By anyone's standards this is not going so well. 'This is difficult stuff' I suggest, 'but we can think it through together'. Matthew is quietly shaking. What on earth is going through his head, and what is my responsibility here? 'If only this was therapy', I think to myself, 'that would be easier'.

My encounter with Matthew took place in the classroom rather than the consulting room. It was one incident among many that made me consider the affinities between the teacher–student dynamic in academic supervision, and the therapist–patient dynamic in the therapeutic relation. The question I was asking myself in this instance – *what is going on for Matthew?* – highlights the rather obvious fact that it is not only the second party in these pairings (i.e. the student or patient) who can feel exposed for her ignorance, and get caught up in the frustrations that ensue. I have taken the Psychosocial Studies Network's conference 'Knowing and Not Knowing: Thinking Psychosocially About Learning and Resistance to Learning' as an opportunity to develop my reflections on this theme in relation to my work as an early career academic and as a psychotherapist in training. I am not concerned here to advance a particular theoretical framework for my thoughts, but rather to identify in broad terms some of the affinities that I have experienced between these two frames of activity. As an exercise in reflective practice, then, this paper comments on my understanding of the ways in which modes of knowing and not-knowing create the unstable grounds for any educative and/or therapeutic encounter. As my opening illustration perhaps already suggests, the challenge of bearing – and bearing witness to – a not-knowing can prove most difficult to tolerate. I am interested in thinking about how the different fields in which I work serve this particular difficulty: Can not-knowing in the classroom be thought about in terms other than deficit? How is the relationship between knowledge and authority differently configured for the teacher and the therapist? How might the desire for knowledge be a help or a hindrance in the educative or therapeutic project? As a teacher and a therapist how can the unknown impact of my speech be thought about? In what ways are the dynamics of distance and intimacy co-fashioned in the educative and/or therapeutic encounter?

Drawing on my own experiences I have identified below three areas that have emerged as common ground between the classroom and the consulting room. I shall consider how the requirement to speak and the requirement to write call for different modes of engagement, and can provoke different types of anxiety. The demand made of students to orally defend their own written work can generate an unproductive level of self-consciousness in which the student appears trapped by her own language. Comparable situations in therapy sessions have given me cause to think about the value of a critical distance from one's own linguistic productions, and techniques for engendering such a distance; I shall explore the function of 'mediating texts' as one such example. I shall then turn to Sigmund Freud's intriguing evocation of the quality of 'aloofness' as that which should colour the patient's engagement with the transference situation. I shall treat Freud's recommendation of aloofness as a mode of critical distance – and a type of impersonality – that can be put to work in the classroom as well as in the consulting room. Finally, and in recognition of my opening vignette, I ask what happens when distance fails; when there seems to be no space for impersonal critique. One way of thinking about the failure of distance is through the lens of shame. Shame comes to the fore when the subject feels herself to have been seen too closely, or to have been exposed as being somehow out-of-place. Here I focus my thought on the contention that the scope for shaming is especially prominent in vocational settings that challenge and interrogate the subject's capacity to know. Taking on board Slavoj Žižek's (2008) provocation that shame is the inevitable affective consequence of being asked a question, I ask how the shaming of the teacher's or therapist's questions might function positively.

Writing and speaking

Staying with Matthew, the student for whom sitting with me in academic supervision appeared to be unbearable, I would like to try to account for the failure of the encounter. In supervision, Matthew and I were due to be talking about his essay on the topic of Freud's theories of sexuality. It would be unreasonable to presume that this topic can be picked up by all students with ease: as a teacher when I speak of psychosexual desire (and introduce the concepts of penis envy, polymorphous perversity, infantile sexuality, the Oedipus complex and the incest taboo, for example), I am asking a lot for my students to speak back to me in the same language. Had we been discussing the status of psychoanalysis as a science, say, Matthew and I may have had a more comfortable supervision. But perhaps not; perhaps it was simply the injunction to speak rather than speaking about sexuality that proved difficult. I've found that students can often write eloquently about a given topic but not necessarily speak about it, and I do not think that this is at all unique to the psychoanalytic subject matter. There is something especially demanding, I would suggest, in asking a student to account for their written work after the event, which is precisely the logic of the supervision system where students and supervisors meet one-on-one and take the student's essay as the catalyst for discussion. The written and spoken word are only loosely related, and it is not always the case that competency in the former is indexed to confidence in the latter. Students demonstrate this frequently through their discomfort, anxiety and confusion at the task of *saying again in speech* what they feel they have already said on the page. But it is precisely in the gap that opens up between these two modes of representation that the lesson itself gets started. Practically, from the perspective of certain educative goals, this gap or disconnect might lead to the student becoming more attentive to the requirements of academic writing (focussing on the clarity of her written expression, and the structure of her argument, for example). However, just as importantly, by scrutinising the distance between her so-called 'authorial intent' and a reader's reception of it, the student may come to a more experiential appreciation of the frustrations of language that psychoanalysis – some traditions more so than others – makes central to its theorising. The student may reflect: 'I don't recognise my meaning in these words'; 'these words do not represent me'; 'I cannot be identical with the words I use to represent myself'; 'I cannot know how my reader will interpret my words which are already distant from me'.

The tension between the written and spoken word can be considered from another angle: if students can resist speaking about their own writing, then a sort of parallel can happen in therapy when a patient expresses the desire to communicate with the analyst via email or letter outside the session. As I read it, the desire to subvert, or outwit, the 'talking cure' in this way could be indicative of the fantasy that there may be a way of being more true to one-self – of representing oneself more fully – if only the conditions of self-narration would allow it. For some, the possibility of expressing oneself through the written word – where time can be taken to arrange and rearrange the order of one's words creating the impression of coherence, exactitude and purpose – is infinitely preferable to being constantly caught short by one's speech. I am reminded of patients who begin their therapy by articulating the wish that it could proceed without words (can there be another way, I ask myself). Perhaps, then, there is something shared between the student who involves herself in the act of deconstructing her own written work, and the patient who undertakes the work of psychotherapy, if only because what is played out in both instances is the experience of being subject to the failures and frustrations of language: whereas the student might say 'I know what I mean, but I can't explain it', or 'when I wrote that I think I meant something else', or 'yes, it's what you said, that's what I meant, but you said it better', the patient is more likely to remain silent.

Mediating texts

Accepting that individual students may find the prospect of speaking (rather than writing) anxiety-inducing, the educational setting has all sorts of 'props' to defend against too much exposure; the central prop being the text itself. With the text comes the introduction of a third element that can intervene in the dyadic relation. In the case of my supervision with Matthew, I was able to say: 'let's turn to the text', where the *subtext* was perhaps: 'let's avert our eyes from each other and find some neutral ground'. Because the student and I now have some autonomous material to address (which exists in a relatively impersonal relation to both of us), one would hope that working directly on the text would immediately reduce the type of anxiety that can be experienced. In the classroom, then, the possibility of a mediating text is always close at hand. There is a parallel observation to be made here with the work of psychotherapy. When a patient comes along with her own text-fragment (whether it be dream material, or a chain of associations that arise in the session) she too is bringing something into the frame that has the potential to act in a mediating capacity. The introduction of this third element in a session may function in all sorts of ways (only one of which could be to alleviate anxiety), but the conditions for *going to work on the text* are, it strikes me, especially precarious. Most critically, in order to explore the text-fragment the patient must already possess the capacity to hold herself at some distance from it.

I am reminded here of one of Freud's discussions of the analytic requirement to manage the patient's 'transference neurosis'. In the third section of *Beyond the Pleasure Principle*, Freud (1920) gives a brief history of the ways in which psychoanalytic technique evolved within the time of his own theorising. He tells us that initially psychoanalytic technique had been an 'art of interpretation' where what was crucial was the analyst's communication of unconscious material to the patient. However, such conscious – we might say 'educative' – communication failed to have therapeutic impact, and so greater attention had to be paid to the patient's *resistances* to his unconscious material. The provocation of the patient's resistances brings into the frame the transference phenomenon, where it is the patient's performative engagement with her resistances (rather than her conscious acknowledgement of them) that ensures the continuing mobilisation of the treatment. As Freud explains it:

> The patient cannot remember the whole of what is repressed in him, and what he cannot remember may be precisely the essential part of it. Thus he acquires no sense of conviction of the correctness of the construction that has been communicated to him. He is obliged to *repeat* the repressed material as a contemporary experience instead of, as the physician would prefer to see, *remembering* it as something belonging to the past ... The ratio between what is remembered and what is reproduced varies from case to case. The physician cannot as a rule spare his patient this phase of the treatment. He must get him to re-experience some portion of his forgotten life, but must see to it, on the other hand, that the patient retains some degree of aloofness, which will enable him, in spite of everything, to recognise that what appears to be reality is in fact only a reflection of a forgotten past. (Freud 1920, 18–19)

The most intriguing point that Freud raises in this passage, I would suggest, is the recommendation that the analyst cultivate the patient's 'aloofness' [*Überlegenheit*] in order that the peculiar power of the transference be seen for what it is (i.e. a repetition or 'reflection' of a past situation).[1] Rather than take aloofness in this context to mean a psychological disposition of superiority, which would surely be interpreted as another form of resistance to the material, I take Freud to be referring to the patient's capacity to distance herself from the transferential material. This is indeed a tall order: the patient is in the throws of the transference but is yet required to maintain sufficient distance (with the analyst's aid) to be able to appreciate the formal qualities of her emotional investments. Leaving to one side the taken-for-granted neutrality of the analyst, Freud's thought seems to be that a degree of distance on the patient's part is a prerequisite for any interpretative work to commence. Resuming my previous comparison, then, for the patient to be able to engage with her own text-fragment in such a way that allows the work of interpretation to be taken up, she must be both invested in the enactment, and able to appreciate its form. I am inclined to think that there is a sort of learning at stake in all of this; that sometimes part of the work is to invite simultaneous investment *and* detachment towards the 'text' in question; to encourage the subject (whether the subject of education and/ or therapy) to aspire to a degree of 'aloofness' with regard to her own material; to encourage her in her capacity as 'reader' of her own material where the very act of reading requires a standing to one side; and, in so doing, to explore the possibility of an *impersonal* relation to the self. I would suggest that in my supervision with Matthew we did not manage to achieve this type of impersonal investment in the material that facilitates critical reading. Importantly, it is this failing that opens the door to shame. However, there is a paradox to be anticipated here (and pursued further below): whilst I would acknowledge that the persistence of a destructive and immobile mode of shame may account for my negative supervision experience with Matthew, I shall also reserve the possibility that the very same shame-dynamics – those of proximity and distance; situatedness and dislocation – can work productively to mobilise the type of impersonality that I suggest is key to critical reflection, and that Freud suggested was necessary to the patient's handling of the transference.

What I have indicated so far is that the substantive topic in question – in this case psychoanalysis and sexuality – may be sufficiently difficult to create an awkward atmosphere in academic supervision, or to provoke a communicative impasse. Furthermore, there are innumerable factors relating to a particular student's psychobiography that are not for me to concern myself with too directly in the classroom. I remarked above that Matthew's apparent distress would have been easier for me to take on board had we been in a therapy context; but in supervision the force of his feelings were not the legitimate object of our discussion. The thought I would like to raise now is that these factors – the particular topic of discussion, and the student's idiosyncratic psychology – can be left to one side as we consider a more general difficulty that pertains to both the classroom and the consulting room.

Shame and the question form

In his *The Sublime Object of Ideology*, Slavoj Žižek ([1989] 2008) makes reference to a book by Aron Bodenheimer entitled *Why? On the Obscenity of Questioning* (*Warum?: Von der Obszönität des Fragens*; Bodenheimer [1984] 2011). Bodenheimer's thesis, Žižek explains, is that there is something obscene in the very act of asking a question, without regard to its content. It is the form of the question as such which is obscene: the question lays open, exposes, denudes its addressee, it invades his sphere of intimacy; this is why the basic, elementary reaction to a question is shame on the bodily level, blushing and lowering our eyes, like a child of whom we ask 'What were you doing?' (Žižek [1989] 2008, 202)

That a question can be felt as a violent imposition is evident in our every-day language practices, consider the following phrases: he was confronted by a barrage of questions; he was subject to an assault of questions; the interviewer saved his most penetrating question till last; he took a battering from the questioner. These mundane examples suggest that a question can insert itself with a force and an uninvited intimacy into the very core of the addressee. The question gets 'inside', so to speak; it insists on being received and hence provokes 'shame on the bodily level'. It is not quite that the question demands an actual *response* (although, as I mentioned above, the injunction to speak can no doubt be a cause of anxiety in itself), it is rather that the question demands a *reception*. The question does its obscene work in advance of – and irrespective of – the answer it elicits.

Žižek ([1989] 2008) holds that the act of 'questioning is the basic proce-dure for the totalitarian intersubjective relationship' (202) because the end goal is not the right answer, or in fact any answer, but rather 'a point at which the answer is not possible, where the word is lacking, where the sub-ject is exposed in his impotence' (202). Hence 'totalitarian power is not a dogmatism which has all the answers; it is, on the contrary, the instance which has all the questions' (203). Clearly, Žižek's treatment of Bodenhei-mer's thesis on the obscenity of the question works in the service of his broader theoretical project. For the purposes of this paper, however, it is necessary only to engage with the claim that the question form is indecent because it seeks to reveal in the addressee a state of impotence and not-knowing. Can it really be the case, we might well ask, that all questions function in this way?

Indeed, the suggestion that the question operates in the service of obscenity and exposure may sit uneasily with those of us who rely on the practice of questioning (alongside listening and other practices of reflection) to perform our vocational identities. Therapists just as much as teachers (or social scientists for that matter) develop expertise in selecting the types of questions they use to engage their addressee. In doing so, no doubt, we also exercise caution with respect to those questions that might be received as destructive impingements on the subject; but Žižek's provocation here is that all questions are indecent so 'caution' is not quite the point. As a teacher and a therapist I have observed my own caution in this regard and retrospectively attributed it to something like care, or concern. But I am reminded of Philip Rieff's (1965, 158) helpful aphorism that 'care is the polite form of desire', and, accordingly, suggest that the question that is withheld in the name of concern or educative/therapeutic wisdom may also function to conceal the desire of the questioner. In which case the shame that inheres in the question form is immediately polyvalent: it is not simply that my question exposes you, for I too am exposed in the asking of it. And, to reiterate, we cannot escape this predicament simply by *taking care* because in crafting my question so as not to expose you, not only do I risk exposing myself (perhaps as someone with an inflated valuation of her own words), but I also risk putting shame into play with the inference that you could be made vulnerable by my less-than-carefully-worded question. The philosopher Alenka Zupančič highlights this possibility when she supplements Bodenheimer's argument by stressing that the obscenity of the question 'does not operate only on the level of exposing the other (the addressee of the question), but also on the level of exposing oneself' (Zupančič 2007, 162–3). However, if all this implies that shame is unavoidable in contexts where questions are asked, it also underscores just how unstable are our economies of knowledge and desire. Shame signals this instability; it communicates and compounds the subject's feelings of being 'caught out', or being seen too intimately by – and with – another. Zupančič glosses this point thus:

> Bodenheimer's definition of obscenity is that it takes place in the conditions where certain parts of my personality – parts that I normally hide from the others or from myself – are revealed directly and without me being prepared for it. I am being exposed without being able to prevent this. In the situation of obscenity, there is an act of exposure on the one side, and the effect of shame on the other. (Zupančič 2007 162)

With the rush of shame, that which would normally remain hidden or even unknown is, if only for a moment, revealed and made explicit. If we can envisage a productive potential in shame's two-way dynamic, it may be as a mechanism for thinking about how the precariousness of one's identity is always implicated in its relations with others.

In their recent work on shame and sexuality, Pajaczkowska and Ward propose that:

> ...shame, the most painfully isolating of emotions, announces the presence of another, the person who shames us and the person before whom we are shamed, and as such it is one of the earliest social feelings ... Shame exists in this double register of self-consciousness-with-others. (Pajaczkowska and Ward 2008, 1)

Because the presence of another is already at work in the moment of shame, isolation cannot be thought about in wholly oppositional terms to sociality. Shame's double register, in other words, implicates both isolation and sociality in the same instance. A further reason for shame's productivity, then, may be that it encourages us to consider the constant and volatile movement between isolation and sociality, including the shameful moments of their collapse into each other.

It is necessary to clarify that the social other does not need to be standing as a physical witness to the scene of shame; just as we can be caught out by our own questions, so too can we feel shame when there is nobody there to see us. Moreover, shame's double register calls into question the very idea of clearly marked boundaries between self and other. We might say that shame is all about boundary disputes: we feel shame when we fall short of ourselves, or when we overstep ourselves, or when another gets too close, or when another remains too distant to recognise us as we want to be seen. Shame keeps the antagonisms of isolation and sociality, distance and proximity, and situatedness and dislocation in conversation (the phenomenon of vicarious or contagious shame indicates just how mobile shame can be). Common to all shame scenarios, though, is the fact that the space of the self that the subject seeks to preserve is in some way trespassed. If we follow Žižek's account then this is felt as a breach or a rupture – i.e. the subject is 'laid open', 'exposed', 'denuded' and 'invaded' – but it is by no means established that this violation is entirely negative (or even unpleasurable). Presumably when the subject is laid open, the prospect of a different freedom comes into play; one where the contours of the subject's very subjectivity may be reimagined. Likewise, if we take the dislocation or 'out-of-placeness' that so often marks the shamed subject we can anticipate certain pleasures in being temporarily estranged (or released) from the resources and convictions that hold a particular self-conception in place. A further way in which shame is productive, then, is in its challenge to the idea that we can be secure in our sense of proprietorship; that we can declare the boundaries of our self-identity to be fixed and stable; and that we can know just what belongs where, or as the over-defended therapist might wish to assert 'that's your stuff, not my stuff'. To put it somewhat differently, we could say that the shameful act of trespass invites us to reconsider our property rights.

Conclusion

We can return now, by way of a conclusion, to my supervision with Matthew. Although I cannot know with certainty that our experiences of the hour we spent together were commensurate, I reflected afterwards on the ways in which a two-way mode of shame may have been created in our supervision. As I intimated above, the shame of shame rebounds: perhaps Matthew read my concern for him as condescension, which presumably would have compounded his self-consciousness; and from my perspective, the possibility that I was even formally responsible for what I took to be a profound discomfort on Matthew's part no doubt heightened my own sense of shame. But critically, in the supervision hour at least, the shame that was operative between us did not get put to good work. Faced with Matthew's silence, I used more language; I explicated the texts we were supposed to be discussing and I asked more questions. In therapy no doubt I would have let the silence stand, uninterrupted. Irrespective of how speculative or tactful my questions were, if we follow the thesis put forward by Bodenheimer and developed by Žižek and Zupančič, then they always had the potential to be received by my addressee as obscene impositions. With their rude proximity, questions threaten the subject's capacity to maintain the type of distance – or aloof impersonality – that is of value both to a learning encounter and to the work of therapy. Distance is diminished at the moment when the question impinges on the subject's space of self. And with this act of trespass, the question infers the possibility that there is another who knows the boundaries of the addressee better than she does; perhaps also, that there is another who is closer to her desire than she is. This inference wounds the ego and risks a defensive withdrawal. But, in principle at least, the breach of the ego is also a release. After all, if, momentarily, the subject has been caught out and feels less than herself, then she is also provoked into reimaging the familiar boundaries of her ego because, unexpectedly, there is another on the scene to account for (i.e. shame is always a 'self-consciousness-with-others'). Moreover, when a question penetrates, and the subject sees the other at a more intimate proximity, the shame she feels ceases to belong exclusively to her because the other who has transgressed on to the place of her desires is, by virtue of this act, obliged to share it with her.

We can think again of Freud's recognition of the importance of managing the transference. In the transference the 'correct' allocation of boundaries between self and other – and between multiple and past selves and others – is a necessary impossibility. For the transference to be set in motion, subject positions have to be, temporarily at least, 'laid open'. The therapeutic relationship is one in which a degree of trespassing on to the grounds of the other is central to the work. What is also central is a degree of not-knowing; if the transference is almost unbearable for the patient, as Freud seems to recognise, then it is because a secure knowledge of who (and what) the other is is unattainable. Such unattainability is, of course, enhanced by the therapist's conscious cultivation of transferred – or displaced – material, but it is also symptomatic of social relations beyond the consulting room. If there is a shame in this, there is also a pleasure. When Freud advises that the therapist cultivate in the patient a quality of 'aloofness' in order that the patient can 'recognise that what appears to be reality is in fact only a reflection of a forgotten past…', he points us to a paradox; the quality of distanced appreciation – or aloof impersonality – emerges from the intimate pains of transference love.

Note

1. I explore further the signification of 'aloof' in this passage in an article co-authored with Barry Sheils entitled 'Tragedy and transference in D.M. Thomas's *The White Hotel*' (Sheils and Walsh 2013).

References

Bodenheimer, A. R. 2011 [1984]. *Warum?: Von Der Obszönität Des Fragens.* Reclam: Ditzingen.

Freud, S. 1920. "Beyond the Pleasure Principle." In *The Standard Edition of the Complete Psychological Works of Sigmund Freud.* vol. 18, edited by J. Strachey and A. Freud, 1–64. London: Hogarth Press and Institute for Psychoanalysis.

Pajaczkowska, C., and I. Ward. 2008. *Shame and Sexuality: Psychoanalysis and Visual Culture.* London: Routledge.

Rieff, P. 1965. *Freud: The Mind of the Moralist.* London: University Paperbacks (Methuen).

Sheils, B., and J. Walsh. 2013. "Tragedy and Transference in D. M. Thomas's the White Hotel." *Psychoanalysis and History* 15 (1): 69–89.

Žižek, S. 2008 [1989]. *The Sublime Object of Ideology.* London: Verso.

Zupančič, A. 2007. "Lying on the Couch: Psychoanalysis and the Question of the Lie." In *Cultures of Lying: Theories and Practice of Lying in Society. Literature, and Film*, edited by Mecke, J., 155–168. Berlin, Galda & Wilch Verlag.

The significance of 'participation' as an educational ideal in education for sustainable development and health education in schools

Jonas Andreasen Lysgaard and Venka Simovska

This article examines the significance of the concept of participation for teacher meaning-making processes in education for sustainable development and health education. In Scandinavian public schools, education for sustainable development and health education focus on a wide palette of societal problems rather than on narrow curricula. Drawing on selected reviews of research literature on education for sustainable development and health education, Lacanian psycho-analysis provides inspiration for our analysis of the concept of participation, and how it is positioned and enacted in these fields of practice. Essentially, we argue that the concept of participation has a dual nature: it serves both as an educational ideal and as a teaching strategy. We also explore how the failure to achieve the ideal of 'true' participation may serve a positive purpose for the teacher; the acknowledgement that participation is not always as genuine as desired establishes a pedagogical situation where ideals of engaging pupils through true participation can continue to exist side by side with clear signs of a less consequential participation.

Introduction

Education is expected to play an important part in preparing present and future generations for the task of addressing environmental and health issues. Much effort has been put into educational practices related to sustaining democratic development; battling illness, climate change and global warming; and emphasising the importance of building inclusive, just and sustainable societies (Klafki 1997; Firth and Smith 2013; UNESCO 2013). This article discusses the notion of participation and its significance for teachers working with education for sustainable development (ESD) and health education (HE) in public primary and lower secondary schools (pupils aged 6–16).

A reoccurring theme within both fields concerns an educational deficit: something is lacking that requires education to help contribute to the making of a better world. Whether there is a need for more democracy, pupils with greater action competence, a larger dose of transformative learning, or more emphasis on participation, debates within education and educational research regularly highlight the absence of what are considered key dimensions (Jensen and Schnack 2006; Læssøe and Öhman 2010; Pavlova 2013). While we support the idea of developing a better understanding of what is *needed*, in this article we focus on the potential *excess* that a concept such as participation is imbued with.

Our aim is to add a new perspective to an already much debated concept by applying a different theoretical framework. When we talk of the concept of participation, we understand it both as a pedagogical practice and as an educational ideal. For the purposes of this paper, our analysis focuses on the concept of participation as found in the research literature linked to ESD and HE in schools, and on exploring the *significance* of these research perspectives and insights. By drawing, on the one hand, on selected literature reviews within ESD and HE, and, on the other, on Lacanian psychoanalytical theories, we suggest a particular perspective on the concept of participation, raising the questions: What is the significance of the ideal of participation within school-based ESD and HE? What role does the ideal of participation play in meaning-making processes for the individual teacher? Is it possible to understand the excess of the concept of participation?

Our argument is primarily a theoretical venture, intended to revisit and add nuance to the understanding of participation as one of the core concepts of ESD and HE in schools. Our point of departure, with reference to continental, critical educational theory (e.g. Klafki 1997; Jensen, Schnack, and Simovska 2000; Schnack 2008), is the understanding that sustainability and health are among the key topics that schools need to address if they are to respond to societal challenges and foster children's competences to deal with these challenges. Further, our assumption is that pedagogical practices related to ESD and HE often share common concerns and values related to social justice, health of the individual, the society and the planet, as well as a focus on participatory and democratic pedagogical approaches. What is crucial then, is understanding and acknowledging the importance of the conditions under which participation is possible in schools and in society, and what these conditions mean for learning.

Although participation is a concept in education that extends beyond the fields of ESD and HE to also include citizenship education, value studies, conflict resolution and so forth, in this article we specifically put the spotlight on ESD and HE. Sustainability and health are understood as concepts that relate to both individual behaviour and the conditions for life involving individual, socio-cultural and societal factors (Reid et al. 2008; Green and Tones 2010; Bonnett 2013; Levy and Zint 2013; Scott 2013; Simovska 2013; Simovska and McNamara 2015). Both concepts belong to discourses characterised by insecure and ever-changing knowledge about the individual, society and the environment, which, from an educational perspective, requires exploration of specific teaching and learning approaches and meaning-making processes.

In fact, from a critical education perspective, the content and the action-oriented understanding of the challenges associated with the promotion of sustainability and health are intimately linked to questions of relevant teaching strategies. In other words, sustainability, health and social justice are regarded as not only concepts which pupils must learn about, but also something that pupils need to experience through the process of education (Klafki 1997; Schnack 2000, 2008). The nature of this experience can be considered as the shared foundation of both practice fields, ESD and HE. They connect in their efforts to develop curriculum approaches that not only emphasise the importance of the complexity of the topic to hand, but also through participatory forms of pedagogic practice.

Framing

In what follows, we discuss a distinct perspective on the concept of participation within ESD and HE in schools, and the significance which the use of this concept can have on two levels: as an educational ideal permeating the fields of ESD and HE, and as a pedagogical strategy offering specific teaching and learning methodologies. We theorise the importance of continuing to apply the concept of participation, and the significance of the concept for teachers by drawing on Lacanian psychoanalysis; a theoretical approach usually seen as an 'outsider' to established ESD and HE research. We start by asking the question: How can the concept of participation be understood as part of the meaning-making processes of the individual teacher involved in ESD and HE? As a first step towards its answering, we consider current perspectives on the concept of participation as found in select literature reviews. The particular reviews were selected as they represent recent systematic attempts to map the different ways in which the concept of participation has been employed within ESD and HE in schools. (It should be noted that the reviews are not employed as an exhaustive representation of research on participation, but rather as highlights of conceptual understandings and empirically grounded discussions of participation in ESD and HE in schools.)

Based on the reviews, we then explore the significance of the concept for the individual teacher from a Lacanian psychoanalytical perspective (Lacan 2004), including the emerging body of neo-Lacanian theories drawing on his work, primarily from Slavoj Žižek and Renata Salecl (Porsgaard 2013). As will be shown, this particular theoretical perspective represents a deviation from those typically employed within ESD and HE and which generally dominate discussions of participation within these fields. Moreover, the Lacanian perspective offers an alternative approach to participation, with the goal of understanding what the individual teacher has to gain from utilising an arguably contested concept such as participation. Strands of psychoanalysis are not the most obvious, convenient, or even 'correct' body of social theory to draw upon, but we do so in an attempt to be inspired by a perspective which, in recent years, has provided a surge of promising and interesting work, but which is usually excluded from ESD and HE (Cooley 2009; Bjerre 2011). Our particular focus in this regard is on how individuals create meaning through the social, rather than a clinical-psychoanalytical approach that seeks to understand the individual unconsciousness and provide a psychodynamic profile of any given teacher. Thus, by applying concepts linked to a distinct strand of psychoanalysis, we attempt to theorise how teachers, as individuals, make sense of the social aspects of participation within ESD and HE.

We continue the paper with a discussion of current perspectives on the concept of participation within ESD and HE, as well as the educational values and ideals related to these conceptualisations. We then outline the key features and arguments of selected recent literature focusing on the use and effectiveness of participation within ESD and HE in schools. Inspired by a Lacanian perspective, we specifically emphasise notions of interpassivity, false activity and pseudo activity as analytical categories. We conclude by arguing that participation as an educational ideal, as well as a pedagogical approach, also needs to be considered and understood from the perspective of the individual teacher's meaning-making, particularly if it is to continue to play a vibrant role in the development of ESD and HE in schools.

The notion of participation as an ideal in ESD and HE

From a Lacanian perspective, an ideal can be understood as a social mechanism which individuals apply in order to install some kind of order and structure into a potentially chaotic situation. The notion of participation, when linked to educational practices, can then be seen as something that adds positive value to processes of learning, and might also offer a structure for educational activities.

In brief, the concept of participation within research and practice of ESD and HE in schools has its roots in the late 1970s when it emerged and quickly became a much discussed and applied principle. This was only strengthened by the adoption of the UN Convention on the Rights of the Child in 1989, and the entailing focus on the issue of children's participation in society and education, including environmental and health education (Rahnema 1992; Hart 1997; Reid et al. 2008; Læssøe 2010; Levy and Zint 2013). As a result, a broad palette of research, educational development initiatives, and publications exploring the concept of participation and its potential to affect the lives of children, as well as their families and wider communities (Simovska 2008).

The term 'participation' has been associated with a number of related words, such as 'taking part', 'involvement', 'consultation' and 'empowerment' (e.g. Simovska 2000, 2007). Taking the dictionary definition (e.g. Merriam-Webster 2014) as a starting point, it is possible to differentiate between two primary modes of meaning-making for the term:

- Participation in the sense of 'taking part in', i.e. 'being present'.
- Participation in the sense of 'having a part or share in something', which can be related to concepts such as 'empowerment' and 'ownership' and refers to one's sense of being taken seriously and being able to make an impact.

Within schools, the term is often directly linked to different understandings of interactivity as an important strategy to improve pupils' motivation for engagement in school and/or community actions in different areas (Simovska 2007, 2012). This is not to be confused with participation rates, i.e. enrolments and attendance, as promoted by the UN Decade of Education for Sustainable Development, or the discourse of the Millennium Development Goals. Participation can also be understood more in terms of the 'voice of youth', grounded in discussions concerning the importance of *listening* to young people. However, both interactivity- and voice-type meanings have been critiqued as positioning participation as *symbolic*, such as when involving children in predesigned activities without necessarily emphasising their influence on these activities. Others have stressed the fundamental importance of participation to notions of citizenship, suggesting *sharing power* in making decisions relating to children's lives (e.g. Hart 2008), but also learning and gaining important competences while participating (e.g. Reid et al. 2008).

As an educational ideal, the concept of participation has been primarily linked to three different understandings of the benefits of engaging with educational activities (Simovska and Jensen 2009):

(1) Participation as a child's right to express their views, to be listened to and to be taken seriously. This argument hinges on the relationship between schools (and other formal and non-formal child settings) and communities creating

space for democratic learning processes which are inclusive in meaningful ways (Hart 1997, 2008).

(2) Participation as beneficial to a child's social and psychological development and thus contributing to better educational outcomes. Among the important potential personal development outcomes of participation, children's empowerment and action competence have been discussed (Schnack 2000, 2008; Carlsson and Simovska 2012).

(3) High hopes are also invested in participation as beneficial to society as a whole, as it potentially strengthens democratic processes and notions of sustainability and health (Simovska 2012). However, it has also been emphasised that while participatory activities do harbour the potential for furthering democratic development, there is an unavoidable tension between democratic processes and environmental/sustainable concerns (e.g. Van Poeck and Vandenabeele 2012).

As such, debates about ESD and HE are ripe with discussions of the importance and the potential of participation as an ideal. Equally, it could also be argued that the notion of participation has been under debate for so long, it risks being reduced to empty rhetoric or even counteracting the intentions behind the concept (Rahnema 1992; Van Poeck and Vandenabeele 2012). Nevertheless, this paper contends that consequential participation, which implies (the ideal of) school children influencing decision-making processes in matters that concern them, constitutes an important dimension of teaching and learning about sustainability and health in schools, and is still a relatively under-researched perspective (Reid et al. 2008; Simovska 2008).

Finally, from a psychoanalytical perspective, the value of participation can be linked with the assumption that the concept functions as a meaning-making tool for the individual subjects (e.g. teachers, pupils, researchers). Before elaborating on this point, in what follows we first look at the ways in which the four selected literature reviews engage with the notion of participation as an educational ideal, and how this ideal is translated into practice.

Researching participation in ESD and HE

In general, it can be argued that the researchers within both ESD and HE have focused either on indicators of participation or on the participatory process itself by analysing its purpose, level, scope, and children's capacity to participate (e.g. Chawla and Heft 2001; Cook, Blanchet-Cohen, and Hart 2004; Simovska 2007, 2012; Reid et al. 2008; Quick and Feldman 2011; de Róiste et al. 2012). We draw particular inspiration from four recent reviews of literature on the participation of children and young people, with a rare emphasis on ESD and/or HE. The reviews have been selected as these are the most recent reviews within the fields, and draw on a wide scope of research literature, with a strong emphasis on understanding and researching the value of participation. Our assumption is that these publications offer a vital window into contemporary perspectives on participation in ESD and HE. Moreover, systematic, high quality reviews in this field are scarce, especially those which value a broad concept of evidence and also include both qualitative studies and theoretically oriented papers.

The four reviews all deal with children's involvement in making decisions in school concerning matters that affect them, and their competences to do so. One of the reviews deals explicitly with notions of participation linked to environmental education and ESD (Levy and Zint 2013), two deal with participation within HE (Griebler et al. 2012; Marent, Forster, and Nowak 2012), while the fourth focuses on children's competences to engage in participatory activities that relate to both ESD and HE (Ljungdahl 2012).

The review conducted by Levy and Zint (2013) focuses on the role of environmental political participation, and offers a fairly critical perspective on the potential of such processes. The authors argue that much of the literature related to environmental education and ESD has very little to offer in terms of furthering pupils' engagement and participation in political activities linked to environmental and sustainability issues. Their review discloses that actual participation in activities of a more political character, inside and outside school, has not been the focus of educational research concerning participation and ESD. Levy and Zint argue that great strides could be made by looking at neighbouring fields of research that draw upon sociology and political science in studying social and political participation. They also claim that the concept of participation could otherwise end up having very little actual impact on the competences of the pupils and even less on society at large.

A more positive perspective is offered by Griebler et al. (2012) and Marent, Forster and Nowak (2012). Both reviews interpret pupil participation as exercising some degree of influence. The two reviews draw similar conclusions: that involving pupils in decision-making processes has a positive impact on their personal and social development, and potentially also on their health and wellbeing. Positive effects are also identified in both reviews with regard to relationships between pupils and adults in the school, and on the school as an organisation, particularly in terms of its psychosocial environment and general atmosphere. Alongside these promising positive effects, negative effects are also identified; for example, pupils feeling disillusioned, not being taken seriously, or not having as real an influence as expected. Marent, Forster and Nowak (2012) conclude on the basis of the various perspectives on participation they identify, that the common denominator is the attempt to provide an in-depth understanding of the complexity of participation, significantly more profound than that offered by an approach centred solely on the use of models and methods. This understanding focuses on participation within the social contexts in which it takes place, and in relation to different connected dimensions such as identity, knowledge, and power, as well as internal differentiation of organisations and movements, including schools, ESD and HE. The application of social theory can, as claimed in different papers included in the review, be beneficial: making explicit or overcoming the normative and ideological framing of participation, deconstructing the reproduction of power relations within knowledge and practice of participatory processes, and generating spaces for joint actions and mutual accountability.

The fourth review (Ljungdahl 2012) focuses on the contested relationships between children's participation and competence development in a range of practice fields, including, but not limited to, ESD, HE, and schools. The question asked in the review is how concepts of children's and young people's participation, competences and competence development are conceptualised, operationalised, and methodologically implemented and assessed in research papers documenting different institutional and non-institutional practices. The review identifies interesting tendencies in the conceptualisation of participation and its relation to competence development. One tendency is to approach participation through children's lack of ability to participate in social practices; that is, participation is viewed from a perspective of deficit correction. Another tendency is reflected in research that regards participation as a method for developing skills. In this literature, participation is conceptualised as taking part, without implying influence or engagement; a one-way causal relationship is assumed between participation and competence development. The third tendency reported, and which comes closest to the understanding of participation in the previous three reviews, and that endorsed in this article, is a perspective including a reciprocal relationship between participation and competence development. This perspective takes a more nuanced approach to the notions of both competence and participation, including contextual, relational and socio-historical dimensions and their dialectic relationships.

Together, the four reviews emphasise that, despite its contested nature, the concept of participation occupies a strong position when discussing issues such as school-based ESD and HE. The reviews also indicate that the concept remains as slippery as ever. Evidently, considerable efforts have been made to qualify different approaches to participation in school practices related to sustainability and health. Alas, the tension between the lure of pseudo-participation and the hardships of consequential participation persists (Hart 1997, 2008; Simovska 2007, 2008). As pointed out by Levy and Zint (2013), it remains very difficult to pinpoint the actual impact of utilising participatory educational practices. Does participation lead to greater involvement in society and in efforts to improve the pupils' own and others' lives in the direction of the educational ideals invested in ESD and HE? Or does the concept of participation get caught up in a focus on methodological strategies that can be used to strengthen narrowly defined teaching practices, while losing sight of the wider purpose of education?

We argue that this tension characterises the role of participation as both an educational ideal and an educational method. In the following, a distinct Lacanian perspective is applied in order to try to understand why practitioners (and researchers) invest so much energy in the concept of participation, even though the ideal of genuine participation seems very hard to achieve and the real impact of using participatory methods in ESD and HE in schools is difficult, if not impossible, to measure. In other words, how can a Lacanian perspective help in unpacking the ways in which the notion of participation adds to the meaning-making processes of those engaging with participatory work within ESD and HE?

The importance of perceptions: a Lacanian take on the perceived

It can be argued that a theme common to the various approaches to participation dwells in the notion that participation is conducive to learning by linking the individual with the importance of acting through the social (Rahnema 1992; Simovska 2008; Læssøe 2010). We, however, adhere to the view that the line between the individual and the social is blurred and that the individual subject's learning is shaped through the social. It is within this social embeddedness that we propose a Lacanian perspective (Lacan 2004), emphasising the importance of the individual subject's (i.e. teacher's) perception of participation as an educational ideal. Discussing how teachers perceive their actions related to engaging pupils in ESD and HE within a framework of Lacanian psychoanalysis stresses the significance of how they create meaning where none might be, and strive to establish a perceived level of rationality as a basis for actions.

The choice of a Lacanian perspective points to the establishment of a link between the subject and language. Our argument is founded on Lacan's argument that: 'the unconscious is structured like a language' (Lacan 2004, 48). In Lacan and Freud's perspective this entails that the unconscious shows through speech. This counters the notion of the unconscious as the domain of irrational drives; something that opposes, and needs to be reeled in by, a rational self. This makes the unconsciousness a site where traumatic truth speaks out. The point is thus not to show an individual the way to accommodate demands of social reality; instead the approach tries to understand how something like 'reality' constitutes itself in the first place. The goal of using Lacanian theory to discuss the concept of participation in ESD and HE is therefore not to disclose some kind of underlying logic that regulates the pedagogical practices of the teachers, but to understand how the notion of participation can be understood as a way of creating meaning, and what the significance of such a meaning-making process might be in teaching.

Building on Lacan, we also contend that our most basic human desire is to be recognised by others. As Kojéve argues:

> Desire is human only if the one desires, not the body, but the Desire of the other ... that is to say, if he wants to be 'desired' or 'loved', or, rather, 'recognized' in his human value ... in other words, all human, anthropogenetic Desire ... is, finally, a function of the desire for 'recognition'. (Kojéve 1969, 6–7)

Put another way, one desires the desire of others, or, paraphrasing Elvis Costello, we all just want to be loved, but, tragically, we do not have access to this other. We can only be ourselves and therefore constantly try to guess what is expected of us and what we could do in order to attain the desire, or recognition, of the other.

Such a Lacanian perspective can have far-reaching implications, but, in our view, the most important aspect is that desire is a social phenomenon. Social processes shape and affect the subject and the desire of the subject. The social is the centre that everything revolves around. Focusing on language and desire is thus focusing on these concepts as something that is created in the social and forms the platform from which the subject is able to partake in the world. This requires a theory that analyses and reflects the processes of subjectification (Laustsen 1999; Biesta 2006), and which emphasises the importance of the social and how the unconscious is structured via the social. It also entails that it remains impossible to gain full knowledge of what goes on in the unconscious and even in the conscious. There is always something which cannot be articulated, which escapes the construction of meaning and returns to the idea of the irreducibility of the unconscious, i.e. the idea that the unconscious is not that which is not known, but that which cannot be known. There is, in other words, always 'a lack' which cannot be fulfilled. This lack is what forces the subject into new, ultimately unsuccessful efforts to identify itself through new paths of consumption, action or opinion. The notion of an ever-present unconscious lack can be understood as a strong motivator for the individual to engage in new activities, and a backdrop for making sense of activities. The perception of one's own opinions, work and desires is thus not a complete mapping of one's innermost beliefs, but a mirroring of what we perceive as the desires of others and what we think they desire of us. In short, our perceptions are driven by an aim to be recognised, seen and, ultimately, loved.

Following this line of thought in discussing the concept of participation in ESD and HE in schools, it can be argued that the teacher is trying to navigate the social based on perceptions of the other's desire, to which the individual subject has no access. The teacher's perceptions are created through and grounded in the social. The emphasis is on how the individual teachers relate to the social and how they construct meaning in the midst of the incoherent, messy field that the social (i.e. ESD and HE in schools) represents. 'Truths' are only perceptions of what the subject believes the other sees as a truth. Messy indeed!

However, this does not mean that anything goes, which leads us to the next claim by Lacan and the next step in our argument.

The lack of an objective underlying truth led Lacan to state that 'les non-dupes errent' (Lacan 1974), which translates as 'those not fooled are mistaken'. Those who are not fooled are indeed the greatest fools. If one takes a step back in order to view 'reality' then one is in very much still stuck in the social with little hope of achieving knowledge transcending the social. Precisely because of the irreducibility of the unconscious and the persistent lack, it is necessary to accept that there is no way of presenting the 'bare facts', but that we will always remain in some sense or other, 'fooled' by social structures, others and ourselves, always carrying a set of pre-existing values and ideas, and having no chance of escaping the social, cultural and historical planes of meaning-making.

Thus the teachers' use of the notion of participation can be understood as part of the effort to structure their social reality in order to install a level of meaning into highly differentiated and elusive educational practices, expected outcomes and ideals about, for example, good health and sustainable development. Through utilising a concept such as pupil participation, the teacher seeks recognition for doing the right thing.

The following discussion, inspired by the research reviews and other literature outlined above, focuses on the possible understanding of the perceptions on participation as indicators of ideals and practices that attempt to cover up an existential lack: a lack that teachers, as individuals, carry in order to create meaning in a tumultuous world of education that aims to address complex societal challenges.

The importance of participation as an ideal

The reviews voice a range of important perspectives on the significance of participation and the reasons for employing the concept within ESD and HE. Two of the reviews emphasise that participation, as dealt with in the research literature, does not only offer distinct advantages when it comes to the effectiveness of educational processes (e.g. Griebler et al. 2012), but reaffirms itself as an educational ideal (e.g. Marent, Forster, and Nowak 2012). In this instance, inspired by critical educational theory, the notion of participation is argued to transcend its positioning primarily as a teaching method and can be viewed as a pervading value in society when promoting notions of a healthy, just and sustainable society (Baillie, Bassett-Smith, and Broughton 2000; Simovska and Jensen 2009). However, while the understanding of participation as an educational ideal is expressed in different ways in the reviews and in the related research literature outlined above, they all include a societal perspective on the *Good* that is inherent to ESD and HE. Returning to the critical potential of applying a Lacanian perspective, one finds that, through Lacan, Žižek can be seen as a stalwart critic of the idealism that the concept of participation seems to be associated with.

Žižek focuses his critique on two different understandings of idealism. Firstly, he criticises the focus on thought and reflexivity as *ideas*, following his interpretation of Marx's critique of the German philosophical idealism of the eighteenth century, as prioritising contemplation ahead of the material struggle against oppression. Secondly, Žižek criticises an idealism harbouring a potential for an *idealising* movement, as an expression of something complete, perfect and good. Both these critiques are centred on the risk that ideals function as pacifiers that instead of seeding emancipatory action, lead to maintenance of the status quo or worse (Žižek 2008, 104).

While the notions of ESD and HE that we draw upon here largely escape Žižek's first level of critique, through their insistence on outreach activities and attention to social injustice and action for change, the second level of critique would appear to hit home in several ways. Two of the selected reviews (Levy and Zint 2013; Marent, Forster, and Nowak 2012) describe how applying the notion of participation to schools can be understood as expressing a desire to move society towards a more idealised position. Similarly, with both ESD and HE, certain perspectives that link participation to pupils' action competence or ability for critical reflection and to initiate change to improve the conditions for sustainability or health (Jensen 1997; Schnack 2008; Carlsson and Simovska 2012) can be seen as representing a move towards the ideals of sustainable development and health equity, respectively. Within ESD in particular, the core concept of sustainability can be seen as describing an ideal (or utopian?) position where the needs of the human race are met, on a local and global scale, without unduly compromising nature and the environment.

In this respect, participation has rightly been criticised for serving many interests in school settings. Drawing inspiration from Hart (1997, 2008), Simovska's work on the continuum between token and genuine participation illustrates how participation can function as icing on an otherwise unappetising cake when trying to push specific agendas; for example behaviour modification and the promotion of 'healthy' lifestyles with little regard for the actual position and power of the pupils involved in such a process (Simovska 2000, 2007), and even less regard for the conditions or social determinants of such a lifestyle. Such work shows that the ideal of genuine participation co-exists with more superficial forms of participation. The notion of participation addresses many different interests and the research referenced in the reviews make a key point of their employment of participatory strategies, regardless of the interests they represent, be they moralistic, or democratic, for example (Levy and Zint 2013; Ljungdahl 2012; Marent, Forster, and Nowak 2012).

To move beyond Žižek's critique, it could be argued that from a Lacanian perspective, the focus on ideals in ESD and HE makes it possible to understand participation as having a core that is often imbued with values. This is not to link participation with hidden agendas, but to argue that the concept of participation within ESD and HE in schools offers the individual teacher more than pedagogical tools. The concept can be co-opted, to exhibit ideological excess; that is there is the distinct possibility of using participation to install an ideal in schools and thus allow the individual teacher to experience, or create, a sense of meaning where none might otherwise be found, intended or reasonably expected.

Participation and interactivity

Considering how the notion of participation offers both educational methodology and a surplus or excess in the form of construction of meaning for the individual teacher, questions of the close link between participation and interactivity comes to the fore. This makes it possible to consider a Lacanian perspective on unconscious functions when it comes to the idealised notion of learning as participation. Lacan suggests what is often a counter-intuitive reading of such a reliance on the notion of interactivity. The Lacanian 'Other' is established through a group, or taking part in activities; this Other, in the form of a group, whether real, virtual or make-believe, can perform several important roles for the individual subject. It can be a vehicle for reaching common goals through interactivity, as discussed in some research within HE (Simovska 2007, 2008), but it can also act instead of the subject. In other words, it is possible for the subject to utilise the Other in such a way that the Other experiences the innermost, spontaneous feelings and attitudes of the subject, instead of the subject (Lacan 2004). To illustrate, Žižek uses the example of hired 'weepers' (women hired to cry at funerals, see La Pastina, Rego, and Straubhaar 2003) to illustrate this point: 'they can perform the spectacle of mourning for the relatives of the deceased, who can devote their time to more profitable endeavours (like dividing the inheritance)' (Žižek 2006, 23). The feelings attached to the activity are still upheld, but the subject is relieved of actually having to live it out. An example of this within ESD and HE would be when teachers, under the guise of participation, make all the important decisions for pupils, while engaging them in playful and 'interactive' activities to provide the 'relevant' knowledge and regulate their behaviour accordingly (Simovska 2007). Another example would be when schools compete and the 'best' ones are rewarded for collecting batteries in the name of recycling and sustainability. Here, the idea is that, through their participation, pupils will learn about important sustainability issues; however, the pupils might be motivated more by the possibility of a reward, for example rewards and resources that flow from when the project is successfully completed, e.g. a school trip, that reinscribes unsustainable practices (Schnack 2008). In both cases, the illusion of participation is upheld while the actual activities might be far from what is envisioned and desired by the teachers. This suggests that the notion of interactivity, and in turn also participation, could be supplemented with its uncanny double interpassivity (Pfaller 2003).

Interpassivity signifies the obverse of interacting with the object (instead of just passively following proceedings), as in the situation in which the object of the activity (e.g. the pupil) takes from the subject (e.g. the teacher) their own passivity, so that it is the object that 'enjoys' the activity instead of the subject, relieving the subject of the duty to 'enjoy' too (Žižek 2006). Of course, participatory and interactive activities should be enjoyable and enjoyed by pupils, the argument goes; but, as the teacher has no guarantee that this actually happens, the perception that the pupil's enjoyment displaces that of the teacher could lead to a situation where no one truly participates in or enjoys the activities, educatively or otherwise.

That is not to say that participatory activities in ESD and HE in schools remove the power of schoolchildren (or teachers) to participate in activities that bring them enjoyment and learning. We want, instead, to draw attention to the double-sided, interactive/interpassive nature of the concepts of participation and interaction that, in effect, open the possibility that both children and teachers assume a position of interpassivity, and relieves both of the duty to be truly interactive. An example of this can be identified in the review by Levy and Zint (2013): they emphasise that research within ESD in schools suggests putting a stronger focus on those participatory methodologies that can be used to involve pupils in issues related to sustainable development. At the same time, there is very little focus on documenting the extent to which children manage to turn these 'learning experiences' into actual engagement with society. Knowledge is presented and children participate in the educational activities, but evidence that this is translated into strategies for altering the conditions of the children's lives is harder to find. The urge to promote notions of sustainability and health in schools is no doubt great, but clinging to the hope that pupils might, sooner or later, take action themselves and bring about change, might lead to disappointment. In effect, through interpassivity, the teacher can remain passive, sitting in the background, while the Other does the work. Instead of pushing for participatory activities that will make it possible for the children to participate in society, the hope is that the children will take action themselves, and instead of being part of a radical shift in power, the 'conflict' or the 'revolution' will address any issues at a later stage. However, as Levy and Zint (2013) rue, a focus on environmental and sustainability issues in schools does not necessarily lead to political participation later on in life.

From a Lacanian perspective, this position can be achieved by the subject (the individual teacher) through interposing another object, the ideal of participation, between him- or herself and the hope for change within ESD and HE. The possibility exists of course that the participatory activities connected to ESD and HE succeeds to some degree; in such circumstances the teacher has arguably remained active through others. Where this is possible, the work of the teacher bears fruit, but chances are that nothing much would happen and the activities that the individual teacher considers possible by engaging the pupils through participation never materialise. Even when such activities do emerge, they have little consequence and lack substantial impact on either sustainability or health. This constitutes a situation where the subject (the individual teacher) is passive through the other; such that the subject concedes the passive aspect (working on new teaching strategies, promoting curriculum, etc.) to the Other.

This leads us to other takes on the notion of interpassivity. The concept of *false activity* or *pseudo activity* stresses that not only is it possible to act in order to change something, it is also possible to act in order to prevent change. In clinical psychoanalysis, this is the typical strategy of the obsessive neurotic. In psychoanalytic treatment, obsessive neurotics talk constantly, flooding the analyst with anecdotes, dreams, insights: their incessant activity is sustained by the underlying fear that, if they stop talking for a moment, the analyst will ask them the question that truly matters – in other words, they talk in order to keep the analyst passive (Evans 2010). Such a conscious strategy to avoid genuine participation by actively pushing pseudo-participation could arguably also pose a threat to participation in ESD and HE, as evident in the reviews outlined above. Levy and Zint discuss how political efficacy is very hard to foster among children, especially when the challenges that they face are hard to grasp and of vast societal importance (Levy and Zint 2013). Yet pushing children to actively engage in society and take a political stance is not simply laudable; it is also extremely complex and potentially frustrating for the individual teacher. This introduces the risk that partaking becomes a more easily achievable goal than actually engaging. The lure of false activity then also becomes a companion to a wide range of efforts to encourage children to participate.

Activities for the sake of the activity itself, with little impact beyond a short episode of general entertainment and attention for the organisation or individual that hosted the activity, is as such a recurring criticism in all the reviews, particularly

Levy and Zint (2013) and Ljungdahl (2012). The review by Griebler et al. (2012) avoids discussing this issue by applying specific criteria for selecting the literature to be included, with one of the important criteria being that participation is interpreted as engagement and influence by pupils. However, even in this case, where the focus is on the desire for an ideal involvement of pupils, the review identifies 'negative' effects when pupils report that they were not listened to or taken seriously.

As such, participation can be seen to have many guises, and not all aspects of ideal notions of learning as participation are covered within a Lacanian understanding of 'interactivity', 'interpassivity', 'false activity' or 'pseudo activity'. However, these concepts do enable an understanding of the unconscious function of these cross-cutting aspects of engaging the pupils via participatory activities. Such activities do not only act as direct realisations of learning potential as perceived by the individual teacher, but also as a way of relating to broader ideals of democracy, sustainability, health and social justice that underpin ESD and HE.

As discussed in all the reviews, participation is understood and applied in a host of different settings, often with the hope of further developing a promising practice. An understanding of how these ideals might lead to activities that, in isolation, have little other impact than preserving the status quo, and why this might be considered desirable, can be drawn from a Lacanian perspective. This does not necessarily entail unsuccessful practices, but it suggests a distinct perspective on parts of the psychoanalytic function of promoting concepts of participation in ESD and HE: taking interpassivity for interactivity can be a way of shielding oneself from dealing with the overall struggle for genuine participation while settling for the less demanding symbolic participation. By applying such a perspective to participatory pedagogies, one does, however, run the risk of only seeing failed attempts, where all efforts to bring out the potential of concepts like participation only manage to gloss over the always possible dark side.

This then, is our critique of a Lacanian perspective; if employed consistently in analysing participatory practices within ESD and HE, there is little to suggest the possibility of positive practices. Equally, we recognise a degree of caution is in order, as there is no reason to suggest that all participatory activities are necessarily embedded in notions of interpassivity, false or pseudo activities. More stridently, it can also be argued that the very notions of interpassivity, false or pseudo activities necessarily fail to explain the full nature of participation, as they remain temporary but nonetheless flawed attempts from psychoanalysis to describe the extremely complex processes of ESD and HE as participatory teaching and learning within the wider, including conscious and deliberate realities of messy and dynamic educational practices in schools.

The dual potential of participation

That said, the mechanisms embedded within the notion of interpassivity do cast light on how teachers ensure they can continue to promote participatory teaching. Even if genuine participation constituted the normal and easily attainable state of affairs in schools, the danger would persist, from a Lacanian perspective, that the individual teacher would have to face up to the miniscule impact of pupils' actions and the continued slide towards unsustainability or ill health, both locally and globally. Believing in the potential of participation, and perhaps seeing interactivity where interpassivity might really be at play, can be seen as a way of establishing a strong base for a persistent belief in the potential of promoting an educational ideal. As emphasised by several of the reviews, participation – and especially 'genuine participation' – is hard to identify in practice, operationalise and measure (Ljungdahl 2012; Marent, Forster, and Nowak 2012). Insisting that some participatory activities and strategies hold special potential for learning, change or emancipation thus helps to translate the actual ideal of participation into actionable approaches. On the one hand, this offers the possibility of working with abstract aims in more concrete and measurable terms and linking them to a familiar context of learning and competence development (Ljungdahl 2012). On the other hand, it also establishes a situation where the exact opposite can happen. The ideals can remain intact with little outcome outside of the context of a given activity, e.g. in project work, frequently of limited duration, focusing on ESD or HE.

This tension, between the effort to shield and protect cherished ideals and the urge to avoid accepting one's failure to live up to them, creates a situation where such ideals are both linked to a context and disconnected from it in case of failure (e.g. Griebler et al. 2012). Meaning-making processes are thus not harmed by negative results of engaging in participatory activities. Arguably, frustrations and lack of success can in this light be understood in a positive manner, as they facilitate a situation where it is possible for the individual teacher to continue participatory efforts instead of withdrawing and questioning whether a chosen (and desired) approach makes any sense.

The reviews, as well as the other literature discussed so far, also indicate that despite the problems and barriers, engagement in ESD and HE participatory practices remain powerful educational tools. By applying a Lacanian perspective however, we emphasise that this educational tool runs the risk of outcomes diametrically opposed to those intended. No matter whether such a dark side of participation is dubbed interpassivity, false activity or pseudo activity, it is important to be aware that it functions as an inescapable shadow, always clinging to attempts at participatory teaching, and at times even obscuring the positive aspects.

Nevertheless, this should not lead to the simple conclusion that we must identify and eradicate interpassivity, false activity or pseudo activity from participatory educational practices within ESD and HE. While that might be a good practical exercise for teachers, we argue that it is important to focus on the significance of this troubling downside to complex concepts like participation. We concur with the Lacanian perspective that the significance lays in the fact that interpassivity or false activity also has a positive dynamic effect for the individual teacher. The acknowledgement that participation is not always consequential or that interactivity is often hard to achieve in teaching and learning processes establishes a situation for the individual teacher where ideals of engaging the pupils through genuine participation can continue to exist side by side with signs of symbolic participation. With actual, 'Real', imperfect educational environments and outcomes being the norm, the utopian potential for a perfect school is maintained. Arguably, without the practice of interpassivity and token participation, the ideal of interactivity and genuine participation could not be maintained.

Epilogue

Criticism and praise of the concept of participation are abundant, yet we hope this discussion has introduced new perspectives to revitalise the debate: Participation is a worthwhile and powerful concept, both as an ideal and as an educational strategy. But we should also try and understand its dark side too, and the role this dark side can play for both teachers and pupils as individual subjects, as well as for the schools as settings, and for broader educational thinking. Participation cannot solve all educational woes, but rests, among other things, on the individual desire to create meaning among the uncertainties that surround education for sustainable development and health education. The individual teachers that take on challenges like ESD and HE and utilise participatory approaches are arguably working hard to create meaning in complex environments such as schools. Curricula, professional identities, institutional requirements and policy frameworks all exercise influence on the teachers' space for choosing pedagogical strategies and on the possibility of understanding these strategies as expressions of a normative ideal.

In other words, the concept of participation harbours significant potential, but as an ideal it rests on notions of the 'good' and 'worthwhile' that are often out of reach, and as an educational tool it clearly clashes with many of the other things actually and necessarily taking place within schools: structures, resources, hierarchies, priorities, assessments, the teacher/pupil relationship, the urge to learn *something* and not just *anything*. All educational ideals face this clash with reality; it does not make participation less important, but we need to be aware of the (in)significance of participation, real or less real, symbolic or genuine, for the individual subjects' meaning-making processes.

When working with research on participation in ESD and HE, a theoretical emphasis on the excess embedded within such an imperfect concept could be seen as a strategy to circumvent the seemingly never-ending race to come up with the 'perfect' concept, and in effect, get rid of the lack or deficit in a given educational field. Again, this should be done in the knowledge that there is no way to transcend the ideal of participation when trying to improve the methodologies surrounding it. There is no 'perfect' version of the concept to be had and, in the spirit of Samuel Beckett, we can only hope to try to push the envelope of participation in ESD and HE, while at the same time recognising that this can only lead us along the path to failure once again, but hopefully failing better.

Disclosure statement
No potential conflict of interest was reported by the authors.

References

Baillie, L., J. Bassett-Smith, and S. Broughton. 2000. "Using Communicative Action in the Primary Prevention of Cancer." *Health Education and Behavior* 27 (4): 442–453.

Biesta, G. 2006. *Beyond Learning. Democratic Education for a Human Future.* Boulder, CO: Paradigm.

Bjerre, H. J. 2011. "Skolen der ikke stopper med at etablere sig." [The School that does not Stop Establishing Itself.] *Slagmark* 62: 33–49.

Bonnett, M. 2013. "Normalizing Catastrophe: Sustainability and Scientism." *Environmental Education Research* 19 (2): 187–197.

Carlsson, M., and V. Simovska. 2012. "Exploring Learning Outcomes of School-based Health Promotion – A Multiple Case Study." *Health Education Research* 27 (3): 437–447.

Chawla, L., and H. Heft. 2001. "Children's Competence and the Ecology of Communities." *Journal of Environmental Psychology* 22 (1–2): 201–216.

Cook, P., N. Blanchet-Cohen, and S. Hart. 2004. *Children as Partners: Child Participation Promoting Social Change.* Victoria: International Institute for Child Rights and Development.

Cooley, A. 2009. "Is Education a Lost Cause? Žižek, Schooling and Universal Emancipation." *Discourse* 30 (4): 381–395.

Evans, D. 2010. *An Introductory Dictionary of Lacanian Psychoanalysis.* London: Routledge.

Firth, R., and M. Smith. 2013. "As the UN Decade of Education for Sustainable Development Comes to an End: What Has It Achieved and What Are the Ways Forward?" *Curriculum Journal* 24 (2): 169–180.

Green, J., and K. Tones. 2010. *Health Promotion: Planning and Strategies.* London: Sage.

Griebler, U., D. Rojatz, V. Simovska, and R. Forster. 2012. *Evidence for Effects of Pupils Participation in Designing, Planning, Implementing and Evaluating School Health Promotion – A Systematic Literature Review.* Vienna: Ludwig Boltzmann Institute Health Promotion Research.

Hart, R. 1997. *Children's Participation, the Theory and Practice of Involving Young Citizens in Community Development and Environmental Care.* London: Earthscan.

Hart, R. 2008. "Stepping Back from 'The Ladder': Reflections on a Model of Participatory Work with Children." In *Participation and Learning*, edited by A. Reid, B. B. Jensen, J. Nikel, and V. Simovska, 19–31. Dordrecht: Springer.

Jensen, B. B. 1997. "A Case of Two Paradigms within Health Education." *Health Education Research* 12 (4): 419–428.

Jensen, B. B., and K. Schnack. 2006. "The Action Competence Approach in Environmental Education." *Environmental Education Research* 12 (3–4): 471–486.

Jensen, B. B., K. Schnack, and V. Simovska, eds. 2000. *Critical Environmental and Health Education: Research Issues and Challenges.* Copenhagen: Danish Royal School of Educational Studies.

Klafki, W. 1997. "Schlüsselprobleme, Epochaltypische [Epoch typical key issues]." In *Lexikon Sachunterricht*, edited by Astrid Kaiser, 321–332. Baltmannsweiler: Schneider Hohengehren.

Kojéve, A. 1969. *Introduction to the Reading of Hegel.* New York: Basic Books.

La Pastina A., C. M. Rego, and J. D. Straubhaar. 2003. "The Centrality of Telenovelas in Latin America's Everyday Life: Past Tendencies, Current Knowledge, and Future Research." *Global Media Journal* 2 (2). http://lass.purduecal.edu/cca/gmj/sp03/gmj-sp03-lapastina-rego-straubhaar.htm.

Lacan, J. 1974. *Les Non-dupes Errent.* Unpublished Seminar, 1973/1974. http://www.scribd.com/doc/48830066/Jacques-Lacan-Seminaire-Livre-XXI-Les-Non-Dupes-Errent.29-3-2012.

Lacan, J. 2004. *The Four Fundamental Concepts of Psycho-analysis.* London: Karnac.

Læssøe, J. 2010. "Education for Sustainable Development." *Participation and Sociocultural Change, Environmental Education Research* 16 (1): 39–57.

Læssøe, J., and J. Öhman. 2010. "Learning as Democratic Action and Communication: Framing Danish and Swedish Environmental and Sustainability Education." *Environmental Education Research* 16 (1): 1–7.

Laustsen, C. B. 1999. "Ideologiske Fantasmer – Politisk filosofi med Jacques Lacan og Slavoj Žižek [Ideological Fantasms – Political Philosophy with Jacques Lacan and Slavoj Žižek]." In *Den ene, Den Anden, Det tredje – Politisk identitet, andethed og fællesskab i moderne Fransk Tænkning* [The One, The Other, The third – Political Identity, Otherness and Community in Modern French Thinking], edited by C. B. Laustsen, and A. Berg-Sørensen, 163–188. Copenhagen: Politisk Revy.

Levy, B., and M. Zint. 2013. "Toward Fostering Environmental Political Participation: Framing an Agenda for Environmental Education Research." *Environmental Education Research* 19 (5): 553–576.

Ljungdahl, A. K. 2012. *Mapping and Reviewing Concepts of Children's and Young Peoples' Competence, Participation and Competence Development.* Lillehammer: Lillehammer University College.

Marent, B., R. Forster, and P. Nowak. 2012. "Theorizing Participation in Health Promotion: A Literature Review." *Social Theory & Health* 10 (2): 188–207.

Merriam-Webster. 2014. *Merriam-Webster Online Dictionary*; accessed March 4, 2014. http://www.merriam-webster.com/

Pavlova, M. 2013. "Towards Using Transformative Education as a Benchmark for Clarifying Differences and Similarities between Environmental Education and Education for Sustainable Development." *Environmental Education Research* 19 (5): 656–672.

Pfaller, R. 2003. *Die Illusionen der anderen: Über das Lustprinzip in der Kultur* [The Illusion of the other: On the enjoyment principle of culture]. Frankfurt: Suhrkamp.

Porsgaard, K. 2013. *What Captivates the Subject?* Aarhus: Aarhus University.

Quick, K., and M. Feldman. 2011. "Distinguishing Participation and Inclusion." *Journal of Planning Education and Research* 31 (3): 272–290.

Rahnema, M. 1992. "Participation." In *The Development Dictionary: A Guide to Knowledge as Power*, edited by W. Sachs, 127–144. London: Zed Press.

Reid, A., B. B. Jensen, J. Nikel, and V. Simovska. 2008. "Participation and Learning: Developing Perspectives on Education and the Environment, Health and Sustainability." In *Participation and Learning: Perspectives on Education and the Environment, Health and Sustainability*, edited by A. Reid, B. B. Jensen, J. Nikel, and V. Simovska, 1–18. Dordrecht: Springer.

de Róiste, A., C. Kelly, M. Molcho, A. Gavin, and S. Gabhainn. 2012. "Is School Participation Good for Children? Associations with Health and Wellbeing." *Health Education* 112 (2): 88–104.

Schnack, K. 2000. "Action Competence as Curriculum Perspective." In *Critical Environmental and Health Education*, edited by B. B. Jensen, K. Schnack, and V. Simovska, 107–126. Copenhagen: The Danish University of Education.

Schnack, K. 2008. "Participation, Education and Democracy: Implications for Environmental Education and Education for Sustainable Development." In *Participation and Learning: Perspectives on Education and the Environment, Health and Sustainability*, edited by A. Reid, B. B. Jensen, J. Nikel, and V. Simovska, 181–196. Dordrecht: Springer.

Scott, W. 2013. "Developing the Sustainable School: Thinking the Issues through." *Curriculum Journal* 24 (2): 181–205.

Simovska, V. 2000. "Exploring Pupil Participation Within Health Education and Health Promoting Schools." In *Critical Environmental and Health Education: Research Issue and Challenges*, edited by B. B. Jensen, K. Schnack and V. Simovska, 29–44. Copenhagen: Royal Danish School of Educational Studies.

Simovska, V. 2007. "The Changing Meanings of Participation in School Based Health Education and Health Promotion: The Participants' Voices." *Health Education Research* 22 (6): 846–879.

Simovska, V. 2008. "Learning in and as Participation: A Case Study from Health Promoting Schools." In *Participation and Learning*, edited by A. Reid, B. B. Jensen, J. Nikel, and V. Simovska, 61–80. Dordrecht: Springer.

Simovska, V. 2012. "Case Study of a Participatory Health Promotion Intervention in School." *Democracy & Education* 20(1), Article 4. http://democracyeducationjournal.org/home/vol20/iss1/4.

Simovska, V. 2013. "Pupil Participation as an Important Dimension of the Health Promotion School: Experience from a European Project." In *The Implementation of Health Promoting Schools*, edited by O. Samdal and L. Rowling, 133–139. London: Routledge Falmer.

Simovska, V., and B. B. Jensen. 2009. *Conceptualizing Participation: The Health of Children and Young People*. Copenhagen: WHO, Regional Office for Europe.

Simovska, V., and P. McNamara, eds. 2015. *Schools for Health and Sustainability*. Dordrecht: Springer.

UNESCO. 2013. *2013. 37 C/4 – 2014–2021. Draft Medium-term Strategy*. Paris: UNESCO.

Van Poeck, K., and J. Vandenabeele. 2012. "Learning from Sustainable Development: Education in the Light of Public Issues." *Environmental Education Research* 18 (4): 541–552.

Žižek, S. 2006. *How to Read Lacan*. London: Granta.

Žižek, S. 2008. *Enjoy Your Symptom!* New York: Routledge.

Learning to fail and learning from failure – ideology at work in a mathematics classroom

Hauke Straehler-Pohl and Alexandre Pais

When actualised in a concrete school, the official discourse of inclusion and equity often encounters a series of obstacles that research strives to identify and address under the imperative to eliminate them. Through the exploration of classroom episodes, teacher interviews and field notes from a German secondary school, we take failure not as a correctable obstacle but as a symptom of the ideology at work in current educational practices. Symptoms, as Žižek (after Lacan) suggested, cannot be eliminated but always (re)emerge since they concern the impossibility of official discourses actualising themselves. We thus argue for a research agenda that learns from failure instead of research concerned with the possible successes that might prospectively be brought into existence, if just the 'right' theory was applied 'correctly'.

Introduction

International organisations (e.g. Organisation for Economic Co-operation and Development (OECD)), professional institutions (e.g. National Council of Teachers of Mathematics 2000) and researchers (see Atweh et al. 2011; Gellert, Jablonka, and Morgan 2010; Herbel-Eisenmann et al. 2012) posit mathematics education as a key element in the development of a socially just and equitable society. It is assumed that a quality mathematics education will allow people to become active participants in a world where mathematics informs and formats many of the decisions that influence our lives (Gellert and Jablonka 2007; Skovsmose 1994). As a result, the main task of mathematics education research has been the development of teaching and learning strategies that can provide a meaningful mathematics for all. Researchers typically see persistent failure in school mathematics as an occurrence contingent on a system that officially aims at equity and freedom (Baldino and Cabral 2006; Pais 2012; Pais and Valero 2012). As such, researchers are often interested in describing successful experiences, showing how learning obstacles can be overcome, instead of analysing episodes of failure (Gutiérrez 2010; Presmeg and Radford 2008; Sriraman and English 2010).

This propensity to report successful experiences partakes in an ideology that Lacan (2008) characterised as *evolutionism*: the belief in a supreme good, in a final goal of progress that guides its course from the very beginning. In the case of mathematics education, the supreme goal is 'mathematics for all', and research has focused on eliminating the obstacles standing in the way of this goal (Lundin 2012; Pais and Valero 2012). The goal itself is seldom questioned – notwithstanding the evidence that mathematics is not for all – and the discourse of equity ends up functioning as a *regulative ideal* rather than an empirically realisable event (Davis 2004). Research is then moved by a desire for what *ought-to-be* in opposition to what *is* (46), thus failing to recognise the concrete conditions of today's schooling. From this perspective, as explored elsewhere (Pais and Valero 2012), the problems encountered by teachers are not didactical in the sense of better ways to teach and learn mathematics, but political, regarding the economic and socio-political implications of schooling. This is especially true at a time when the official rhetoric of the curriculum – which emphasises the high goals of equity and global access – contrasts with the economic demands on education (competition, employability, pressure to succeed in global assessment, etc.). Indeed, insofar as mathematics education research has to address the problems of practitioners, it cannot afford to dismiss the real conditions of their work.

Against this background, we present a study of educational failure. We set our investigation in a secondary school that can be thought of as *marginalised* or *underprivileged*, and analyse two classroom episodes that led to students' exclusion from learning mathematics. If we followed the *evolutionistic* thesis, we would be expected to formulate strategies to overcome the problems that led to students' failure. These could be formulated in terms of teacher education (e.g. a different way of interacting with the students), the curriculum (e.g. more challenging tasks) or classroom organisation (e.g. project or group work instead of blackboard-centred and individual work). However, we will instead analyse the classroom episodes *as they are* since our interest is not in providing solutions for the problems of practice, but in pinpointing the ideological injunctions at work in the way teachers and students interact in the classroom. By analysing things as they are (instead of how they 'should' be), we seek to make visible the incongruence between the official discourse and the lived experiences of students and teachers.

We focus our analysis on the way students 'decide' to participate (or not) in the activities proposed by their teachers. We argue that the ideological frame is set in such a way that failure cannot be attributed to anything other than individuals making the wrong choices. However, as we shall see, these are false choices, since they lack a crucial precondition of choice: the freedom to choose. On the side of the student, we will show that, whether or not they 'choose' to participate in classroom activities, the outcome will be failure in school mathematics. On the side of the teacher, we will reveal the fallacy of the belief that she could have transformed failure into success by making choices that were more aligned to the regulative ideal of school mathematics. The analysis of the cases we present leads us to conclude that the production of failure is a structural problem, escaping the realm of an evolutionist mathematics education.

The necessity of failure and the ideology of research

As a point of departure for our analysis we claim that failure is an integral part of the economy of schooling (Bowles and Gintis 1977; Baldino and Cabral 2006; Lave and McDermott 2002; Pais 2012). We conceptualise schools as a *credit system*, which school mathematics is a part of (Vinner 1997) and which operates through *selection* and *accreditation*. Mathematics is thus posited as an economically valuable resource under the condition of scarceness. In order to load such economic value, an accreditation of mathematical competence requires a momentum of distinction. The value of the ones who fail is appropriated by the ones who pass as surplus-value. As failure is inherent in the logic of the credit system, it appears no longer as a contingent phenomenon, but can be posited as a *necessary* condition for schooling: 'in order to perpetuate the process of production/seizure of surplus value, a certain amount of failure is necessary' (Baldino 1998, 77). Therefore, 'failure of students means success of the institution' (Baldino and Cabral 2006, 34).

To acknowledge that failure is a necessity of current schooling is not easy for those who work in it. To be able to operate efficiently and become a productive cog in the machine of schooling, one needs to believe that the final goals for which we all strive are equity, social justice, inclusion and the like. The discrepancy between the regulative ideal, which exalts the supreme goals of democracy, and its actualisation in a life-world context is a central concern of *ideology critique* (Žižek 2008a). In the Lacan-Žižek axis, ideology is conceived as a defence against some traumatic real, a 'fantasy-screen' (Žižek 2008b, 7) focused on restoring order to a situation that otherwise seems chaotic or impossible. A fantasy provides a rationale for failure, that is, a meaningful way of dealing with a traumatic situation. Failure – without the screen of ideology – is chaotic, impossible, or even unbearable for an individual teacher, researcher or policy maker.

The fantasy-screen of ideology provides a rationale for these uncontrollable experiences. When confronted with the worldwide problem of failure in school mathematics and the societal demand for 'mathematics for all', research establishes an explanatory scheme within which an approach to the problem is proposed (Baldino and Cabral 2006; Pais 2012, 2013). Although the particular constellation of the fantasy narrative changes from one research thematic to another, the figure of 'failure' functions as that which simultaneously thwarts the realisation of the ideal goal of a universally meaningful mathematics and compels the articulation of an entire discourse concealing the necessity of failure itself (hence providing researchers a frame within which to develop their work). As such, experiences of failure function as symptoms (Žižek 2008a) of mathematics education. The exploration of these symptoms reveals the impotence of current educational systems to deal with exclusion.

To paraphrase Žižek (2008a, 161), when one is dealing with a universal principle, such as the high goals of equity and 'mathematics for all', one invariably assumes that it is possible to apply this principle to every particular element, so that the principle's empirical non-realisation – the fact that people continue to fail in school mathematics – is seen as a matter of contingent circumstances. A symptom, however, is an element which, while appearing as a contingency, is in fact essential to the universal principle that it breaches. In Žižek's words, it is an element in which:

> – although the non-realisation of the universal principle in it appears to hinge on contingent circumstances – has to remain an exception, that is, the point of suspension of the universal principle: if the universal principle were to apply also to this point, the universal system itself would disintegrate. (Žižek 2008a, 161)

When it is claimed that everyone should be provided with a meaningful mathematics education, this official goal conceals the obscenity of a school system that year after year 'rightfully' excludes thousands of students from the possibility of pursuing higher studies or a place in the society of abundance. This happens under the official discourse of an inclusionary and democratic schooling. It is in this discrepancy between the official discourse and its (failed) actualisation that ideology is made operational. Within the official discourse, what is *necessary* is the abstract motto of 'mathematics for all', all the exceptions to this rule (the ones who fail) being seen as contingencies. However, in our analysis, what is *necessary* is precisely the existence of those who fail, the abstract proclamation being a purely contingent result of the frenetic activity of individuals (researchers, practitioners, politicians) who believe in it. Failure as a symptom indicates that the condition of impossibility of realising the goal is simultaneously its condition of possibility. The antagonistic character of social reality – the crude reality that in order for some to succeed others have to fail – is the *necessary* Real which needs to be concealed so that the illusion of productive research and equitable schooling can be kept. The figure of 'failure' – which encompasses the marginalised, the excluded, the truant – has to remain an exception; and the universality preached by the official discourse masks the symptomatic character of exclusion, the fact that the true universality at work in schooling is the need to produce failure.

One of the ways the system has of constructing exclusion as a contingent occurrence is to treat it as an individual choice. Apparently, students are confronted with the choice of participating in the official discourse by means of active engagement in the classroom activities. However, as we shall see, there are places where this is a false choice since, even when students choose to participate, their choice leads to exclusion. As Žižek (2006, 348) puts it, '[t]his appearance of choice, however, should not deceive us: it is the mode of appearance of its very opposite: of the absence of any real choice with regard to the fundamental structure of society'. In our case, this appearance of choice – to participate in classroom activities – disavows the absence of any real choice regarding the possibilities these students have of pursuing a valuable education. The system initiates students into blaming failure on their own choices for the sake of keeping the appearance of a free and equal school system.

The place and the layout of a free and equal school system

Traditionally, the German school system was organised federally and streamed students after primary school into three different school-types according to their supposedly 'innate' ability.[1] This streaming was done in different ways with teachers and/or parents being able to shade decisions based on a student's average marks. However, the three streams were organised hierarchically with only the highest stream providing access to an academic education.

According to the official rhetoric, the stratification of streams allowed the effective design of classes for students according to their different 'innate' abilities. While in practice 'ability' meant achievement in literacy, mathematics and science, it still lacks any scientific operationalisation or justification. Rather, it is grounded in a historically grown common sense of different 'forms of ability' (Rösner 2007). According to this common sense there is 'academic ability' as opposed to 'practical ability'. While the high stream supposedly optimised learning conditions for 'academically able' learners, the low stream provided an environment supposedly optimitised for 'practically able' learners. The middle stream appeared as a hybrid that supposedly nourished both forms of ability. The administrative moral imperative that assured that such stratification would not collide with the democratic principle of equity, but could operate within it, was that 'without consideration of rank and assets of parents, the educational pathway has to stay open *which accords with his or her ability*' (Kultusministerkonferenz, cited in Pietsch and Stubbe 2007, 428, emphasis added). Together with the common sense of different abilities, this moral imperative provided the rationale for maintaining the fantasy of a free and equal school system despite the explicitly selective and stratifying organisation of schooling in Germany. Thus, while the structure of the German school system might make it easier to expose the systematic occurrence of failure, the system still provides an ideological fantasy-screen that deceives the observer about the nature and role of failure.

The data

This paper is based on the re-analysis of data from the project 'Emergence of Disparity in Mathematics Classrooms' with which one of us was involved (Knipping et al. 2008). As this project had its main focus on the social interactions that discursively produce mathematical knowledge and consciousness, data collection was made mainly through *videography*. The mathematics classes in which we undertook our research were in one seventh grade (first year of secondary school) in Berlin, Germany, just after the summer holidays of 2009. Before the summer holidays, all the students in the research class had finished their primary schools with a recommendation that they attend the lowest of the three available ability-streams in secondary school. During the first three weeks of the school year, we captured all mathematics lessons (14) in one classroom using a camera recording a long shot. While two teachers were present most of the time, one of the two teachers was responsible for the organisation of the mathematics classes.[2] In addition, we carried out in-depth interviews with the teacher leading the class and took field notes. There were 14 students in the class. The students in this study can be considered underprivileged given the social segregation that results from where they live, their background as members of a cultural minority, having German as a second language and by the institutional selectivity of the German streaming school system. A considerable number of the students in the class had already had to repeat one or two school years in primary school. Eight of the 14 students had Sinti and Romani backgrounds; the remaining six students were second- or higher-generation descendants of Turkish and Arabic immigrants. None of the students spoke German as a first language.

The analysis we present here is different from that in the original project; rather than analyse students' or teachers' interactions, here we seek to pinpoint how ideology is operationalised through these interactions. Thus, when we undertake an interpretation of a teacher's or student's actions and speech, it is a *theoretical reading of a social reality*. We do not claim to 'truthfully' represent the psychic situation of any real existing human being, but rather posit their activity within – and as a symptom of – broader structural arrangements which we then theorise. Therefore, we deliberately chose key incidents that would allow us to explicate the theoretical significance that we attributed to the whole data corpus. In our cases, and within the Lacan-Žižek theorisation we are deploying here, these key incidents allows us to address the system's points of *extimacy* (Lacan 2008), that is, the features that are simultaneously part of the school system (all the episodes we analyse occurred in regular mathematics classes) and strange to this same system (since they report experiences of undesirable failure and are thus extrinsic to the broader educational discourse of equity and access for all). In other words, the failure we analyse through these key incidents is something strange to the system of equity in which schooling is based, yet it is at the heart of this same system.

The episodes and their (psychoanalytical) interpretation

Elsewhere we have described the pedagogy enacted in the classrooms we observed as one that 'in order not to overcharge – infantilizes students and – in order to enable classroom management – objectifies students … Learning in such mathematics classrooms' we suggested 'adds to the underprivileged conditions that these learners face' (Straehler-Pohl and Gellert 2011, 198). Classroom interactions were set up in such a way that, as observers, we could identify very few opportunities to acquire mathematical knowledge. A deeper analysis, using Bernstein's theory of pedagogic codes, revealed that the pedagogy in this classroom was almost completely free from the 'instructional discourse' (Bernstein 2000, 32) that creates specialised skills. What remained was an excessive 'regulative discourse' (32) that was concerned with the regulation of the students' position in the social order so that, in the end, 'students are locked into an identity of failed primary school mathematical knowers' (Straehler-Pohl 2012). Against this background, participating in the classroom activities seemed inevitably to lead students towards failure in learning mathematics. In the following analysis, we present the cases of two students who 'decided' not to participate in the activities in the way that the majority of their peers did. We then contrast these students' (non-)participation with the ideological positioning of the teacher. The case of these students, although seen by the teachers as contingent occurrences that might be overcome through sanctions such as expelling the students from the classroom, will then be analysed as symptoms of schooling.

The case of Melinda

Melinda's participation in the classroom was characterised by a total refusal of the teachers' authority (most of the time two teachers were present in class). At the beginning of the first mathematics class in this new school, each of the students was asked to complete the sentence, 'I am feeling ___, because ____'. Though still not acquainted with the second teacher, Melinda articulated the following: 'I am feeling bad because today we have class with this teacher [pointing at the second teacher]'. During the course of the mathematical activity (working '887 − 339' at the blackboard), Melinda spent quite some time talking to Mariella, her classmate, in a foreign language. This was mostly ignored by the teacher, although twice she calmly admonished her. When Mariella was asked to finish the task at the blackboard, Melinda shouted at Mariella: 'what are you doing bitch?' Although clearly stated and quite loud, this interruption remained unsanctioned. However, a few minutes later, Melinda 'collected' (teacher's word) her third, calmly spoken, admonishment and was excluded from the classroom for the rest of the day. The following day, the mathematics class took a similar course, resulting in Melinda again being excluded. On the third day, Melinda did not reappear: she had been expelled from school. As she was still of compulsory school-age she would have been directed towards another low-streamed school in the neighbourhood.

The case of Hatice

On the third day of the researcher's observations, Hatice, who was already known to the teachers as a truant, appeared in class for the first time. In class, Hatice was quietly doing the calculations demanded of her by the work sheet (such as '9700 − 300'). Hatice was among three students who succeeded in finishing their work sheets. The next time Hatice appeared in class, she completed three work sheets in 20 minutes including 186 'simple multiplication exercises'. The fourth sheet, one given to Hatice 'as a reinforcement' (teacher's words), stated at the top of the page that 'it is now getting harder and harder', and concluded at the bottom: 'when you have solved all the problems correctly – then you are the king of computations' (see Figure 1). When Hatice came back to her seat and started filling in the solutions on the work sheet, the second teacher asked her to 'read the instructions first'. However, there were no instructions for the first 54 calculations. Ignoring Hatice's confusion, the teacher commanded, 'read!' Hatice did not show up to any of the rest of the observed lessons.

Interpretation

Both Melinda's and Hatice's behaviour resulted in their physical exclusion from the class, either by expulsion or by truancy. Yet their actions were fundamentally different, if not opposite. Melinda seems to have staged her opposition *against* the institution of the school and its norms: she insisted on making use of her mother tongue, which is forbidden in class; on

It is getting harder and harder - number range up
to 10.000. Watch the tens!

1. $4509 + 2 =$	$3490 + 20 =$	$8970 + 40 =$
$3804 + 7 =$	$7180 + 70 =$	$1990 + 50 =$
$7205 + 9 =$	$2570 + 90 =$	$5980 + 60 =$
2. $3400 + 760 =$	$2780 + 45 =$	$3247 + 80 =$
$8900 + 480 =$	$1460 + 52 =$	$1199 + 20 =$
$7600 + 690 =$	$9690 + 69 =$	$7881 + 40 =$
3. $2800 + 754 =$	$7997 + 4 =$	$5600 + 2800 =$
$6700 + 986 =$	$4995 + 9 =$	$4800 + 2400 =$
$8900 + 211 =$	$1999 + 8 =$	$1900 + 2700 =$
4. $5000 - 50 =$	$3200 - 60 =$	$4200 - 400 =$
$8000 - 80 =$	$6100 - 90 =$	$7300 - 900 =$
$2000 - 10 =$	$9300 - 70 =$	$8100 - 600 =$
5. $8000 - 8 =$	$5200 - 7 =$	$2482 - 6 =$
$2000 - 4 =$	$1700 - 4 =$	$8113 - 5 =$
$6000 - 5 =$	$9800 - 1 =$	$3685 - 9 =$
6. $3200 - 23 =$	$8000 - 45 =$	$9010 - 40 =$
$4400 - 98 =$	$3000 - 21 =$	$6020 - 80 =$
$7900 - 11 =$	$5000 - 83 =$	$4030 - 60 =$

7. Write all the exercises in the form of packages and compute them!

4000	4500	1740	2375	+	2	20	200
6000	5800	7690	9764	-	3	30	300

When you have solved all the tasks correctly -

then you are the king of computations.

Figure 1.   Worksheet (translated from German).

speaking whenever she wanted to; and finally she swore at a fellow student
and did not respect the teacher's authority. Melinda thus operated in ways
that teachers may believe justifies the way they organise their classes: effective learning is not possible because of students' bad behaviour and thus
mathematics instruction has to be suspended in favour of social regulation.
The teacher succeeded in constructing Melinda's resistance as a matter of
her own choice. While the teacher stayed calm and delivered quiet admon-
ishments as some sort of countdown that Melinda could have accepted
('three strikes and you're out'), she *decided* to ignore them. We can interpret the teacher's 'counting down' as a *false activity* (Žižek 2007, 26).
Installing this countdown, the teacher does not act in order to change something (in particular the fact that students are not learning mathematics), but
instead acts to prevent change: once Melinda was expelled from the classroom community, business could go on as usual. Melinda thus appeared to
be a contingent individual obstacle; once all 'Melindas' have been expelled,
mathematics learning will occur.

On the other hand, Hatice seems to stage her opposition *in line* with the official discourse of the institution of school. She remained quiet, worked effectively and solved her tasks correctly. However, this form of behaviour deviated so strongly from what the teachers expected of a student in her position that it ended up being not rewarded but rather reprimanded. The reason for the reprimand may lie in the resourcefulness shown by Hatice: through her behaviour she laid bare the teachers' ridiculously low expectations regarding the learning of mathematics, and, as a consequence, how irrelevant school was for her future. When the teacher prohibited Hatice from doing the activity quickly, it appears that her intention was not so much to disturb Hatice's participation, to inhibit her from achieving what was indeed expected from her, but to mask the fact that students like Hatice are not supposed to behave/succeed like this.

It would seem that students such as Hatice might have greater potential to do well in schools since, instead of aligning themselves with the implicit demand to fail, they follow the letter of the 'law' and, in Hatice's case, she actually performed well in the classroom. However, her industry *could* also reveal the contradictoriness and hopelessness of her situation and threaten the effectiveness of the organisation of classes. This threat did not go unnoticed by the teachers, who reacted by reprimanding Hatice for her behaviour. In the next section we problematise the role of the teachers. From the perspective of an evolutionistic thesis, the teachers' pedagogy could be seen as the primary *contingent obstacle* to a meaningful mathematics education, yet we will provide a deeper insight into the teacher's perspective in order to highlight how we see her activity, not as contingent, but as articulated by ideology.

The teacher's perspective

> In the break between the two math-lessons, Mrs Streller [the lead teacher] sits down at her desk and immediately starts talking … To me, it sounds almost like a confession, the way she gets the frustration off her chest … When she started working at this school thirty years ago at the age of twenty-six, she said, she came home crying regularly. This does not happen anymore. However, the reason is not that the situation has changed; the situation, she says, is getting steadily worse. But it has changed, because she herself has 'dulled'. She doesn't care anymore about a lot of things, as she learnt to ignore when students swear at her or others … She sees herself rather as a social worker, as a substitute mother, actually anything rather than a transmitter of knowledge. Transmitting knowledge appears to be unwinnable anyway, she says … Many of the students would not reach beyond the attainment of third-graders at the end of class nine. In this class, she estimates, maybe four or five students would manage to leave school with a low-stream graduation. (Hauke Straehler-Pohl, extract from field notes, 16 September 2009)

When I started, right after finishing my teaching degree, I really came home crying. I said to myself, you will never ever go there again; my teacher education was a waste. (Extract 1, interview with Mrs Streller, November 2009)

Then they [the experienced teachers] said to me: 'No, you can't do a dictation [in German class] like that. You have to write the text on the board, word by word and let them copy.' I said: 'Well, I can't write a dictation on the board. What kind of dictation is that?', 'Well, just do it ... and you will see', they said. And still [after trying], children were only getting [marks] fours, fives and sixes, even though the whole text was written on the board... (Extract 2, interview with Mrs Streller, November 2009)[3]

Well I do not necessarily always want to have only stress with my students, I want to experience some nice things. (Extract 3, interview with Mrs Streller, November 2009)

If I force them and even more and even more ... then they won't get it anyway. They become nervous and fed up with it, yes? Why should I do math after all then? It leads nowhere ... And then I would, if I was alone, I would say, well lets go into the playground for 10 minutes yes, and count flowers or collect 10 leaves or well yes, just to make a little change ... The disadvantage is, when there are two teachers in the room, you never know well would my colleague agree with that or does he think it's stupid?, because you ... also with colleagues, you have not chosen all of your colleagues. (Extract 4, interview with Mrs Streller, November 2009)

Interpretation

The image of the teacher (from the two incidents with the students) as a cold and punitive figure does not match either the teacher's reflective discourse (interview) or the researcher's impressions of the teacher's spontaneous discourse (field notes above). The teacher explicitly reported her emotional reactions when she was hit by the discrepancy between the idealised school ('everything you studied') and what was actually going on in her new workplace. This led her to revaluate her role as a teacher. She reported this experience as a serious threat (extract 1 and field notes) that required her to develop a phantasmic defence (becoming 'dull', field notes).

As previously mentioned, a fantasy provides a narrative for failure, one that covers over the traumatic experience of having to fail someone. When confronted with the failed union between the ideal and actual school, the teacher operates – or rather *partakes in* – an ideology that allows her to continue her work. We suggest that the community constituted by her more experienced colleagues played a crucial role in this process: they provided the ideological material that allowed her to fill the gap between the official discourse and the concrete conditions of schooling. This ideological material was not the official discourse of equity, but the underlying belief, shared by all members of the community, that the official discourse is indeed a *lie*. In order for the new teacher to be part of the community, the public rule (assuring equity through meaningful mathematics instruction) was not a sufficient means for identification. It had to be supplemented by a clandestine 'unwritten' rule that constituted the true 'spirit of the community':

> What 'holds together' a community most deeply is not so much identification with the Law that regulates the community's 'normal' everyday circuit, but rather *identification with a specific form of transgression of the Law, of the Law's suspension* (in psychoanalytical terms, with a specific form of *enjoyment*). (Žižek 2005, 55, emphasis in the original)

The way the new teacher found to cope with the gap between the Symbolic reality and the Real of schooling was by identifying herself with practices that she knew would not lead to the high goals of the Law. Identification with the community is always based upon some shared guilt or, more precisely, upon what Žižek (2005, 55) calls the *fetischistic disavowal of this guilt*: I know very well these students will never make it; nevertheless I keep acting as if they can. The teacher's fantasy of pursuing the superior aims of education enables her to repress the traumatic insight that all she is doing is actually working against these aims. Moreover, the teacher deals with the guilt resulting from having given up her desire (for a truly emancipatory education) through a philanthropic idealisation of herself as a 'substitute mother' (field notes) or an advocate for these poor children (extract 4). This humanistic position allows her to ideally construct herself in opposition to her colleagues (extract 4). This move, although perceived by the teacher as a 'step away from' from the ideology that she criticises in her colleagues, rather signals her total immersion in it:

> an ideological identification exerts a true hold on us precisely when we maintain an awareness that we are not fully identical to it, that there is a rich human person beneath it: 'not all is ideology, beneath the ideological mask, I am also a human person' is *the very form of ideology*, its 'practical efficiency'. (Žižek 2008a, 27, emphasis in the original)

Ideology is effective not because subjects consciously adhere to its values, but because they keep performing the external ideological ritual, in this case, promoting low-level activities among the students, using excessive regulatory strategies, etc., even as they publicly maintain a distance from its values.

Within the Lacan-Žižek axis, the attachment to something we know is 'wrong' can only be explained in terms of *jouissance*, or, in its anglicised form, *enjoyment*: although the ideology has been exposed, we do not change our behaviour because *we enjoy it*. As the teacher is aware, she has to find some pleasures in her job (extract 3). However, as it appears impossible to fulfil the desires framed by the official discourse of mathematics education, she has to find *jouissance* somewhere else. As mentioned in the quote from Žižek above, what a subject enjoys when deprived of a full identification with the Law is the transgression of this Law itself. This is the domain of the *superego* which 'emerges where the Law – the public Law, the Law articulated in the public discourse – fails; at this point of failure, the public Law is compelled to search for support in an *illegal* enjoyment' (Žižek 2005, 54, emphasis in the original). In this sense, superego is the 'obscene underside' that necessarily redoubles and accompanies the 'public' Law. It represents the true spirit of the community yet simultaneously violates the explicit rules of community life. While the symbolic Law provides meaning (based on the high goals of equity and inclusion), the superego provides enjoyment that serves as the unacknowledged support of meaning (56). An ideological edifice 'bribes' subjects into accepting renunciation by way of offering enjoyment. Concluding from the case studies, we posit the enjoyment of the teacher not in the official Law, but in the entire set of regulative measures that she puts forward to control the classroom. This happens even though, or rather, precisely because, these measures keep the students in a situation of imminent failure. The teacher sees these regulative measures as being for the students' own good, thus failing to acknowledge her own enjoyment in this ordeal.

The forced choice

Apparently the 'choice' that students face regarding school mathematics is between participating in the classroom activities and refusing to participate. However, the argument we present in this paper is that in certain mathematics classes, the choice is not an 'individual' choice between participation and non-participation, but between two modes of 'non-participation'. The first mode offers the choice of a straightforward non-participation by abandonment or exclusion from the school system. In the second mode, the alternative is to participate in classroom activities that contribute to an understanding of one's own ignorance of mathematics. This implies participating in one's own stigmatisation and exclusion from access to socially valued vocational and educational opportunities. Although the majority of students explicitly participated in the classroom activities, the narrow-mindedly mechanical and arbitrary activities guaranteed that the outcomes of this learning will not provide students with the skills and knowledge to open up further educational or vocational options. Thus, students' decisions to participate in classroom activities result in their non-participation in further education, in much the same way as the direct decision not to participate. As such, the choice is a false choice, since either way students are paving the way to their own exclusion from a consensually valued form of life. At best, students can postpone the materialisation of an already-determined exclusion.

At stake here is what Žižek (2008a, 38) calls the *choix forcé*, which directly concerns the relation of a subject to her or his community: 'every belonging to a society involves a paradoxical point at which the subject is ordered to embrace freely, as the result of his choice, what is anyway imposed on him' (36). In our case, what the school community indicated, both to the novice teacher and to the students, was that they had freedom to choose, but only on condition that they chose the right thing, that is, on the condition that they chose to operate between the official discourse and the obscene unwritten rules of the superego. The role of the unwritten rules was to restrain the field of choice by prohibiting the possibilities allowed for, guaranteed even, by the public Law (38). Taken together, the cases of Hatice and Melinda can be read as a message from the teachers to the other students that subtly undermined their freedom of choice and established the *choix forcé*. In the case of Melinda the message was: you are free to choose to participate in the activities or not. However, be sure that you will lose your membership of the community if you decide not to. In the case of Hatice the message was: even when you choose to participate, do it in the way that we expect you to, that is, play the role of the 'deficient' student who cannot go beyond ineffectual and stultifying tasks. In both cases, the students were forced to choose what had already been given to them.

Can things be different? As we discussed previously apropos the teacher, fantasy designates the unwritten framework that tells us how we are to understand the letter of the Law (Žižek 2008a, 38). In this sense, Hatice's behaviour (not accepting the unwritten rule of the community: behaving in an orderly manner and correctly solving the exercises set by the teachers) posed a threat to the teacher's fantasy. As Žižek points out, 'the truly subversive thing is not to disregard the explicit letter of the Law on behalf of the underlying fantasies, but to *stick to this letter against the fantasy which sustains it*' (38, emphasis in the original). However, as discussed above, a shared lie is an incomparably more effective bond for a group than the truth. What keeps the class together is not a sense of emancipation, of fulfilling the Law, but a shared sense of failure. This is how Hatice, by following the Law, excluded herself from the community. She literally treated the forced choice as a *true choice* suspending the phantasmic frame of unwritten rules which told her how to choose freely, and chose the impossible: to actually learn mathematics.

Perhaps the truly revolutionary act would be for students to behave like Hatice, to fully identify themselves with the public Law and demand a serious and rigorous mathematics education from their teachers. Žižek (2008a, 29) calls this gesture one of *overidentification*, which consists of taking the system more seriously than it takes itself. He explains that 'an ideological edifice can be undermined by a too-literal identification, which is why its successful functioning requires a minimal distance from its explicit rules' (29). A student like Melinda does not present any threat to the teacher. On the contrary, her behaviour justifies teachers' arguments that there are some students for whom pedagogic efforts are not worthwhile: *even though we know we deny our students a meaningful mathematical experience, we do it for their own good since they lack any sense of discipline.* A student such as Hatice, on the other hand, by erasing the minimal difference between the Law and its underside, presents a real threat to the teacher's libidinal economy. The only way the teacher has to deal with Hatice's act is through blind challenge: 'read it'!

Final remarks

As the title of our paper indicates, our aim was twofold. Firstly, through the exploration of classroom episodes we aimed to explore failure as a necessary feature of current schooling. A critique of ideology provided us with the means to undermine the fantasy-screen built around the issue of choice. This allowed us, secondly, to frame our analysis within a broader critique of a certain research approach to mathematics education that we characterise as evolutionistic. To do this we built on the assumption that the failure evident in the key incidents was not an empirical obstacle to the actualisation of the ideal, but a symptom of the functioning of the school system based in this ideal. The objective was to demonstrate how putting failure in its place – as a necessity of the system instead of a contingent obstacle – can improve our understanding of it (and its unequal distribution). We have thereby shown what we might gain if we dared to escape the regulative imperative of an optimistic evolutionism and make 'failure' itself the object of educational research.

Our analysis reveals the risks involved in considering educational failure as an unpleasant obstacle on the didactic road towards salvation. Describing things in terms of what *ought-to-be* instead of what *is* requires us to refrain from seeing failure in its totality, and to compartmentalise it into contingent variables that allow us to formulate narratives of modification for each variable. However, as we have shown, such an action ignores the life-world contexts of those involved and, thus, of those who necessarily would be involved in the *change* that research wants to bring about. By maintaining the demand to disregard totalities in favour of contingent variables, much educational research becomes what we have described above as a false activity: instead of unfolding a potential for a real change, it creates the conditions for things to remain the same. This happens by creating the imperative to research the *conditions for success* which creates a blind spot around the *conditions for failure*. A research agenda that could unfold this potential for change would need to take serious account of the stratification of failure and success inherent in the current meritocratic organisation of schools. Research would not only have to ask questions such as 'Why do students fail to succeed?' or 'Why do teachers fail to make students succeed?' or 'Why does teacher education fail to make teachers make students succeed?', etc., but juxtapose these questions with their antagonist: 'Why does school succeed by making students fail?'

The first essential step towards such a research agenda is to acknowledge the apparently pervasive function of school as a *credit system* (Baldino and Cabral 1998; Baldino 1998; Pais 2013; Vinner 1997). In order for such a credit system to work effectively within the official discourse of a democratic society, it needs to portray itself as a place where equal students meet freely and an 'invisible hand' guarantees that the competition of individuals' egos work for the common good. An analytic approach such as ours makes visible that merit in this credit system is possible only in relation to the demerit of others, i.e. the notion of personal merit is only possible as long as others fail. However, our analysis of the German school system, which abstains from efforts to disguise its functions of selection and accreditation, has shown that only accepting schools as credit systems does not suffice to undermine effectively such ideology. Our analysis has pointed to the more subtle ways in which ideology works by making individuals (mis)recognise their choices as their own, as free choices – especially when these choices imply failure. However, as we have seen in the cases of Melinda and Hatice, refusing to produce according to demand results in being barred from the school(ed) community. Thus, it becomes imperative that individuals read failure as the result of fair competition among equals and repress the traumatic truth that they fail so that others can succeed. Our theorisation has illustrated how schools need to obscure this 'truth' in order to retain their central role in maintaining apparently democratic and inclusive societies. Our analysis has shown the need for more research that focuses on the subtle ways in which this 'truth' is performed in the actual contexts of students and teachers. We claim that this kind of research is necessary to expose how failure is entangled within a meritocratic school system.

The reader may be left wondering to what extent our analysis has been a product of the contingent (and by now even historical) organisation of the German school system as an overtly streaming system. We would like to close our article with a question: Are less explicitly segregated school systems not just more effective in veiling the 'subversive supplement' of necessary failure and thus maintaining the fantasy of an exclusively democratic and inclusive endeavour?

Notes

1. The educational system is organised federally, each Bundesländ (province) having its own educational laws. In some provinces, the decision on to which school-stream a student is sent is based on the average marks in the final report cards; in some provinces, the classroom teacher gives an obligatory suggestion

(parents can just deviate downwards); in some Bundesländer, the classroom teacher gives an optional suggestion and the final decision is made by the parents.
2. Schools receive a budget of additional teacher resources, assigned according to variables such as the number of second-language learners, students with learning disabilities, etc. As almost all of the relevant variables were high at this school, the school could, in the majority of cases, afford to allocate two teachers to each class for the main subjects.
3. In Germany, marks are given on a scale from one to six with one being the best mark, five being a 'fail'. Giving a six is reserved for marking a 'complete' failure, such as a refusal to take part.

References

Atweh, B., M. Graven, W. Secada, and P. Valero eds. 2011. *Mapping Equity and Quality in Mathematics Education*. Dordrecht: Springer.

Baldino, R. 1998. "School and Surplus-Value: Contribution from a Third-World Country." In *Proceedings of the First International Conference on Mathematics Education and Society (MES1)*, edited by P. Gates, 73–81. Nottingham: Centre for the Study of Mathematics Education.

Baldino, R., and T. Cabral. 1998. "Lacan and the School's Credit System." In *Proceedings of 22nd Conference of the International Group for the Psychology of Mathematics Education (PME22)*. Vol. 2, edited by A. Olivier and K. Newstead, 56–63. Stellenbosch, South Africa: University of Stellenbosch.

Baldino, R., and T. Cabral. 2006. "Inclusion and Diversity from Hegel-Lacan Point of View: Do We Desire Our Desire for Change?" *International Journal of Science and Mathematics Education* 4: 19–43.

Bernstein, B. 2000. *Pedagogy, Symbolic Control and Identity: Theory, Research, Critique*. Rev ed. Lanham: Rowman & Littlefield.

Bowles, S., and H. Gintis. 1977. *Schooling in Capitalist America*. Educational Reform and the Contradictions of Economic Life. New York: Basic books.

Davis, Z. 2004. The Debt to Pleasure. the Subject and Knowledge in Pedagogic Discourse. In *Reading Bernstein, Researching Bernstein*, edited by J. Muller, B. Davies, A. Morais, 44–57. London: Routledge Falmer.

Gellert, U., and E. Jablonka. 2007. *Mathematization and Demathematization: Social, Philosophical and Educational Ramifications*. Rotterdam: Sense.

Gellert, U., E. Jablonka, C., Morgan. Eds. 2010. *Mathematics Education and Society. Proceedings of the Sixth International Mathematics Education Conference. 20th - 25th March 2010, Berlin, Germany*. Berlin: Freie Universität Berlin.

Gutiérrez, R. 2010. "The Sociopolitical Turn in Mathematics Education." *Journal for Research in Mathematics Education* 41: 1–32.

Herbel-Eisenmann, B., J. Choppin, D. Wagner, and D. Pimm. eds. 2012. *Equity in Discourse for Mathematics Education. Theories, Practices, and Policies*. Dordrecht: Springer.

Knipping, C., D. A. Reid, U. Gellertand E. Jablonka. 2008. The Emergence of Disparity in Mathematics Classrooms. In *Proceedings of the Fifth International Mathematics Education and Society Conference*, edited by, J. F. Matos, P. Valero and K. Yasukawa, 320–329. Lisbon: Centro de Investigação em Educação, Universidade de Lisboa.

Lacan, J. 2008. *The Ethics of Psychoanalysis: the Seminar of Jacques Lacan Book VII*. New York: Taylor and Francis. (Orig. pub. 1986)

Lave, J., and R. McDermott. 2002. *Estranged Learning. Outlines* 1: 19–48.

Lundin, S. 2012. "Hating School, Loving Mathematics: on the Ideological Function of Critique and Reform in Mathematics Education." *Educational Studies in Mathematics* 80 (1-2): 73–85.

National Council of Teachers of Mathematics (NCTM). 2000. *Principles and Standards for School Mathematics.* Reston, VA: NCTM.

Pais, A. 2012. "A Critical Approach to Equity in Mathematics Education." In *Opening the Cage: Critique and Politics of Mathematics Education,* edited by O. Skovsmose and B. Greer, 49–91. Rotterdam: Sense.

Pais, A.. 2013. *An Ideology Critique of the Use-Value of Mathematics. Educational Studies in Mathematics.* doi: 10.1007/s10649-013-9484-4.

Pais, A., and P. Valero. 2012. "Researching Research: Mathematics Education in the Political." *Educational Studies in Mathematics* 80 (1-2): 9–24.

Pietsch, M., and T. Stubbe. 2007. "Inequality in the Transition from Primary to Secondary School: School Choices and Educational Disparities in Germany." *European Educational Research Journal* 6 (4): 424–445.

Presmeg, N., and L. Radford. 2008. On Semiotics and Subjectivity: A Response to Tony Brown's "Signifying 'students', 'teachers', and 'mathematics': a Reading of a Special Issue". *Educational Studies in Mathematics,* 69, 265–276.

Rösner, E. 2007. *Hauptschule Am Ende. Ein Nachruf.* Münster: Waxmann.

Skovsmose, O. 1994. *Towards a Philosophy of Critical Mathematics Education.* Dordrecht: Kluwer.

Sriraman, B., and L. English. 2010. "Surveying Theories and Philosophies of Mathematics Education." In *Theories of Mathematics Education: Seeking New Frontiers,* edited by B. Sriraman and L. English. Heidelberg: Springer.

Straehler-Pohl, H. 2012. *Devaluing Knowledge: School Mathematics in a Context of Segregation.* Aix-en-Provence, France: Paper presented at the Seventh Basil Bernstein Symposium.

Straehler-Pohl, H., and U. Gellert. 2011. Learning Mathematics as a "Practically Able" Learner: an Instance of Institutional Denial of Access. *Quaderni Di Ricerca in Didattica / Mathematics (QRDM) Quaderno,* 22 (1): 195–199.

Vinner, S. 1997. From Intuition to Inhibition – Mathematics Education and Other Endangered Species. In *Proceedings of the 21th Conference of the International Group for Psychology of Mathematics Education (PME21),* ed. E.Pehkonen Vol. 1, 63–78. Lahti, Finland.

Zizek, S. 2007. *How to Read Lacan.* New York: Norton & Company.

Žižek, S. 2005. *The Metastases of Enjoyment: Six Essays on Women and Causality.* London: Verso. (Orig. pub. 1995)

Žižek, S. 2006. *The Parallax View.* MIT Press.

Žižek, S. 2008a. *The Plague of Fantasies.* London: Verso (Orig. pub. 1997).

Žižek, S. 2008b. *The Ticklish Subject.* London: Verso. (Orig. pub. 1999).

An ideology critique of global citizenship education

Alexandre Pais and Marta Costa

ABSTRACT

In the last two decades, global citizenship education (GCE) has become a catchphrase used by international and national educational agencies, as well as researchers, to delineate the increasing internationalisation of education, framed as an answer to the growing globalisation and the high values of citizenship. These developments, however, have created issues, due to the presence of two conflicting discourses. While the discourse of critical democracy highlights the importance of ethical values, social responsibility and active citizenry, a neoliberal discourse privileges instead a market-rationale, focused on self-investment and enhanced profits. These two discourses are not separated; they rather appear side by side, causing a confusing effect. This article aims to analyse GCE as an ideology, unveiling not only its hidden (discursive) content but also the role played by non-discursive elements in guaranteeing the coexistence of antagonistic discourses. It will be argued that not only the critical democratic discourse does not offer any resistance or threat to the neoliberal structuring of higher education, but also this discourse can function as an apologetic narrative that exculpates all of us who still want to work in universities, notwithstanding our dissatisfaction with their current commodification.

Introduction

The United Nations Educational Scientific and Cultural Organisation (UNESCO) recently posited *global citizenship education* (GCE)[1] as one of the strategic areas of work of the United Education Programme (2014–2017), and one of the three priorities of the United Nations Secretary-General's 'Global Education First Initiative' launched in September 2012.[2] In the document 'Global Citizenship Education: An Emerging Perspective' (2013), UNESCO provides the rationale for the implementation of global citizenship education across different countries. This gesture epitomises nearly two decades of relentless internationalisation of higher education, framed as an answer to the growing globalisation and the elevated goals of citizenship. This document appears at a time when many educational institutions around the globe are adopting global citizenship education as a foundation around which to organise their curricular activities (Andreotti, Biesta & Ahenakew, 2015; Jorgenson & Shultz, 2012; Shultz, Abdi, & Richardson, 2011; Yang, 2003).

This adoption, however, has not been without its problems. Whereas the official discourse (as presented in the UNESCO's strategy, for instance) anchors global citizenship education in the high values of social justice, solidarity, diversity and communitarian engagement, the implementation of this discourse into schools and higher education institutions seems to be thwarted by neoliberal practices, marked by a market rationality and the idea of an 'entrepreneurial citizen' (Burbules & Torres, 2000; Camicia & Franklin, 2011; Popkewitz, 2007). At stake here is the tension between two discourses, as recently identified by Camicia and Franklin (2011): one focused on individual achievements and self-investment (neoliberalism), and another one focused on active, responsible citizenship (critical democracy). These two different discourses are not separated; rather, they appear side by side, causing a confusing effect: 'students are being prepared to participate as global citizens, but the meaning of this citizenship is complicated by a tension and blending between neoliberal and critical democratic discourses' (p. 321).

How is the blending being made and what are its outcomes? The research carried out by Camicia and Franklin (2011) suggests that nowadays the neoliberal discourse overpowers the critical democratic one, thus the necessity for the development of truly critical democratic practices in global citizenship education that could provide a countervailing force to the neoliberal discourses (p. 321). However, we will argue that the critical democratic discourse has instead an important ideological role in justifying the increasing commodification of higher education. Global citizenship education is precisely what makes it possible to harmonise these two apparently contradictory discourses into a narrative that disavows this contradiction. Not only the critical democratic discourse does not opposes the neoliberal structuring of higher education, but also this discourse can easily function as a fantasy that exculpates all of us who still want to work in universities, notwithstanding our dissatisfaction with their current commodification. What this narrative thus conceals is the crude impossibility of achieving the lofty values of critical democracy under the rule of today's capitalism.

In order to posit both discourses as necessary and complementary parts of the increasing commodification of education, we will rely on the contemporary theorisations on ideology by Slavoj Žižek. Whereas traditional ideology critique seeks to unravel the particular interests behind a given ideological statement, by analysing its inconsistencies in order to pierce the actual mode of its functioning (e.g. Marx & Engels, 1932), it does so in an ineffective way since – and this is the main contribution of Žižek to ideology critique – it neglects the relation of ideology with what Lacan (2007) called *jouissance* or, in its anglicised form, *enjoyment*. What secures a given ideological edifice, what binds us to explicit ideologies, is not so much a rational decision, but a mode of enjoyment. Many academics have been criticizing the progressive marketisation of education, making visible the impact of neoliberalism and globalisation on higher education, where bureaucrats, special interest groups and profit-driven corporate programs prevail over democratic tenets (e.g. Apple, 2006; Biesta, 2009; Brown, 2011). It has become a common place among academics to complain about the pressure to produce publications and score points in the academic ranking, as well as the constant pressures to find external funding and alliances with the private sector. Nonetheless, we all struggle to publish as much as we can and to play the funding game in a profitable manner. We do so in spite of better knowledge. The crucial question about ideology is thus not to be posited in terms of knowledge – what people need to know in order to break the ideological spell – but in terms of enjoyment: what do people enjoy that prevents them from changing? The attachment to something we know is 'wrong' can only be explained in terms of enjoyment: after the ideology has been exposed, we still do not change our behaviour because we enjoy it.

What do researchers enjoy that keeps them attached to the belief that global citizenship education can be a way to save education from neoliberal tenets? Global citizenship education is a favoured term for many funding agencies, and an energetic field of current educational research. Contrary to Camicia and Franklin's (2011, p. 321) observation that the discourse of critical democracy is becoming increasingly rare, a literature review as well as an analysis of the rhetoric used by national agencies, non-governmental institutions and universities to describe global citizenship education shows that this discourse has instead become quite popular in the last two decades (e.g. Murray, 2006; Oxfam, 2003; Shultz et al., 2011). This makes global citizenship education a privileged area of research among educational sciences, with all the concomitant benefits of funding, working conditions and possibilities for research. Global citizenship education, although it might rest on the principles of critical democracy, is still going to be implemented in highly commoditised schools and universities, by people who are immersed in the dynamics of capitalist economics.

These contradictions in GCE have raised concerns for some researchers, who have been arguing for the need for studies to adopt a more critical and theoretical approach to the underlying assumptions of GCE (e.g. Andreotti, 2006; Mannion, Biesta, Priestley, & Ross, 2011; Marshall, 2011; Pashby, 2011). This article aims to contribute to our current understanding of educational policy, by analysing some of the relevant contemporary research on GCE. We begin by describing the *neoliberal* and *critical democratic* facets of GCE, and their entanglements. We then use elements of Žižek's philosophy to situate the content of these programmes, particularly the ones steaming from a critical democratic approach, against the background of global education. We argue that the discourse of GCE functions as an 'empty signifier', wherein antagonisms that pertain current education can be foreclosed and harmonised. Such a gesture allows us to have *hope* amidst an inherently exclusionary educational system; yet, it cancels any serious engagement with what are the concrete circumstances of today's schooling.

Competing discourses

The call for education to develop a more global orientation and to endow people with the knowledge, competences and attitudes that will prepare them for dealing with global issues is not new (e.g. Fujikane, 2003; Palmer, 1998; Parker, 2007). However, over the last decade, many of these diverse and dispersed projects have become crystallised under the overall umbrella of global citizenship education. Not only are educational institutions adopting global citizenship education as a main referent in their curricular and pedagogical activities, the amount of educational research dedicated to global citizenship education has also grown significantly in the last decade. We have today special issues of journals (e.g. Andreotti, 2011; Murray, 2006), anthologies (Banks, 2004; Noddings, 2004; O'Sullivan & Pashby, 2008; Peters, Britton, & Blee, 2008; Shultz et al., 2011; White & Openshaw, 2005) and handbooks (e.g. Lewin, 2009), dedicated to the thematic of global citizenship education.[3] These publications, by gathering the work of important scholars and encompassing different understandings and approaches to global citizenship education, provide us with significant material to analyse the ideology pertaining to global citizenship education. In this article, we are interested in investigating the role played by two (often) opposite discourses that emerge when discussing the concept and the implications of global citizenship education.

The naming of these discourses may vary, but they all deal with the Marxian notion of *class struggle*, displayed in divisions such as communism and capitalism, left- and right-wing politics. These terms have been disappearing from the academic scene, where researchers prefer to use other terminologies such as *critical democracy* and *neoliberalism* (Camicia & Franklin, 2011), *ethically driven* and *market-driven* (Khoo, 2011), *social justice* and *technical-economic* agendas (Marshall, 2011), *globalist* and *internationalist* missions (Cambridge & Thompson, 2004),[4] *critical* and *soft* agendas (Andreotti, 2006), to refer to the binary at work in the way global citizenship education is perceived. No matter how they are named, these two discourses work as competing forces in the struggle to define the content and the practical implications of global citizenship education (Andreotti, 2006; Camicia & Franklin, 2011). In what follows, we will briefly analyse what these discourses encompass and how they are present in today's research. We will use Camicia and Franklin (2011) naming for the sake of categorisation.

The neoliberal discourse

Neoliberalism – or in Marxian terms, *capitalism* – concerns not only economy. Its functioning has taken over all areas of life through the 'economisation' of non-economic spheres and practices (Brown, 2015; Jameson, 1991; Žižek, 1989) – starting with the restructuring of the state through a business model (Brown, 2006) and the subsequent undoing of basic elements of democracy, ending with the transformation of its citizens (Brown, 2015). Brown (2015) adopts Foucault's idea of the 'homo oeconomicus' (Foucault, 2004, cited in Brown, 2015, p. 56) to describe today's citizens as spectres of human capital, who 'approach everything as a market and [know] only market conduct' (p. 39).

Underlying the neoliberal agenda is the idea that education should prepare people for an already given world. The purpose of education is not framed in terms of criticising, raising questions, imagining alternatives for today's political arrangements, but to optimise a system that is seen as the ultimate horizon for human sociability (e.g. Fukuyama, 1992). Problems are recognised, but perceived as malfunctions of an otherwise good system that needs to be improved. The aim is to educate people to become more competitive, entrepreneurial and individualistic (Brown, 2015). Questions about the world in which people are supposed to be active are not posed within a neoliberal educational frame. The problem is how to prepare people to fit in and succeed in *this* world (Jorgenson & Schultz, 2012, p. 11). As a result, universities have become 'increasingly corporate in physical appearance, financial structure, evaluation metrics, management style, personnel, advertising and promotions' (Brown, 2011, p. 35). This is what Giroux (2010) called a 'business engaged in education', where students act as consumers, conceiving higher education as a 'personal investment (...) construed mainly in terms of earning capacity' (Brown, 2011, p. 23). Lurking in the background is the idea that education should have as its main purpose the raising of economic competitiveness (Shalberg, 2006).

Scholars have been indicating the presence of this discourse in global citizenship education programmes (e.g. Biesta, 2009; Khoo, 2011). Khoo (2011) refers to the increasing influence of market-driven scenarios in education to signal how the logic of banking, profitability and national dominance in global markets has been eroding the existence of ethical scenarios that engage with alternative agendas based on human rights and ethical globalisation. Biesta (2011) has developed a critique on the way ideas such as 'active citizenship' approach the idea of a 'citizen' from the needs of the current sociopolitical order, by specifying the 'kinds of activities and "investments" that individuals need to make so that the specific socio-political order can be reproduced' (p. 38). These investments aim to foster cosmopolitan capital (Marshall, 2011), and to maintain the global status quo by promoting the globalisation of the capitalist economy and by serving the interests of global economic and cultural imperialism (Sleeter, 2003).

The critical democratic discourse

While the neoliberal discourse highlights the values of the market for the structuring of human relations, the discourse of critical democracy emphasises instead the principles of social justice, diversity, equality and deliberative democracy (as it is present in the works of Jürgen Habermas, for instance). As stressed by Camicia and Franklin (2011), critical democracy 'is based upon a deep commitment to multiculturalism, critical awareness of global power asymmetries, emancipation and social justice' (p. 314).

A significant part of the criticisms made to the neoliberal agenda in global citizenship education comes from a postcolonialist perspective (e.g. Andreotti, 2006, 2011; Parmenter, 2011). Authors have been criticising the western strategy that informs global citizenship education, arguing for 'decoloniality' and 'diversality' (Andreotti, 2011). Indeed, despite the positive and seemingly inclusiveness of the concept of global citizenship education, the fact remains that global citizenship education is indeed a very local and restricted concept. As exposed by Parmenter's (2011) study – an exhaustive mapping of the literature addressing global citizenship education from 1977 to 2009 – the geographic affiliation of the 263 authors of the articles showed how the transnational literature on global citizenship education is 'massively dominated by western, English speaking states' (p. 62). The United States of America, the United Kingdom, Australia and Canada combined represent 85% of the institutional affiliations of the articles. Belgium, Hong Kong and Japan accounted for 6% of the articles. Countries like Cyprus, South Africa and India represented only each 1% of the literature on global citizenship education. Jefferess (2008) argues that global citizenship comes attached to a privileged social background, making it an exclusive concept that separates the ones who are in the position of helping and the ones in need of help. The idea of helping and being responsible for the other turns the other into 'an object of benevolence' (Jefferess, 2008, p. 28). Moreover, global citizenship education is delivered by a 'white, liberal elite' (Heilman 2009, cited in Standish, 2014, p.182). It appears that the idea of global citizenship, although portraying a global community, is in reality privileging a very particular group of people.

A critical democratic reading of global citizenship education emphasizes the promotion of a sense of belonging to a larger community, through the encouragement of new ways of understanding and interacting with others, both at local and global levels (UNESCO, 2013, p. 4). The critical-democratic discourse in global citizenship defines a global citizen as someone who belongs to a global community, and whose responsibility is not limited to a specific area, but extended to a universal one (Jefferess, 2008). As such, global citizenship is seen as a way of transcending the boundaries created by each country, to enhance universal human rights (Dower, 2003, cited in Khoo, 2011), global interconnectedness (Torres, n.d, cited in UNESCO, 2014) and global ethical responsibility (Jefferess, 2008).

Contrary to the unproblematic approach to the world conveyed by neoliberalism, critical democracy presupposes a critical engagement with the world. The current political, social, cultural and economic situation is seen as problematic, where new forms of colonialism emerge, economic and representative inequality arises, and environmental issues presses us to reformulate old practices. For critical democracy, the world is a mess, and global citizenship education is a way of turning the current situation into a more social just one. The way critical democratic perspectives conceive the level of transformation available is however problematic, and can easily be aligned with neoliberal tenets as we explore later in the article. As researchers have noticed (e.g. Hunter, White, & Godbey, 2006; Jorgenson & Shultz, 2012; Marshall, 2011; Sleeter, 2003), while in policy and practice, has emerged to challenge the economic foci of education, the result seems to be a reproduction of the same system global citizenship education seeks to transform.

Critical democracy as an antidote to neoliberalism

These two discourses, although apparently opposing each other, often appear side by side in global citizenship education programmes, making them 'increasingly indistinguishable' (Marshall, 2011, p. 419). As an example of this blending, Camicia and Franklin (2011) analysed the 'Teach First' programme (Teach First, 2015), a project where successful graduates teach for 2 years in low-income areas around England and Wales. The overall rhetoric of the programme is one of mitigating inequality by increasing access, achievement and aspirations of people from disadvantaged areas, thus pointing to the democratic orientation of this project. However, the entire structuring of the programme based on public–private partnerships indicates the presence of a neoliberal practice. It is as if teaching and its egalitarian purposes are not ends in themselves, but 'temporary ventures and practice fields for the more important realm of the market' (Camicia & Franklin, 2011, p. 320). The authors conclude that the two discourses become somehow fused, to the detriment of the critical democratic discourse that is overpowered by the logic of neoliberalism present in the programme.

Different global citizenship scholars have noted the eroding of the critical democratic discourse in favour of the neoliberal one (e.g. Camicia & Franklin, 2011; Khoo, 2011). As mentioned by Khoo (2011, p. 350),

> current global conditions are highlighting the contradictions of internationalisation more starkly than ever, as financial pressures are pushing higher education institutions towards marketised, competitive and unethical interpretations of internationalisation, while ethical and cooperative development policies and programmes for mutual learning and benefit are eroded.

As a way to struggle against this neoliberal trend, researchers advocate a logic of compensation, wherein critical democratic and emancipatory discourses and practices compensate for the overriding influence of neoliberalism in education (Camicia &

Franklin, 2011; Huckle, 2004; Johnson, Boyer, & Brown, 2011; Jorgenson & Shultz, 2012). As mentioned by Jorgenson and Shultz (2012, p. 1),

> as global citizenship educators grapple with and respond to the global unevenness of internationalization, the legacies of colonialism, and ideologies that support a system that benefits the few at the expense of the many, educators look to global citizenship education efforts to open educational spaces for working for a more just and peaceful world.

Authors from a critical democratic vein advocate a stronger critical democratic discourse, so that this discourse can function as a counterforce to the now dominant neoliberal one (Blum & Bourn, 2013; Thanosawan & Laws, 2013). Although acknowledging the intertwined way in which these two discourses appear, researchers tend to posit both discourses as opposite, and invite us to choose the side of critical democracy. However, could it be that these two apparently contrasting agendas are not opposite but together form a 'composite' (Balarin, 2011, p. 361), that strengthens (instead of alleviating) the neoliberal agenda?

The place of enunciation

At stake here is the gap between the *enunciated content* of a certain educational programme and its actualisation in a concrete setting, that is, its *place of enunciation*. Enunciated content and place of enunciation are Lacanian terms, which are used by Žižek to explore how the explicit rejection of an ideological hegemony can well involve the full endorsement of this same hegemony on the level of the position of enunciation (Žižek, 1997). The content of a statement can be analysed by focusing on the explicit message being conveyed by the subject. For instance, in the case of researchers who advocate critical democracy as a counter-force to the neoliberal educational agenda, the enunciated content of their statements can be hardly criticised in itself. Who would raise against the high goals of democracy, justice, diversity, sustainability and decoloniality? The problem arises when this same discourse is analysed not in itself, but as an act performed by a particular speaker or writer at a specific time and place. The place of enunciation is the place from where the subject speaks, the place where the high-goals of global citizenship education are going to be realised. Critical democratic approaches to global citizenship education do not exist in a political vacuum; rather they occur within a wider society that is 'reproducing powerful corporate cosmopolitan ideals entrenched in a set of neoliberal and knowledge-economy norms' (Marshall, 2011, p. 424). As noticed by Balarin (2011), global citizenship discourses rarely recognise that this presumed 'empirical reality' is entrenched within a system where social injustice is not an error to be corrected, but an essential requirement of the system. As Glass (2000) reminds us, 'wittingly or not, schools rank, sort, and merge masses into an ideological order that unfairly reproduces an unjust status quo' (p. 278).

The critical democratic discourse in global citizenship education seeks to uncover the processes that hide difference, create inequalities and maintain exploitation. It is assumed that through pedagogical endeavours such as critical literacy and reflectivity, students can analyse their own positions in complex structures, with a view to changing them and their attendant assumptions, identities, attitudes and power relations (Andreotti, 2011). Some authors argue that global citizenship education is capable of instilling a collaborative work ethic among students (Taylor, 1996; Villegas & Lucas, 2002), an understanding of citizenship that recasts autonomy and liberty (Hiskes, 1998), and orients our practices towards more humane and less antagonistic forms of educational policy and planning (Papastephanou, 2003). Such a display of students' engagement with education, however alluring in prospect, conceals a major question: What will make students work collaboratively and ethically towards a common goal amidst a school system that grades individually? The problem arises when we conceive education not as the realisation of a collectively motivated goal through continuous ethical commitment, but as the strictly individualistic goal of passing the course or achieving the highest grade. The school system is inherently individualistic, and this feature is obliterated in global citizenship education through the illusion that students are indeed working for a collective purpose. The antagonism that perpetrates schooling is disavowed by the fantasy of a collective of learners that does not match the real conditions of today's educational system.

A programme of global citizenship education designed by researchers is not the same as the concrete practice of global citizenship education in educational institutions. What makes them different are the different worlds they inhabit. A student is first and foremost a student, frequenting a specific place called school, with particular rules and organisation of labour. Research acumens such as critical literacy, reflexivity, collaborative ethical work are going to be implemented in schools – the place of enunciation. The latter determines the true content of these proposals, so that, in the end, it becomes difficult to imagine how these suggestions can change any of the core features of the 'school's credit system' (Pais, 2012, p. 69). To believe that our enunciated intentions are going to be implemented in schools without some kind of 'misrecognition' is to neglect the crucial role that the place of enunciation – the entire political field structuring education – has in attributing meaning that was not intended by the subject. So the question to be posed is as follows: What prevents global citizenship education, particularly within a critical democratic vein, from becoming commoditised, and thus utterly determined by the place of enunciation?

Ideology: taming the contradiction

As we've previously seen, authors that advocate a critical democratic approach see global citizenship education as an opportunity to counteract the pernicious influence of neoliberal policies and practices in today's education. Others, however, do not see any contradiction between the two discourses, and argue for a complementary relation between both (e.g. Held & McGrew, 2003; Johnson et al., 2011; Jorgenson & Shultz, 2012). According to Johnson et al. (2011), GCE is vital for the 'continued competitiveness of national economies and national security' (p. 516), and this endeavour complements the more humanistic goals of a critical approach to GCE:

> In the end, then, those on the left can support this agenda for 'normative', humanistic reasons, while those more on the right can support a global studies agenda for security purposes. As a result, effective global education should be something that can be supported regardless of political orientation or nationality. (pp. 516-517)

Likewise, Held and McGrew (2003) argue that the interdependence of markets, technology, ideas and solidarity can enrich people's lives where there is an emphasis on shared values and a shared commitment to the development of all people. Here the combination of the two discourses appears side by side, seen as non-contradictory.

Common to both discourses, is the idea that GCE is the path that contemporary education must follow if the purpose is to achieve a better world. Any contradictions that emerge from the confrontation of both discourses are disavowed, either by assuming that there is in fact no contradiction (as in the case of *soft* (Andreotti, 2016) approaches to GCE) or that the contradiction can be dealt with by focusing on identity change[5] (as in *critical* approaches to GCE). The latter is particularly evident in the UNESCO (2013) discourse. Although there is an awareness of the tensions between different agendas for GCE, noticeable in the way the document raises questions such as 'whether global citizenship education should promote global community outcomes or outcomes for individual learners' (p. 5); 'how to promote, simultaneously, global solidarity and individual national competitiveness?' (p. 5); and 'how to bring together local and global identities and interests?' (p. 5); the document does not deal with any of these problematic questions. Instead, they are dismissed by the narrative that 'research and dialogue could facilitate the reconciliation of local and global identities and interests. Furthermore, in the perspective of diversity, the tensions can also be seen as a value' (p. 5). The solution for these tensions is conceived in terms of research and dialogue. That is, instead of being understood as the core contradictions undermining the ideal of a global world, these tensions are instead portrayed as empirical obstacles, possible to overcome through expert research and dialogue between conscious people.

At stake here is the way we conceptualise the contradictions that pertain to social reality. According to Mouffe (2005), opposite conflicting categories such as 'left' and 'right', 'individual' and 'collective', or 'solidarity' and 'competitiveness' have descended into a centralised acceptance of capitalism as the ontologised modus operandi of today's world. As stated by Mouffe (2005),

> Nowadays politics operates supposedly on a neutral terrain and solutions are available that could satisfy everybody. Relations of power and their constitutive role in society are obliterated and the conflicts that they entail reduced to a simple competition of interests that can be harmonized through dialogue. (p. 111)

Indeed, this new all-encompassing category of people – the Citizen – stands precisely for this imaginary space of (neo)liberal-democracy where there is no antagonism: equal people discussing towards a common consensus. Against this view, Mouffe (2005) argues for the ruthless antagonistic constitution of the political field. This was the groundbreaking step taken by Ernesto Laclau and Chantal Mouffe in their book *Hegemony and Socialist Strategy*. Against a liberal-corporative view of society based in the idea of *consensus*, they assert the constitutive status of *social antagonism*. According to them, the appeal for a consensus always implies a hegemonic act, by means of excluding the dissident voices, i.e. the ones who have to be excluded so that consensus could be reached (Laclau & Mouffe, 1995). As explored by Mouffe (2005), in liberal-democracy the troubled 'other' is heard insofar as it is the voice tending to the consensus, the voice expected to be heard. According to her, the decisive achievement for democracy today is to recover the radical meaning of the *Political* – not as a utopian space of distributive justice (Rawls, 1999) or unpolluted communication (Habermas, 1984) – but a place of disagreement.

Slavoj Žižek has been further developing Laclau and Mouffe's insights on the political, through a revitalisation of the Marxian notion of ideology. Within the

Lacan-Žižek axis ideology is conceived as a defence against a traumatic real, a 'fantasy-screen' (Žižek, 1997, p. 7) focused on restoring order to a situation that otherwise seems chaotic or impossible: a 'totality set in effacing the traces of its own impossibility' (p. 50). The discourse on global citizenship education can be conceived as an ideological formation set in order to dilute the contradictions inhering in the role of schools and universities. As explored by Mannion et al. (2011), drawing on the work of Laclau and Mouffe (1995), global citizenship education functions as a 'nodal point' that attempts to 'fix meaning and bring together different discourses' (p. 444). Global citizenship education allows for the continuing commodification of higher education, but wrapped around a discourse of critical democracy and emancipation, so that the contradictions between community solidarity and individual competition, or between collective identity and individual identity are dismissed. This way, global citizenship education functions as a kind of 'empty container for the multitude of mutually exclusive meanings' (Žižek, 1997, p. 75). As an empty container, global citizenship education means that both critical, emancipatory education *and* market-oriented, reactionary education can work together in achieving the high goals of global citizenship education.

Ideology: a defence against the real of our enjoyment

Along these lines, not only are certain epistemological transitions currently unworkable, they provide the ideological material for critical researchers to continue following their radical educational agendas without posing any threat to the same system they criticise. Important here is the difference between the attitude that a certain educational proposal assumes towards the dominant relations of production, and the position of this same proposal within these relations of production. As posed by Žižek (1997), referring to the work of Walter Benjamin, 'a product whose explicit attitude is very critical towards the dominant relations of production often fits the frame of these relations perfectly' (p. 56). Going along with the ideology of global citizenship education brings enjoyment. It creates an entire educational and academic industry (from higher education programmes and funding schemes to conferences, journals, or international assessment mechanisms such as Programme for International Student Assessment) aimed at broadcasting the values of globalisation and citizenship across the world. This industry brings many of us a salary, partnerships, funding opportunities, academic excursions and other means of enjoyment. However uncomfortably, all of us who work in the academia somehow take advantage of the branding of universities as global institutions. Students, on the other hand, might be well aware that workshops on 'how to write a Curriculum Vitae', 'network effectively' or 'be successful in interviews' (Manchester Metropolitan University, 2015) have little to do with the higher goals of global citizenship, but still they undertake the programme. Possessing these skills might give them little in terms of global citizenship, but will potentially place them ahead of other contesters for future jobs, which will allow them to achieve a better social status and ultimately a richer bank account – in other words, it allows them to enjoy all the little pleasures that populate a capitalist economy. In both cases, the real of capital is present, structuring people's actions, hindering us from acting according to what we know. It is important to remark that what we usually call ideology – the 'hidden' agenda that reduces global citizenship education to a mechanism of accountability, employability and credit – is not 'ideological' but *real* in the precise Lacanian sense: something that does not depend on my idea of it.

Against this background, we can argue that the ideology of 'global citizenship education' is a defence against the real of our enjoyment: we need to know that the education for which we all strive is based on 'a sense of belonging to the global community and common humanity, with its presumed members experiencing solidarity and collective identity among themselves and collective responsibility at global level' (UNESCO, 2013, p. 3), so that we can accept the unequal, increasingly competitive reality in which we all work as educators. That is, the discourse on global citizenship education allows to perceive ourselves as ethical people, struggling for common goals through solidary efforts, while, at the same time, carrying on living our 'homo oeconomicus' lives. As argued by Žižek (1997), 'in contemporary consumerist societies, we, the subjects, are no longer interpelled on behalf of some ideological identity, but directly as subjects of pleasures, so that the implied ideological identity is invisible' (p. 11). What remains understated in the discourse around global citizenship education is the eminent subordination of education to the needs of the market. By buying into the critical-democratic discourse that encompasses, we can perceive ourselves as followers of a great cause, while the implied message delivered between the lines concerns the enjoyment with which we will be bribed if we subject ourselves to the cause. This is a case of what Žižek (1994) calls *fetishist disavowal* (Žižek, 1994): we know very well what is happening around the world, that globalisation actually means to impose the interests of a few to the lives of all, that democracy is in crisis, and that inequality pervades all societies; nevertheless, we continue to support the high goals of citizenship and globalisation. Standish (2014) argues that far from being altruistic, global citizenship is a self-serving practice, where citizenship means self-investment to increase self-value. Moreover, it assures that everybody has a place in the system: neoliberalists who are completely attuned with the depiction of schools and universities as businesses centred on knowledge (the so-called 'knowledge economy'), and critical researchers who can build their careers criticising and imagining alternative possibilities.

Conclusion

Both soft and critical GCE programmes (Andreotti, 2006) pose education as a crucial dimension, either in producing the enterprising individuals who will be successful in the globalised world, or in producing the individuals that counteract this neoliberal tendency. While the ones that advocate a soft approach to GCE do not see a contradiction between GCE and current educational policies, the critical researchers, on the other hand, see GCE as an opportunity to counteract the current neoliberal hegemony that characterises education. GCE is then posited as the enterprise that will bring about a change towards more ethical, solidarity and democratic practices in education. Although recognising the constraints that the objective reality of schools and universities pose to the development of this programme, not much is said about the concrete circumstances that have to be met so that such an emancipatory programme can be successfully implemented. This is partly because critical approaches to GCE conceive individuals as the loci of change, as if students and teachers were disposed to work collectively. Both agendas thus perform a very important role within today's neoliberalism: they provide us with rationales for action, thus keeping us occupied, while at the same time inhibiting a structural analysis and a possibility of a change beyond individual agency.

Some will say that such an awareness of the problem is too pessimistic and only takes us to a deadlock. As mentioned by O'Connor and Zeichner (2011), 'without infusing the message of hope into the curriculum, teachers risk fuelling overwhelming feelings of cynicism, frustration and fear among students, leading them to feel "cognitively overwhelmed" and paralysed to take action' (p. 532). Although acknowledging the endemic nature of exclusion in education, we need to believe that the goal for which we all strive is equality and freedom (that the presupposition of the system is a 'good' one), so that we can accept the unequal reality in which we live (Pais, 2013). We need to have 'hope', and infuse the message in anyone that crosses our path. Otherwise, we risk frustration and paralysis. The ethos of scientific research today makes plain that empty words are not enough; we must set to work, do it instead of just talking about it. What we need, some say, is engagement in action, quick solutions ready to be implemented, evaluated and, eventually, discarded, so that the entire process can start again. We argue that this pressure to produce 'solution-based' research is part of an ideological injunction to keep us occupied with specific research, while neglecting research that is not immediately concerned with providing solutions but rather to complicate the usual ways we approach problems. Some would say that such an approach to research will lead us into a state of paralysis, lost in an endless discussion from which no practical solutions, no 'insights for action' will emerge. Our response is that the true act sometimes could be a purely 'inactive' one. We strongly believe that sometimes the best way to act is to stop 'acting' – in the sense of doing research that immediately implies some kind of action – and ruminate. Žižek (2006) expresses this attitude as follows:

> The threat today is not passivity but pseudo-activity, the urge to "be active", to "partici-pate", to mask the Nothingness of what goes on. People intervene all the time, "do something"; academics participate in meaningless "debates", and so forth, and the truly difficult thing is to step back, to withdraw from all this. Those in power often prefer even a "critical" participation, a dialogue, to silence – just to engage us in "dialogue", to make sure our ominous passivity is broken. (p. 334)

If the theorization we advanced leads to paralysis it will not be the worst of evils. It would be worse to keep the current state of affairs, wherein resources are disbursed in innocuous research, which has not been proved to have the solutions for the core educational problems of our time. Indeed, if teachers refuse to participate in school promotion, and if researchers reserve more time for contemplation instead of complying with market demands for *fast research*, perhaps paralysis would have a very disruptive effect. As put by Žižek earlier, the worst threat for the system today is not 'activism', but passivity: the refusal to comply with more of the same.

A final word begs to be said about our own position as researchers,[6] particularly concerning the enjoyment that we, as authors, are also gaining from writing and publishing this article. After all, we also take advantage of the increasing importance given to GCE to develop this piece of research. Is there any difference between this research and the critical research in GCE that we criticise in this article? Or, more tersely, is there any difference between our enjoyments? The answer is no. We, the authors, are as much part of the problem as everyone else working today in higher education. If there is a difference, it consists in the realisation that we are indeed part of the problem; and avoid taking refuge in the fantasy of a critical GCE. Our critique sought to show how GCE is brought to its end not when it finally succeeds – guaranteeing a meaningful global education for all – but when that which seems its fatal obstacle – neoliberalism – is experienced as its ultimate goal. Instead of running after the demand of making GCE more equitable, social just, democratic, and developing increasingly refined stratagems to better implement it in schools and higher education institutions, perhaps we should acknowledge the crude reality that education is not for all, that schools are places of selection and teachers are agents of exclusion. These are the conditions of today's schooling, and research cannot afford dismissing them as being beyond its field of action.

Notes

1. For the sake of the fluency of the text, we use the acronym only in some paragraphs.
2. The other two being 'to put every child in school' and to 'improve the quality of learning' (http://www.unesco.org/new/en/gefi/).
3. Moreover, different subfields of educational research (such as Science Education, Mathematics Education, Teacher Education, etc.) have also been adopting global citizenship education has a main referent for thinking subject-matter educational issues (e.g. Skovsmose & Valero, 2008; Vesterinen, Tolppanen, & Aksela, 2016).
4. There appears to be different understandings in research of what internationalisation and globalisation signify in terms of the political agendas they imply. For instance, while for Cambridge and Thompson (2004) internalisation is associated with a concern for greater human rights and global justice, and globalisation is more on the side of human capital theory and the neoliberal agenda; for Jorgenson and Shultz (2012), they signify the opposite, with internationalisation a name for the promotion of neoliberal and corporatist views of education, linked to what is usually called 'knowledge society'.
5. Promotors of global citizenship education within a critical democratic vein often privilege the transformation of identities and take a normative approach to education (Balarin, 2011; Mannion et al., 2011; Marshall, 2011; Pashby, 2011). Although recognising the political and economic dimension of the problem, the solutions proposed are often centred on changing 'mentalities'. Moreover, this discourse assumes that students and teachers are locally autonomous and well equipped with a faculty of choice (Jahng, 2013), which allows them to pursue their own critical global citizenship education programmes in spite of all constraints. This way, critical democratic discourses of global citizenship education, while embedded in a rhetoric of improving global power inequities, remain rooted in humanistic discourses that privilege individual change over structural transformation (Mannion, Biesta, Priestley & Ross, 2011; Pashby, 2011). This erosion of the public sphere in favour of the private sphere, where people are expected to voluntarily 'do the right thing', is common to neoliberal and critical democratic approaches to global citizenship education.
6. We thank one of the anonymous reviewers for enticing us to write this final remark.

Disclosure statement

No potential conflict of interest was reported by the authors.

References

Andreotti, V. (2006). Soft versus critical global citizenship education. *Police & Practice: A Development Education Review, 3,* 40–51.

Andreotti, V. (2011). (Towards) decoloniality and diversality in global citizenship education. *Globalisation, Societies and Education, 9*(3–4), 381–397. doi:10.1080/14767724.2011.605323

Andreotti, V., Gert, B., & Ahenakew, C. (2015). Between the nation and the globe: Education for global mindedness in Finland. *Globalisation, Societies and Education, 13*(2), 246–259. doi:10.1080/14767724.2014.934073

Apple, M. (2006). *Educating the "right" way: Markets, standards, god and inequality.* Oxon: Routledge.

Balarin, M. (2011). Global citizenship and marginalisation: Contributions towards a political economy of global citizenship. *Globalisation, Societies and Education, 9*(3–4), 355–366. doi:10.1080/14767724.2011.605321

Banks, J. (2004). *Diversity and citizenship education: Global perspectives.* San Francisco, CA: John Wiley & Sons.

Biesta, G. (2009). Education in the age of measurement: On the need to reconnect with the question of the purpose of education. *Educational Assessment, Evaluation and Accountability, 21,* 33–46. doi:10.1007/s11092-008-9064-9

Biesta, G. (2011). *Learning democracy in school and society: Education, lifelong learning, and the politics of citizenship.* Rotterdam: Sense Publishers.

Blum, N., & Bourn, D. (2013). Global perspectives for global professionals in the UK: Engaging students within engineering and health. *Compare, 33*(1), 37–55.

Brown, W. (2006). American nightmare: Neoliberalism, neoconservatism, and de-democratisation. *Political Theory, 34*(6), 690–714. doi:10.1177/0090591706293016

Brown, W. (2011). The end of educated democracy. *Representations, 116*(1), 19–41. doi:10.1525/rep.2011.116.1.19

Brown, W. (2015). *Undoing the demos: Neoliberalism's stealth revolution.* New York, NY: Zone Books.

Burbules, N., & Torres, C. (2000). *Globalisation and education: Critical perspectives.* New York, NY: Routledge.

Cambridge, J., & Thompson, J. (2004). Internationalism and globalisation as contexts for international education. *Compare: A Journal of Comparative and International Education, 32*(2), 161–175.

Camicia, S., & Franklin, B. (2011). What type of global community and citizenship? Tangled discourses of neoliberalism and critical democracy in curriculum and its reform. *Globalisation, Societies and Education, 9*(3–4), 311–322. doi:10.1080/14767724.2011.605303

Fujikane, H. (2003). Approaches to global education in the United States, the United Kingdom and Japan. *International Review of Education, 49*(1–2), 133–152. doi:10.1023/A:1022994613635

Fukuyama, F. (1992). *The end of history and the last man.* New York, NY: Free Press.

Giroux, H. (2010). Bare pedagogy and the scourge of neoliberalism: Rethinking higher education as a democratic public sphere. *The Educational Forum, 74,* 184–196. doi:10.1080/00131725.2010.483897

Glass, R. D. (2000). Education and the ethics of democratic citizenship. *Studies in Philosophy and Education, 19*(3), 275–296. doi:10.1023/A:1005267212544

Habermas, J. (1984). *A theory of communicative action vol. 1.* Boston, MS: Beacon Press.

Held, D., & McGrew, A. (2003). *The global transformations reader.* Cambridge: Polity Press.

Hiskes, R. (1998). *Democracy, risk, and community: Technological hazards and the evolution of liberalism.* New York, NY: Oxford University Press.

Huckle, J. (2004). Citizenship education for sustainable development in initial teacher training. Retrieved from http://www.citized.info/?r_menu_induction&strand_0

Hunter, W., White, G. P., & Godbey, G. C. (2006). What does it mean to be globally competent? *Journal of Studies in International Education, 10*(3), 267–285. doi:10.1177/1028315306286930

Jahng, K. (2013). Conceptualizing kindergarten education in South Korea: A postcolonial approach. *Asia Pacific Journal of Education, 33*(1), 81–96. doi:10.1080/02188791.2012.751898

Jameson, F. (1991). *Post-modernism, or, the cultural logic of late capitalism*. London: Verso.

Jefferess, D. (2008). Global citizenship and the cultural politics of benevolence. *Critical Literacy: Theories and Practices, 2*(1), 27–36.

Johnson, P., Boyer, M., & Brown, S. (2011). Vital interests: Cultivating global competition in the international studies classroom. *Globalisation, Societies and Education, 9*(3–4), 503–519. doi:10.1080/14767724.2011.605331

Jorgenson, S., & Shultz, L. (2012). Global citizenship education (GCE) in post-secondary institutions: What is protected and what is hidden under the umbrella of GCE? *Journal of Global Citizenship & Equity Education, 2*(1).

Khoo, S. (2011). Ethical globalisation or privileged internationalisation? Exploring global citizenship and internationalisation in Irish and Canadian universities. *Globalisation, Societies and Education, 9*(3–4), 337–353. doi:10.1080/14767724.2011.605320

Lacan, J. (2007). *The other side of psychoanalysis: The seminar of Jacques Lacan book XVII*. New York, NY: Norton & Company.

Laclau, E., & Mouffe, C. (1995). *Hegemony and socialist strategy*. London: Verso.

Lewin, R. (2009). *The handbook of practice and research in study abroad: Higher education and the quest for global citizenship*. New York, NY: Routledge.

Manchester Metropolitan University. (2015). *Global Futures*. Retrieved from http://www.mmu.ac.uk/students/futures/global.php

Mannion, G., Biesta, G., Priestley, M., & Ross, H. (2011). The global dimension in education and education for global citizenship: Genealogy and critique. *Globalisation, Societies and Education., 9*(3–4), 443–456. doi:10.1080/14767724.2011.605327

Marshall, H. (2011). Instrumentalism, ideals and imaginaries: Theorising the contested space of global citizenship education in schools. *Globalisation, Societies and Education, 9*(3–4), 411–462. doi:10.1080/14767724.2011.605325

Marx, K., & Engels, F. (1932). A critique of the German ideology. *Marx/Engels Internet Archive*. Retrieved June 11, 2016, from www.marxists.org

Mouffe, C. (2005). *The democratic paradox*. London: Verso.

Murray, S. (2006). Editorial. *Policy & Practice: A Development Education Review, 3*, 1–4.

Noddings, N. (2004). *Educating citizens for global awareness*. New York, NY: Teachers College Press.

O'Connor, K., & Zeichner, K. (2011). Preparing US teachers for critical global education. *Globalisation, Societies and Education, 9*(3–4), 521–536. doi:10.1080/14767724.2011.605333

O'Sullivan, M., & Pashby, K. (2008). *Citizenship education in the era of globalisation: Canadian perspectives*. Rotterdam: Sense Publishers.

Oxfam. (2003). *Education for global citizenship*. London: Oxfam Publishing.

Pais, A. (2012). A critical approach to equity in mathematics education. In O. Skovsmose & B. Greer (Eds.), *Opening the cage: Critique and politics of mathematics education*. Rotterdam: Sense Publishers.

Pais, A. (2013). An ideology critique of the use-value of mathematics. *Educational Studies in Mathematics, 84*(1), 15–34. doi:10.1007/s10649-013-9484-4

Palmer, J. A. (1998). *Environmental education in the 21st century: Theory, practice, progress, and promise*. London: Routledge.

Papastephanou, M. (2003). Forgiving and requesting forgiveness. *Journal of Philosophy of Education, 37*(3), 503–524. doi:10.1111/1467-9752.00341

Parker, W. C. (2007). 'International education' in U.S. schools: The second wave. *Washington State Kappan, 1*, 4–7.

Parmenter, L. (2011). Power and place in the discourse of global citizenship education. *Globalisation, Societies and Education, 9*(3–4), 367–380. doi:10.1080/14767724.2011.605322

Pashby, K. (2011). Cultivating global citizens: Planting new seeds or pruning the perennials? Looking for the citizen-subject in global citizenship education theory. *Globalisation, Societies and Education, 9*(3–4), 427–442. doi:10.1080/14767724.2011.605326

Peters, M., Britton, A., & Blee, H. (2008). *Global citizenship education: Philosophy, theory and practice.* Rotterdam: Sense Publishers.

Popkewitz, T. (2007). Alchemies and governing: Or, questions about the questions we ask. *Education, Philosophy and Theory, 39*(1), 64–83. doi:10.1111/j.1469-5812.2007.00240.x

Rawls, J. (1999). *A theory of justice.* Oxford: Oxford University Press.

Shalberg, P. (2006). Education reform for raising economic competitiveness. *Journal of Educational Change, 7*(4), 259–287. doi:10.1007/s10833-005-4884-6

Shultz, L., Abdi, A., & Richardson, G. (2011). *Global citizenship education in postsecondary institutions: Theories, practices, policies.* New York, NY: Peter Lang.

Skovsmose, O., & Valero, P. (2008). Democratic access to powerful mathematical ideas. In L. D. English (Ed.), *Handbook of international research in mathematics education. Directions for the 21st century* (2nd ed., pp. 415–438). Mahwah, NJ: Erlbaum.

Sleeter, C. (2003). Teaching globalization. *Multicultural Perspectives, 5*(2), 3–9. doi:10.1207/S15327892MCP0502_2

Standish, A. (2014). What is global education and where is it taking us? *The Curriculum Journal, 25*(2), 166–186. doi:10.1080/09585176.2013.870081

Taylor, H. (1996). Practical suggestions for teaching global education. In *Eric digests* (pp. 1–7).

Teach First. (2015). Retrieved from https://www.teachfirst.org.uk/

Thanosawan, P., & Laws, K. (2013). Global citizenship: Differing perspectives within two Thai higher education institutions. *Journal of Higher Education Policy and Management, 35*(3), 293–304. doi:10.1080/1360080X.2013.786861

UNESCO. (2013). *Global citizenship education: An emerging perspective.* Retrieved from http://unesdoc.unesco.org/images/0022/002241/224115E.pdf

UNESCO. (2014). *Global citizenship education: Preparing learners for the challenges of the 21st century.* Paris: UNESCO.

Vesterinen, V., Tolppanen, S., & Aksela, M. (2016). Toward citizenship science education: What students do to make the world a better place? *International Journal of Science Education, 38*(1), 30–50. doi:10.1080/09500693.2015.1125035

Villegas, A., & Lucas, T. (2002). Preparing culturally responsive teachers: Rethinking the curriculum. *Journal of Teacher Education, 53*(1), 20–32. doi:10.1177/0022487102053001003

White, C., & Openshaw, R. (2005). *Democracy and the crossroads: International perspectives on critical global citizenship education.* Oxford: Lexington Books.

Yang, R. (2003). Globalisation and higher education development: A critical analysis. *International Review of Education, 49*(3–4), 269–291. doi:10.1023/A:1025303303245

Žižek, S. (1989). *The sublime object of ideology.* London: Verso.

Žižek, S. (1994). How did Marx invent the symptom? In S. Žižek (Ed.), *Mapping ideology.* London: Verso.

Žižek, S. (1997). *The plague of fantasies.* London: Verso.

Žižek, S. (2006). *The parallax view.* Cambridge, MA: MIT Press.

Recognising desire: a psychosocial approach to understanding education policy implementation and effect

Alex Moore

It is argued that in order to understand the ways in which teachers experience their work—including the idiosyncratic ways in which they respond to and implement mandated education policy—it is necessary to take account both of sociological and of psychological issues. The paper draws on original research with practising and beginning teachers, and on theories of social and psychic induction, to illustrate the potential benefits of this bipartisan approach for both teachers and researchers. Recognising the significance of (but somewhat arbitrary distinction between) structure and agency in teachers' practical and ideological positions, it is suggested that teachers' responses to local and central policy changes are governed by a mix of pragmatism, social determinism and often hidden desires. It is the often under-acknowledged strength of desire that may tip teachers into accepting and implementing policies with which they are not ideologically comfortable.

Introduction: sociological and psychoanalytical perspectives on educational enquiry

In this paper I want to suggest that in order to arrive at more complex and therefore more helpful understandings of the learning and experiences of teachers, and specifically their role as local mediators of centrally mandated policies, we need to combine approaches and perspectives that may be perceived as strictly sociological with approaches and perspectives that may be perceived as more strictly psychological. In particular, we need to set beside our sociological understandings of the workings of society, including the manner in which public policy affects or comes into conflict with individual behaviours, understandings drawn from the field of *psycho-analysis*, if we are to gain a fuller understanding of the relationships between individual agency and social structure and of the ways in which the social world is experienced and acted upon by individuals.

Such an approach, which, after Hogget and others (e.g. Layton, 2004; Hoggett, 2004), I will refer to as a psychosocial approach to understanding and researching about education and schooling, not only moves us forward in our understandings of education as a set of socio-psychological customs and practices, but, in so doing, suggests new theories of education and schooling that are likely to have relevance to a number of abiding pedagogical and curricular concerns. This is not to argue for some kind of 'third-way' synthesis between sociological and psycho-analytical perspectives in understanding social phenomena, but rather to suggest the advantage of adopting complementary vantage points from which to view the 'messy complexity' (Goodson & Walker, 1991, p. xii) of social life (including, centrally to this paper, *classroom* life) and the ways in which 'a personal life can be penetrated by the social and the practical' (Thomas, 1995, p. 5). As Hoggett (2004, p. 84), writing about psychoanalysis and politics, puts this in aptly autobiographical terms:

> I've spent most of my adult life trying to find out how things fit together—private and public, psychoanalysis and politics, care and justice. They don't. That is not to say that their curvature, at many points, doesn't coordinate perfectly but, if these are pieces of a jigsaw then the puzzle can't be solved.

Hoggett's notion of 'coming together by not-fittingness' (2004, p. 75) is particularly helpful here, suggesting, in relation to policy research, the benefits of greater collaboration across the disciplines of sociology/social studies and psychology/psycho-analysis which neither necessitates an unacceptable compromise nor promises to provide definitive and easy answers to perceived conundrums. If such approaches to the study of human beings in culture and society are not entirely new, they are, nevertheless, relatively uncommon in relation to other disciplinary approaches, and are particularly and surprisingly uncommon in research related to understanding teachers' experiences of classroom life. (For notable exceptions, see, however, the studies of *student* teachers undertaken by Britzman, 1989, 1991; Britzman & Pitt, 1996; Mitchell & Weber, 1996; Boler, 1999.)

The empirical base

In promoting my argument, I shall draw for illustration on the two research studies that prompted it in the first place. The first of these was an ongoing study—an *Autobiography Project*—involving student teachers on a one-year PGCE (postgraduate certificate of education) course at a British university (Moore & Atkinson, 1998; Moore, 2004). This study, which was subsequently developed at another British university into a study of reflective practice in student teachers (Moore & Ash, 2002), involved recordings and notes from conversations with 80 student teachers—mostly training to become secondary school English teachers—over a period of eight years, based on important issues and experiences identified by the students themselves in the process of keeping teaching-practice journals. The emphasis in these conversations was on encouraging the student teachers to talk about and understand their current experiences in the context of previous experiences they had had at school, at home or in other arenas of their social lives. The second study, the *Teacher Identities Project* (Halpin *et al.*, 2000; Moore *et al.*, 2002), on which I shall draw rather more heavily, comprised recorded and analysed semi-structured interviews with 70 practising schoolteachers and eight school principals across six secondary schools and three primary schools in the Greater London (UK) area. The aim of this study was to learn more about the ways in which teachers experienced and organised their working lives in the context of rapid and substantial educational policy developments driven by central government, and what cultural, practical and (in the event) psychic resources they drew upon in making those responses. We were particularly interested in this study to learn more about how teachers responded to policies that they did not particularly approve of, and how initially 'unpopular' policies came, nevertheless, to be put into practice at school and classroom level.

Given the ethical implications of reporting on interview-based research (in addition to issues concerning reliability and validity), it is important to say a word or two about the manner in which the two studies were conducted and in particular about the relationship between the researchers, the research and the 'researched'.

The first thing that needs to be said is that from the outset, though it was understood that the researchers would take responsibility for analysing the data, making connections across the sample and reporting and sharing findings, both studies were presented and (if our respondent feedback is to be believed) experienced as essentially collaborative in nature. While one aim of the studies was to contribute more generally to understandings of professional experience and the local reception and implementation of public policy, it was also intended that participation in the study would have the potential to contribute more directly to the professional development and understandings of those involved. That this was in no small measure achieved was evidenced by respondents frequently indicating at the end of their interviews, often after the tape-recorder had been switched off, that they felt they had articulated—or, in some cases, even thought—things for the first time, and by positive comments received when transcripts were returned to respondents for checking and validation and during group interviews (held at the end of each study) in which participants discussed what they felt they had learned from taking part in the research. It was interesting in this regard that a number of participants—including one of those ('Graeme') quoted in this paper—were very keen that their experiences and feelings should be shared with a wider audience so that (to quote Graeme) they 'did not feel isolated'. Comments such as 'Wow ... that was interesting. I'd like to hear that [played back]' and 'I don't think I've ever spoken about a lot of that before' provided an interesting reflection of the suggestion put forward by several of the student teachers in the *Autobiography Project* that a major aid to *reflection on practice* was having an interested professional to 'act as a sounding board' or to 'bounce ideas off'.

Common ground

The teams carrying out each of the studies I have referred to were primarily 'socio-logical' in orientation. However, in both cases there were researchers with strong interests in bringing psychoanalytical approaches and perspectives to our understand-ings of teachers' experiences and practice. It was clear from the start of each study that, far from resulting in tensions or directional disagreements among the research teams, these diverse perspectives were both complementary and productive, shedding particularly useful light when it came to analysing the personal, 'in-head' debates carried out by practitioners as they sought to position themselves (Coldron & Smith, 1999) in relation to mandated policy change.

This complementarity initially came as something of a surprise to us; for though we were aware of some theoretical and analytical synergies between the two disciplines, and in particular of developments in the relatively small, relatively recent but ever expanding field of the sociology of the *emotions* (e.g. Bendelow & Williams, 1998; Barbalet, 2002), we had anticipated a far greater difference than proved to be the case in the areas of *focus and emphasis* in the collection and analysis of our data. In particular, we had been concerned, as a group, that although both disciplines were interested in issues of structure and agency, the sociology of education had traditionally prioritised the 'external' structure, whereas the traditional emphasis in psycho-analysis, notwith-standing Lacan's (1977, 1979) notions of the structured unconscious or Freud's occa-sional references to the impact of specific socio-economic conditions on the individual psyche, had been on 'internal' agency. In relation to the sociology of *education*, for example, traditional themes had been the roles and functions of education (including its role in the socialisation of the young); issues of achievement and underachievement (often, in connection with class, gender, race and ethnicity); school processes and structures; and (more recently) policy and policy effects—all firmly rooted in explan-atory paradigms concerned with developing critical understandings of the social and economic circumstances within which education takes place, and its relationships with the wider social systems. Psychoanalysis, by contrast, even when used metaphorically or derivatively, had tended to concern itself with wider issues of the development, expression and repression of *desire* in the individual psyche, rarely—given its more immediate concern with familial and sexual relationships—venturing into the specific circumstances of schools and classrooms. (The most notable exception to this is prob-ably the work of Anna Freud (1979). See also, however, Gallop, 1995; Britzman & Pitt, 1996.)

Charting the psycho-social journey: the socio-economic order

The overlaps and (to refer back to Hoggett) coordinations between the disciplines were apparent in many aspects of our collective understandings of the data, not least in exploring the kinds of macro-micro policy dynamics elaborated elsewhere by, for exam-ple, Ball *et al.* (1992), Fulcher (1998) and Codd (1999), and in exploring the concept of policy as *discourse* within which and at whose margins the individual voices of practitioners struggle to assert themselves (Ball, 1993). The overlap which was to prove particularly striking and useful, however, and which offered us the strongest guidance when it came to data analysis, was a common interest in the life-journeys undertaken by individual human beings from a pre-social, pre-symbolic state of being into a pre-existing socio-symbolic and socialis-*ing* world: a journey which starts in infancy but continues, if (very often) with less obviously consequential effects, throughout a human life. The sociological perspectives of Bourdieu and the psychoanalytical perspectives of Freud and Lacan were of particular interest and use to us here.

For Bourdieu, the pre-existing social world into which the individual subject is born is described chiefly in terms of 'fields' (Bourdieu, 1971, 1977, 1990; Moore, 2000), these being the social 'spaces', structures, systems and organisations, infused with power relations, in which we live out our lives: social spaces which are characterised by having '[their]dominant and [their] dominated, [their] struggle for usurpation or exclusion, [their] mechanisms of reproduction' (Wacquant, 1989, p. 41). From the moment we are born, Bourdieu suggests, we *internalise* these structures, systems and organisations in the processes of socialisation; however, we make our internalisations differently according to the socio-economic position we initially occupy *in* the various fields. If I am born into a relatively well-off home, my internalisation is likely to be very different from that of someone born into a relatively poor home, and my expectations of success—and of the degree of control and influence I may have *over* the structures, systems and organisations—are also likely to be different. Bourdieu's term 'habitus' describes these internalisations: it is the habitus—the internalised, inner 'disposition', so deeply embedded (like Freudian repression) as to make us unaware of its existence—that effectively decides for us who we think we are, where we think we belong, and what might be reasonable expectations and ambitions for ourselves in the social order.

In terms of understanding the implementation and effects of educational policy at the local level (that is to say, in its impact on and mediation by classroom teachers and school principals), analyses such as that of Bourdieu's, which 'locate' the individual practitioner within relations of power and perceived social positionings, have much to offer. They may, for example, help practitioners and students of educational policy to understand how and why mandated policy is received, experienced and worked upon by practitioners often in quite different ways from one another—and indeed why, by and large, resistance to unpopular policy is less widespread and effective than might be expected given the large numbers of teachers involved and their potential political leverage. It was of interest in our own studies to note the very high incidence of respondents telling us (to quote two respondents typical of many): '*It's not my place* to oppose policy just because I don't like it: I can certainly try and work around it, and I do—but there's not much point arguing against it' (Ken, Head of high-school Humanities Department, *Teacher Identities Project*); 'There's no point opposing these things "out there": we can't change anything, even if we wanted to; it's just a waste of time and effort' (Mary, newly-qualified elementary-school teacher, *Teacher Identities Project*). It was equally interesting that very few teachers or student teachers openly criticised such matters as the selection of curriculum content (from, for example, the point of view of cultural bias), tending to express far greater concern about the amount of work they were being asked to do or the number of curricular items and skills they were expected to cover in an unreasonably short space of time, and how personal ambitions, too, were often linked quite markedly to perceived positions and possibilities within the social order. (For a fuller account, see Moore, 2004.)

It is not just (pre-)dispositions, of course, that account for these responses. As Billig *et al.* (1988, p. 44) and Hewitson (2004) have pointed out, teachers are constantly having to make pragmatic choices in the light of purely practical circumstances (to do with resources, the legal *requirement* to follow mandated policy, home and family circumstances, the nature of one's students, and a simple understanding of the prevailing socio-economic situation within which our work is located). These same practical considerations will be present in—and again contribute to explanations of— teachers' compliance with mandated policy change even where (as is often the case if our research is typical) there may be deeply-felt *ideological* tensions and clashes (i.e. between the individual teacher's or school's pedagogical or curricular convictions and those embedded implicitly or explicitly in imposed policy). As Billig *et al.* argue, teachers' positionings and ways of experiencing and responding to professional life are seldom internally consistent discursively, for:

> Teachers do not have the luxury of being able to formulate and adhere to some theory or position on education, with only another theorist's arguments to question its validity. They have to accomplish the practical task of teaching, which requires getting the job done through whatever conceptions and methods work best, under practical constraints that include physical resources, numbers of pupils, nature of pupils, time constraints, set syllabuses and so on. (Billig *et al.*, 1988, p. 46)

We might safely assume that when teachers embody in their practice educational aims and purposes with which they may be less than happy, their preparedness to do so may result as much from an understanding of legal requirements or a respect for democratic processes as from an internalised view of their own relative powerlessness within the system.

Recognising desire: psychoanalytical perspectives on educational enquiry

Bourdieu's conceptualisations of field and habitus, and research that explores the impact of the contingent on professionals' practice, clearly have the potential to help us to understand individual responses to social structures and events and to throw light on why and how different people experience and respond to the 'same' systems and public policies in different ways (that is to say, a recognition and understanding of the *idiosyncratic*). What such accounts tend to emphasise, however, are the collective and individual responses and experiences themselves, rather than where those responses and experiences 'come from'. That is to say, they tend to sustain the locus of the investigation *within* considerations of the readily observable mechanisms and structures of the socio-economic order rather than on what individual actors may have brought *to* that order and therefore on some of the less easily observed constraints on individuals' experiences and responses to social events (including those embedded in the linguistic structures through which experience is shared and mediated). This is true even of Bourdieu's account of the *habitus*, which prioritises the processes and mechanisms by which 'habitual' positions and dispositions are sustained by and within social 'fields' over the actions, perceptions and experiences of the social actors within it.

What is missing from these accounts is precisely the element of *desire* that is so fundamental to *psychoanalytical* understandings of human experience and interaction and that dominates the extensive writings of professional psychoanalysts such as Freud and Lacan. Of particular interest to the teams undertaking the *Autobiography* and *Teacher Identities* projects were:

- Lacan's (1977, 1979) emphasis on the power and effects of *language* in the infant's journey into and within the social/symbolic order (where connections with the discursive approaches of sociologists such as Ball (1993) were most obvious), and
- Freud's (1991) emphasis on the repression of desires, linked in turn to concepts of repetition and transference, that are recognised (unconsciously) by the individual as unacceptable in the social world.

It is important to clarify that 'repetition'—described by Freud (1968, p. 454) as 'new editions of old conflicts'—is here understood as the ways in which social sites (such as classrooms and school staffrooms) provide opportunities and invitations for people to 'play out' or 're-enact' previously unresolved social/emotional conflicts, including the assumption of specific 'roles' (that of child, parent, jilted lover, and so forth) that they have previously assumed in other situations. The related concept of 'transference' (Freud, 1991) describes the more particular process whereby one individual is addressed, perceived and responded to as if they were another (absent) person implicated in some previously unresolved conflict (e.g. a parent, a child, a jilting lover). To use Freud's own account, in which he applies the concept to the relationship between the analyst and the analysand, transference involves 'new editions of impulses and phantasies which are aroused and made conscious during the progress of the analysis [but which have the] peculiarity ... that they replace some earlier person by the person of the physician' (quoted in Klein, 1975, p. 48).

Anna Freud has famously argued that emotionally charged school classrooms, infused with relations of power and reflections of familial roles, are *particularly* apt to become sites of repetition and transference (the 'physician', for example, being paralleled by the headteacher, a particular colleague, a particular child and so on). Her suggestion is that if teachers are genuinely to seek to become effective in what they do, or to develop fuller understandings of how they react to things and whether those reactions can become less obstructive, they have a responsibility *to acknowledge and to try to understand such psychic operations*. To quote Britzman and Pitt's helpful summary of this position:

> The classroom invites transferential relations because, for teachers, it is such a familiar place, one that seems to welcome re-enactments of childhood memories. Indeed, recent writing about pedagogy suggests that transference shapes how teachers respond and listen to students, and how students respond and listen to teachers. ... [T]eachers' encounters

> with students may return them involuntarily and still unconsciously to scenes from their individual biographies. ... Such an exploration requires that teachers consider how they understand students through their own subjective conflicts. ... The heart of the matter ... is the ethical obligation teachers have to learn about their own conflicts and to control the re-enactment of old conflicts that appear in the guise of new pedagogical encounters. (Britzman & Pitt, 1996, pp. 117, 118)

This notion of adopting familiar roles and positions or re-enacting unresolved tensions from the past—or from the 'outside' of teaching (i.e. roles *currently* adopted in relation to tensions that are currently problematic and unresolved in the teacher's ongoing social and perhaps family life)—and of actively but unconsciously seeking out 'new sites for old conflicts' proved particularly helpful to many of the student teachers taking part in our *Autobiography Project* (Moore, 2004). Through participation in this reflexive project (reported in Moore & Atkinson, 1998), several of these student teachers came to understand some of their less constructive responses to classroom and staffroom conflicts in terms of adopting the perspective and persona of (in particular) a son, daughter, sibling or partner—an understanding which did not magically remove any unwelcome emotions arising from the conflict but helped the students to 'move on' from the conflict through bringing to it an alternative perspective. The *Autobiography Project* and subsequent *Reflective Practice Project* also shed light for the research teams on how the element of desire operates in relation to professional practice and experience, and why it is important to include it in our considerations and understandings of classroom experience, whether we are a teacher, a researcher or indeed a policy-maker. To quote one of the respondents in the student-teacher studies, raising an issue which was subsequently to prove very helpful in making sense of the testimonies of more experienced teachers in the *Teacher Identities Project*:

> With teaching, it's not just how you see yourself, it's about how you see how other people see you: how you see yourself being seen. ... What you inevitably end up doing is looking at the pupils and judging yourself through them. The children are in your head all the time. (Mizzi: student teacher)

For many student teachers, this anxiety about how one was being 'seen' was more specifically tied down to a desire to be liked and respected in the classroom:

> I wanted to be liked by the children. ... At the start, I was intimidated by them and my aim then was to fight back: if I get them to like me, they won't intimidate me, they'll like me. (Carrie, student teacher)

> Part of what I realised was that I'd had this feeling of kind of being watched all the time—as if there was some expectation of classroom performance that I was constantly not living up to. It helped talking about this too, and realising I wasn't the only one experiencing things this way. Another bit, related to that, was that I actually wanted the kids to be 'more personal' to me, if that makes any sense. I think I needed to be liked and respected, and strange as it seems now I'd never actually understood that myself—how my need was contributing to the overall problem. (Marlene, student teacher)

While some student teachers had initially responded to this desire through an effort to combine 'being nice' with 'being effective', others claimed to have adopted a protective 'persona' strategy, almost giving up on the project of being liked 'for themselves' and presenting instead a public front for their students to respond to. While such a strategy went some way to resolving 'the popularity issue' (as Marlene called it) by effectively removing it, it was not without considerable personal cost to the practitioner. As another student teacher, Celia, put it:

> It's a bit of a persona in a way and not really wanting that persona to be too far away from who I [really] am, because then it feels like you are having a role all day long and I think that's very hard work, having to actually pretend to be someone different. (Celia, student teacher, Reflective Practice Project)

This desire—sometimes articulated, sometimes not—to be liked/loved/approved of by our fellow human beings, and the related insecurity that we may not merit or receive such liking/love/approval, was not just a feature of the responses of the student teachers we spoke to; it also contributed repeatedly and in no small measure to the responses to policy directives that we heard about during our interviews with *practising* teachers, to which I shall turn next.

Bill: not rocking the boat

In order to give a flavour of how the psycho-social approach to our research worked in practice, I want to focus in some detail on two of the respondents in our teacher identities study, Bill and Graeme—both mature teachers with several years' experience currently working at the same inner-city comprehensive school. Bill and Graeme had both told us that they had experienced great changes in education over the past 25 years and both had expressed some ambivalence towards recent government policy and recent organisational decisions taken by their school, some of which had clearly been, at least in part, prompted *by* government policy. I have chosen Bill as an example of one of many teachers who had adopted what we came to see as a consciously pragmatic orientation to such central and local policy developments (Moore *et al.*, 2002a, b), underpinned, however, by a psychic (and largely unacknowledged or trivialised) need to secure and maintain personal approval (Mulkay, 1988). I have chosen Graeme as an example of one of many teachers whose earlier (including childhood) experiences were clearly affecting their current perceptions and experiences in ways that these practitioners appeared, at the start of the study, to have been only superficially aware of but that had played a not inconsiderable part in determining the manner of their experienc*ing* of mandated policy and their classroom implementations of it.

The first of the respondents, Bill, was an assistant principal. At the time of interview, he was in his mid-50s and had been teaching for nearly 30 years. In line with current national revivals in streaming and setting and in stricter dress codes, Bill's school had recently moved away from mixed-ability teaching towards more widespread setting of students according to ability, and had changed from being a non-uniform school to one in which the wearing of school uniform was compulsory.

Bill's attitude toward each of these developments had remained ambivalent. While the decision to adopt school uniform, had, he told us, been taken very democratically, involving teachers, parents and pupils, he had openly opposed it at the time on the grounds that the existence of school uniform was likely to create even more problems—including more staff-pupil conflicts—than it would solve. Even though this view was based on Bill's own experience of having moved from a uniform-school to a non-uniform-school, he had, by the time of our interview, come to accept that 'probably, overall, [introducing uniform] was the right thing'. His subsequent, elaborate defence of his position, however, suggested a continuing lack of comfort with this personal shift of view as, indeed, with his shifting ground over mixed-ability teaching:

> I think we had to go for uniform because of the rivalry, the competitiveness—and parents overtly wanted it ... I think probably overall it was the right thing. You know, I think it was because of a sense of identity. We made the uniform friendly. Most of the parents like it. Some of the kids didn't, but most of them did ... . I think it's very hard to know in the long run. You know, our intake has gone up, and we are much more popular. That might be one of the reasons ... . I think it might lead to an improvement in exam results, and a good [government inspection report]— you know—because those things do have an effect, quite a large effect, out there. But I'm still not ... . Again, I suppose it's like the mixed-ability thing: I'm willing to go along with whatever we agree democratically. But I was not one of the people necessarily in favour.

Bill, it seemed, had done what many teachers are compelled to do when confronted by enforced change with which they are not in agreement: he had put his initial feelings and views to one side, and gone along with the change reluctantly; rendering his immediate professional experience less happy, perhaps, but simultaneously offering him his only hope of long-term survival. In order to justify his change of position, and perhaps to express his discomfort with it or to render it more acceptable (to himself or to others), Bill interestingly explained his shift of attitude with reference to an ideology of *democracy* that he clearly felt he and others would approve of: i.e. 'I was not one of the people necessarily in favour ... [but] I'm willing to go along with whatever we agree democratically.'

Bill's understandable capitulation to a policy that he does not like is, in itself, of interest and importance, and examples such as this have much to tell us about the increasingly coercive effects of public policy on resistant individuals as policy becomes part of institutional hegemony. As Coldron and Smith (1999, p. 711) in their account of how practitioners 'actively locate' themselves in 'social space' argue, external policies which 'impose greater degrees of uniformity and conformity' threaten to '*impoverish* the notion of active location, restricting the number of potential positions the teacher might assume' (1999, p. 711, emphasis added; see also Ball & Goodson, 1985, p. 2). However, in order more fully to understand the *mechanisms* of such forms of local policy enactment, it is important to recognise and understand the part played by the individual psyche, and the ways in which the psyche interacts with—and perhaps is manipulated by—the policy imperative. In this regard, Bill's testimony immediately brings to mind Billig's (1997) discussion of the predisposition we have to regulate our feelings in order to fit in with situational norms, and our shared understanding of the potentially damaging impact of conflicting demands. It might also, depending on the reading we take, illustrate the same writer's comments

(1997, p. 143) on how individuals will '[resolve] a neurotic conflict through fantasies about the ideal self' (in Bill's case, the consistent democrat).

Whichever interpretation we prefer, Bill sends out a clear message in reflecting on his initially reluctant support for school uniform and ability-setting, that he did not want to rock the institutional boat: a position reflected elsewhere and repeatedly throughout his interview, through references to himself as 'a pretty reasonable bloke', as 'liking to get on with everybody regardless of their educational views', as being a 'middle-of-the road sort of socialist', and (indeed) of 'not liking to rock the boat'. In the discussions leading up to the local policy changes that he is most concerned to talk about (setting by ability and the introduction of school uniform), reflected on in an interview in which he is prepared to allow his continuing ambivalence to show through, Bill seems to have been compelled to subordinate one set of feelings—to do with educational and political ideology—to another set, to do with not wanting to lose popularity through giving offence to the developing ideological and symbolic order of the school: that is to say—though at first sight the reverse may seem true—in the struggle between ideology and desire, it is desire (the desire for popularity, for acceptance, for personal and institutional equilibrium) that wins. Billig (1997, p. 146) expresses this in considerations of conversation analysis and discursive psychology: 'It is as if speakers find themselves inhabiting a normative structure which is more powerful than their individual feelings and to which they have to conform for interaction to proceed.' (See also Mulkay's (1988, p. 79) argument concerning the avoidance of disagreement.)

The relationship between ideology and desire is, of course, notoriously difficult to chart, especially when desire is understood in its repressed (and repressive) form rather than, as I have done here, in its more accessible guises. (For one of the more interesting attempts to do this, see Zizek, 1989.) Certainly, space allows for no such enterprise here. I want to suggest, however, that it is in this 'have to conform'—this sense of compulsion—that the desire can be found: that is, the desire both resists the symbolic/ideological order and simultaneously urges obedience to it. To apply our *initial* (essentially sociological) analysis to an understanding of Bill's response, we might say that here is an example of the victory of a dominant over a non-dominant ideology—one that we might find examples of across a wide range of practitioner experience. Without in any way wishing to undermine such an analysis, our second analytical pass suggests that we are also seeing a triumph of desire—with, of course, its own history in the biography of the individual—over ideology, and that in order to see the 'whole picture' we need to visit both of these analytical perspectives. This might lead us, among other directions, to the view that without the presence of individual desire, with its tendency both to resistance and to compliance, the local implementation of public policy, especially where this appears to involve the imposition of an oppositional ideology, might be significantly harder to achieve.

Graeme: the return of the past

The second of the two teachers I have chosen to discuss in some detail, Graeme, had been in teaching for nearly 25 years—a career spent at just two secondary schools in the same area of a major city. Having qualified at a small training college in the 1970s, Graeme had begun his career as an English and Drama teacher, and continued to work within the English Department at his current school. After six years of teaching, however, he had opted to specialise in the pastoral aspects of education, and had been a Head of Year ever since.

Having experienced what he called an 'appalling' education himself, Graeme had rather drifted into teaching with a tentative vision of ensuring that some students at least got a better deal out of the system than he had. In interview, Graeme maintained that his own school experiences—in particular, the more negative ones—had helped him to understand his own students' feelings and needs, especially in Years 9 and 10 when they were going through 'the strains and stresses of puberty'. This feeling of being able to empathise with his students had helped to keep Graeme in a job that, for many years, he had 'enjoyed tremendously'. Recently, however, he had become disillusioned with teaching, finding it increasingly less rewarding to teach the younger students, and he was now, at the age of 49, looking for a move out of the profession altogether.

Our early analysis of Graeme's testimony had, as with Bill, focussed on essentially sociological issues from an essentially sociological perspective; in particular, an interest in the ways in which mandated policy becomes internalised and/or transformed within schools by teachers and school principals. We were interested in comparing the extent and effects of such internalisations and transformations across a range of schools and classrooms, and drew for support largely on the work of McLaughlin (1991), Ball (1997) and Gerwirtz and Ball (2000) related to 'reorientation' changes (temporary or compromise adjustments to structures and practices) and 'colonisation' changes (more permanent alterations to a teacher's or school's ethos and philosophy) brought about through the effects of public policy change (see also Moore *et al.*, 2002a, b). Within this theoretical paradigm, Graeme's story had been one of increasing disillusionment brought about by increased bureaucracy, by the insistence of a results and performance culture, by changes in teacher-parent and teacher-student relationships and by a de-emphasis on what Graeme called 'the socialisation aspect [of education] ... the preparation for life'—all leading to an enforced teaching style away from (to quote Graeme) a 'progressive', 'liberal' approach towards a 'more reactionary', 'more abrasive' one. In short, Graeme had self-presented as an interesting example of a classroom practitioner putting policy into practice at considerable— and highly visible—cost to his own immediate job satisfaction: a process he was finding so difficult as to make him want to quit the profession altogether.

While such a perspective again revealed much about the manner in and extent to which public policy becomes operationalised locally, highlighting some if its more insidious characteristics (Moore, 2004), it was clear that another perspective would be required if we were to make a meaningful stab at answering an additional question that had become increasingly hard to ignore during the process of our data gathering and analysis: that is to say, 'Why is it that teachers adopt the different strategies that they do in their negotiations with policy mandates, and how is it that some teachers— *regardless of their initial ideological positioning* —find the process far more difficult (or far easier) than others?' In this case, what was it *about Graeme* that had made him so desperate, so unwilling to continue to do as he was told, when others in his school of a similar ideological disposition had been willing to carry on? (It is important to point out here that Graeme's difficulty was not just about a clash of ideologies; nor was it indicative of a generally defeatist attitude. Graeme could 'talk pragmatism' as well as the next teacher, and, like Bill, was also able to justify setted teaching and school uniform—neither of which he had originally supported—through reference to local issues of results and behaviour.)

In order to begin to answer this question, we felt that we needed to think more about Graeme *the person*—and more about Graeme's *life*. Fortunately, we already had a good deal of information about this from Graeme's response to an initial question put to all our interviewees in the *Teacher Identities Project*, 'What brought you into teaching?' This question had initially been included as something of an 'ease-in' to the interview, and we had been sceptical to the possibility that it might yield much usable data given our more pressing research imperatives. We had been surprised, however, to find that respondents actually had a great deal to say, often providing many unsolicited details of their personal circumstances and aspirations, and in some cases responding almost as if in a confessional—details which (as in the case of Graeme) were often to prove particularly helpful in explaining some of the experiences and orientations discussed later on in the interview. Graeme's response offers a particularly illuminating and accessible example of the kind of 'soul-baring' undertaken by many of our respondents. This extract is taken from the very beginning of Graeme's interview:

Interviewer:	I wonder if you could say something about what brought you into teaching and what motivated you to become a teacher in the first place—and perhaps when you made that decision?
Graeme:	Well I dropped out of the sixth form at school and had five years wandering, doing all sorts of jobs of this and that, selling things and getting a motor cycle. Eventually a friend who was going into teaching suggested that I might be good at it. I thought about it and having had such an appalling school experience myself, which I hated, I think that led me to think perhaps I would like to make it better for others. That's what took me into it: I think it was that eventually.
Interviewer:	Was it bad teachers, or—?
Graeme:	No my own school. It was different things. It was to do with [family circumstances] and the fact that I was sent to a boarding school that I hated [...] and a whole lot of things. And they put me back a year because [of] my attainment, and with that my confidence totally went after that. I was twelve. I had done very well at school and suddenly I am sent to somewhere where I am told I am not doing well and that was it. I did no 'O' levels, started the sixth form and couldn't stand it any longer and dropped out.
Interviewer:	Those negative experiences—you say they helped you?
Graeme:	Those negative experiences have helped me as a teacher I am sure.
Interviewer:	Is that in the way you respond to the kids?
Graeme:	I think the way I respond to them, yes, because I do understand to an extent, I understand all that they feel.

One of the more interesting aspects of Graeme's testimony is that while he recognises the impact of his own experiences of schooling on his desire to become a teacher himself—and a particular *kind* of teacher—he does not appear to make the same kind of connection between his experiences of schooling and his decision to *leave* teaching. When asked to explain this latter decision, he tends to concentrate on the clashes between his own preferred teaching style and the style that he feels is being imposed on him from a variety of 'outside' forces—seemingly overlooking the 'inside' force that is also at work. Graeme's situation brings to mind not only Sigmund Freud's conceptualisations of repetition and transference, but the exemplary study of Anna Freud of how transference and repetition work in practice. This study, summarised by Britzman and Pitt (1996, p. 118), tells of a governess employed to help three children with their academic work. The governess quickly fixed on the middle child, deemed by his parents to be the least able, formed a close attachment with him, and raised his achievement to a remarkable degree. No sooner had the child demonstrated his academic success, however, than the governess resigned her post, appearing to lose interest in the child altogether. Explaining the governess's behaviour, Britzman and Pitt (1996, p. 118) continue:

> Her identification with this child was due to feelings of being ignored and misunderstood in her own childhood. She came to see how her devotion for teaching this child—a devotion Anna Freud names as 'rescue fantasy'—turned to envy when the child became successful ... [T]he child served as a representation of a condensed version of her own childhood.

Given Graeme's observations about his own childhood, it is not fanciful to begin to understand his own difficulties at least partly within these same contexts of repetition and transference. That is to say, what is at stake for Graeme is not simply a threatened ideological/educational stance, but a threatened *re-enactment*: indeed, a threatened *expiation* of sorts and, hence, a threatened purpose that lies beyond stories of wanting to contribute something useful to society. From this perspective, the key observations in the snippet of conversation cited above are 'I would like to make it better for others' and 'I understand all that they feel': in other words, just like the governess in Anna Freud's study, Graeme's students had as much of a *function* in Graeme's professional life as he had in their socio-academic lives: they, too, 'served as a representation of a condensed version of [his] own childhood'—and in rescuing theirs, Graeme was, effectively, rescuing his own.

I do not want to undermine either Graeme's altruism or his devotion and sense of vocation by suggesting that he had entered the teaching profession for purely 'selfish' or instrumental reasons; merely that a broader approach to understanding professional experience, including that of practitioners *like* Graeme, who are experiencing serious difficulties, may provide important contexts for those experiences and understandings and may even suggest possible resolutions. If we adopt the viewpoint suggested in the previous paragraph, we can suggest that Graeme's genuinely felt aspirations for his students connect very strongly—and semi-consciously—to the brutality of his own schooling and a need to expiate that brutality: so that when he finds himself pushed by factors in the 'external' social world (e.g. changes in public behaviour and in government education policies) towards replicating that *same* brutality, he does all that he feels he can do: he decides to resign. The decision may thus be understood not simply as an inability to change habits and accept change (in Graeme's words, becoming 'a bit of a dinosaur'), but in terms of a far more fundamental threat to the teacher's very 'identity'.

Recognising the emotional: understanding compliant and resistant responses

This paper has argued that the individual social actor's journey into and within the socio-symbolic world is simultaneously a journey into and a positioning within the socio-economic order (an order of laws and regulations, of power relations and hierarchical 'locations') and a journey into and a positioning within the psychic order (an order concerned with the allowance, control and denial of desire). The navigation of this journey—undertaken within the contingent context of practicality/practicability and the idiosyncratic context of initial and ongoing social induction—is germane to the individual's subsequent sense of identity and is of critical importance in the ways in which we continue to experience and to understand social situations, interactions and events including those situated within our professional and 'public' lives. To understand the journey and its effects in the fields of educational policy and practice suggests the importance of a joint focus on—but at the same time a breaking down of the semiotic boundaries between—both agency and structure. In particular, it argues for research into the idiosyncratic ways in which blunt, 'universal' policy is received and worked upon by those charged with its implementation (Ball, 1993). This requires a recognition that teachers (no less, indeed, than their students) are constantly positioning and repositioning themselves in relation both to the practicalities of their daily work and to the demands of their 'inner selves': that is to say, these positionings and repositionings occur in neither a social nor a psychic 'vacuum' (Hartnett & Carr, 1995; Smyth, 1995).

There is a growing body of literature (e.g. Britzman & Pitt, 1996; Boler, 1999) suggesting that the emotional—that *desire*—is too often left out of our understandings of classroom practice and experience, and that this omission can be detrimental both to our development as reflective individuals and to the development of our practice— a view elaborated elsewhere by Zizek (1989) in relation to our desire for approval in the eyes of others. Critically, the overlooking of this dimension seriously hampers our understanding of—and subsequent ability to respond constructively to—those other issues concerning practical (re)orienations in relation to dominant hegemonic views of teaching and schooling and to dominant policy perspectives on teaching and schooling. From the practitioner's point of view, it can also prove critical in determining not so much the manner in which public policy is implemented at the local level but in the sense that the practitioner makes of the more negative and troublesome aspects of their work experiences and the extent to which these do or do not prove 'fatal'. Hoggett (2004, p. 84) has suggested in this respect that '[W]e must learn to enjoy our [internal and external] conflicts; it is only when we are afraid of them that our troubles begin.' While this may be easier said than done, one is left wondering, in respect of the experiences of Graeme (above), whether or not a more reflexive consideration of his difficulties, carried out within a more supportive professional environment, might have helped him to reach the same kind of equilibrium achieved by his colleague Bill and others, whereby he could have continued in work that he clearly saw as important without completely sacrificing either his motivation or his ideals. This is not, of course, to argue the case for compliance: far from it. For such reflexivity and support might also—though with more attendant difficulties, perhaps—have suggested a more genuinely *resistant* response in place of Bill's compliant one, the latter simply having demanded a cost too high for Graeme to be prepared to pay.

References

Ball, S. J. (1993) What is policy? Texts, trajectories and toolboxes, *Discourse*, 13(2), 10–17.

Ball, S. J., Bowe, R. & Gold, A. (1992) *Reforming education and changing schools* (London, Routledge).

Ball, S. (1997) Policy sociology and critical social research: a personal review of recent education policy and policy research, *British Educational Research Journal*, 23(3), 257–274.

Ball, S. & Goodson, I. (1985) Understanding teachers: concepts and contexts, in: S. Ball & I. Goodson (Eds) *Teachers' lives and careers* (London, Falmer Press), 1–26.

Barbalet, J. (Ed.) (2002) *Emotions and sociology* (London, Blackwell).

Bendelow, G. & Williams, S. G. (Eds) (1998) *Emotions in social life: critical themes and contemporary issues* (London, Routledge).

Billig, M. (1997) The dialogic unconscious: psychoanalysis, discursive psychology and the nature of repression, *British Journal of Social Psychology*, 36, 139–159.

Billig, M., Condor, S., Edwards, D., Gane, M., Middleton, D. & Radley, A. (1988) *Ideological dilemmas: a social psychology of everyday thinking* (London, Sage).

Boler, M. (1999) *Feeling power: emotions and education* (New York and London, Routledge).

Bourdieu, P. (1971) Intellectual field and creative project, in: M. F. D. Young (Ed.) *Knowledge and control* (London, Collier-Macmillan), 161–188.

Bourdieu, P. (1977) *Outline of a theory of practice* (Cambridge, Cambridge University Press).

Bourdieu, P. (1990) *The logic of practice* (Cambridge, Polity Press).

Britzman, D. (1989) Who has the floor? Curriculum, teaching and the English student teacher's struggle for voice, *Curriculum Inquiry*, 19(2), 143–162.

Britzman, D. (1991) *Practice makes practice* (Albany, SUNY).

Britzman, D. & Pitt, A. (1996) Pedagogy and transference: casting the past of learning into the presence of teaching, *Theory into Practice*, 35(2), 117–123.

Codd, J. A. (1999) The construction and deconstruction of educational policy documents, in: J. Marshall & M. Peters (Eds) *Education policy* (Cheltenham, UK/Northampton, MA, Edward Elgar Publishing), 19–31.

Coldron, J. & Smith, R. (1999) Active location in teachers' construction of their professional identities, *Journal of Curriculum Studies*, 31, 711–726.

Freud, A. (1979) *Psycho-analysis for teachers and parents* (Trans. B. Low) (New York, W. W. Norton).

Freud, S. (1968) Introductory lectures on psycho-analysis, part three, in: *Standard Edition*, vol. 17 (Trans. J. Strachey) (London, Hogarth Press).

Freud, S. (1991) *The essentials of psycho-analysis* (London, Penguin).

Fulcher, G. (1998) *Disabling policies? A comparative approach to education policy and disability* (Sheffield, Philip Armstrong Publications).

Gallop, J. (Ed.) (1995) *Pedagogy: the question of impersonation* (Bloomington, IN, University Press).

Gewirtz, S. & Ball, S. J. (2000) From 'Welfarism' to 'New Managerialism': shifting discourses of school headship in the education marketplace, *Discourse*, 21(3), 253–268.

Goodson, I. F. & Walker, R. (1991) *Biography, identity and schooling* (London, Falmer Press).

Halpin, D. & Moore, A., with Edwards, G., George, R. & Jones, C. (2000) Maintaining, reconstructing and creating tradition in education, *Oxford Review of Education*, 26(2), 133–144.

Hartnett, A. & Carr, W. (1995) Education, teacher development and the struggle for democracy, in: J. Smyth (Ed.) *Introduction to critical discourses on teacher development* (London, Cassell), 39–54.

Hewitson, R. (2004) A critical ethnographic account of teacher professional development in a devolved high school setting. PhD thesis, Flinders University, Adelaide, South Australia.

Hoggett, P. (2004) Strange attractors: politics and psychoanalysis, *Psychoanalysis, Culture and Society*, 9, 74–86.

Kelly, A. V. (1999) *Curriculum: theory and practice* (London, Paul Chapman Publishing).

Klein, M. (1975) *Envy and gratitude and other works 1946–1963* (London, Hogarth Press/the Institute of Psycho-Analysis).

Lacan, J. (1977) *Ecrits* (London, Tavistock Publications).

Lacan, J. (1979) *The four fundamental concepts of psycho-analysis* (London, Penguin).

Layton, L. (2004) A fork in the royal road: on 'defining' the unconscious and its stakes for social theory, *Psychoanalysis, Culture and Society*, 9, 33–51.

McLaughlin, R. (1991) Can the information systems for the NHS internal market work?, *Public Money and Management*, Autumn, 37–41.

Mitchell, C. & Weber, S. (1996) *Reinventing ourselves as teachers: private and social acts of memory and imagination* (London, Falmer).

Moore, A. (2000) *Teaching and learning: pedagogy, curriculum and culture* (London, RoutledgeFalmer).

Moore, A. (2004) *The good teacher: dominant discourses in teaching and teacher education* (London, RoutledegeFalmer).

Moore, A. & Ash, A. (2002) Developing reflective practice in beginning teachers: helps, hindrances and the role of the critical o/Other. Research paper presented at the *British Educational Research Association Annual Conference*, University of Exeter, September.

Moore, A. & Atkinson, D. (1998) Charisma, competence and teacher education, *Discourse*, 19(2), 171–181.

Moore, A., Edwards, G., Halpin, D. & George, R. (2002a) Compliance, resistance and pragmatism: the (re)construction of schoolteacher identities in a period of intensive educational reform, *British Educational Research Journal*, 28(4), 551–565.

Moore, A., George, R. & Halpin, D. (2002b) The developing role of the headteacher in English schools: management, leadership and pragmatism, *Educational Management and Administration*, 30(2), 177–190.

Mulkay, M. (1988) *On humour* (Cambridge, Cambridge University Press).

Smyth, J. (Ed.) (1995) *Introduction to critical discourses on teacher development* (London, Cassell).

Thomas, D. (1995) Treasonable or trustworthy text: reflections on teacher narrative studies, in: D. Thomas (Ed.) *Teachers' stories* (Buckingham, Open University Press), 1–23.

Wacquant, L. J. D. (1989) Towards a reflexive sociology: a workshop with Pierre Bourdieu, *Sociological Theory*, 7.

Zizek, S. (1989) *The sublime object of ideology* (London, Verso).

Psychical contexts of subjectivity and performative practices of remuneration: teaching assistants' narratives of work

Claudia Lapping and Jason Glynos

ABSTRACT

A range of sociological work has theorized neoliberal regulative regimes, suggesting the contradictions contained in the enactment of policy and foregrounding the painful effects of these processes on subjectivities produced within performative school cultures. This paper contributes to this body of work by tracing the movement of desire in teaching assistants' subjective relations to workplace practices of remuneration. We do this through an analysis of a series of group- and individual-free associative interviews with teaching assistants working in primary schools. Drawing on a Lacanian account of the way processes of identification channel affect, as desire, through signifying chains within a discursive field, we explore the associative chains of meaning that overdetermine the subjectivities produced within performative practices of remuneration. We suggest that the complex and contradictory chains of signification embodied in the school environment constitute a space where fragile teaching assistant subjectivities reiterate previous relations to an ambiguous Other.

Introduction: theorizing the production of remunerative practices and relations to work

Debate about pay and remuneration in the media is often sensationalized in relation to the high pay of executives, sports stars, and celebrities on the one hand, in relation to those receiving below minimum wage on the other, or, alternatively, in polarized responses to workers striking in a variety of private and public sector organizations. It is perhaps tempting to dismiss out of hand the sensationalized, truncated, and often inconsistent stances on pay and remuneration circulating in the popular media and in our everyday discourse; and the extent to which these debates affect policy or practice is difficult to determine. However, popular narratives of justification, as well as common deliberative dynamics, and the terms of specific political debates re-emerge in the everyday interactions that constitute relations to pay and remuneration. The appearance or disappearance of these discursive elements can contain important clues about how regimes of remuneration are sustained and how they might be transformed. This paper foregrounds one approach to interpreting these clues: an approach that enables us to examine the unconscious processes that tie individual subjects into the remuneration regime of a particular sector, and to trace moments of potential fissure. We do this through an analysis of a series of group- and individual-free associative interviews with teaching assistants working in primary schools.

Contemporary developments in the neoliberal and financialized political economy have been identified with contradictory moments in our beliefs and practices about wealth (Langley 2008; Peck 2009; Davies 2014). Political discourse provides an illustration of these contradictory articulations. A moment of economic prosperity in 1998 made credible the widely reported claim that Peter Mandelson, a senior UK Labour politician, had said that he was 'intensely relaxed about people getting filthy rich'. If nothing else, this demonstrates in a rather brazen manner how regimes of pay and remuneration come to be taken for granted when other economic indicators provide an opportunity for complacency and wishful thinking. This complacency might be understood as a form of exuberance, an idealizing affective response that ignores complexities elided by narrowly defined indicators. In contrast, in a post-2008 financial crisis context, pay and remuneration have moved onto the political agenda, as a point around which to unify public outrage, and also, increasingly, as the focus for specific policy proposals to regulate, for example, executive pay or zero-hours contracts (Resolution Foundation 2013). There is thus clear evidence of a shift in political relations to existing regimes of pay and remuneration within what might be thought of as the same 'neoliberal' political economy. One interpretation of this shift might be that the sense of precarity following the crisis created a need for an alternative object of moral condemnation. A question remains, though, about whether and under what conditions this kind of shift might be mobilized as a resource to unsettle or 'reactivate' the fundamental economic assumptions upon which the legitimacy of these regimes is grounded.

Moments of exuberance and precarity can also be traced within the education system, and, for the purposes of this paper, in the figure of the teaching assistant. Teaching assistants traditionally supported teachers with a range of tasks to ensure the smooth running of the classroom, but have increasingly taken on roles directly related to curriculum delivery. Often their work is aligned with dedicated funding streams targeting individual or small groups of children identified as suitable for additional support. Under New Labour, a series of reforms diverted proceeds of prosperity into the school system to regulate and optimize the working time of teachers. One initiative was the introduction of a statutory right for teachers to be allocated ring-fenced time for 'planning, preparation and assessment' (PPA) (Times Education Supplement FAQ 2005). The diverted funds, and additional regulatory changes, allowed schools to pay appropriately trained 'Higher Level Teaching Assistants' (HLTAs) to cover classes, to enable teachers to take up their PPA time. New Labour also supported the introduction of work-based 'Foundation Degrees': programs of undergraduate-level study that enabled students who might not otherwise access higher education to build on skills and knowledge developed in the workplace. Foundation Degrees for teaching assistants enabled many who had found employment in schools despite lack of qualifications, frequently women who hadn't had opportunities to study earlier in life, to return to education. This could in turn lead to a full degree and, ultimately, qualification as a teacher. While offering new opportunities for progression for a significantly marginalized sector of the workforce, these reforms added to the complexity of the categorizing system within the work place, which now graded teaching assistants from NVQs level 1–3 through to HLTA and potentially autonomous classroom practitioner; and at the same time provoked opposition from teaching unions, who felt that the promotion of teaching assistants to cover PPA time undermined the professional status of teachers. Nevertheless, there was a certain exuberance both about the recognition of teachers' need for planning time and about the development of new routes for equity in access to educational and professional opportunities. Under the austerity regime that followed the 2008 financial crash, the more exuberant elements of this scenario have themselves been revealed as fragile and precarious.

Changes in teachers' conditions of pay provide one illustration of the precarious aspect of exuberant remunerative reforms. During the period of austerity, a variety of longstanding mechanisms for ensuring transparency within a national pay system were revoked as schools were given more autonomy in practices of remuneration (National Union of Teachers 2013). At the same time, intensified mechanisms of accountability, in the form of performance related pay linked to pupil achievement, replaced attempts made in the period of prosperity to offer scales of progression that recognized the value of classroom practice (ibid). Thus, an exuberant moment of apparent universalism and recognition of professional knowledge quickly evaporated. The NUT action in opposition to these changes was one element of the context of the project reported in this paper.

As many others have noted, these instances of shifting discourses and regulative practices of pay and remuneration can be theorized in a variety of ways. Walkerdine and Bansel (2010) point to the opposition between Giddens' understanding of late modernity as offering opportunities for a 'reflexive project of the self' and Rose's suggestion that this imperative to choose is itself a construction, an obligation to be free that is demanded of subjects of neoliberal technologies (495). McGimpsey (2017) notes that liberal and neoliberal policy shifts have been described as exemplifying successive formations of 'the state', and that this kind of analysis projects an idea of the state as 'a comprehensive and comprehendible unity' (67). The coherence this implies is questioned in analyses that view policy initiatives as constitutive of, rather than responsive to, a cause or a problem: McGimpsey suggests that 'austerity functioned discursively to shift the locus of the crisis from private debt and reckless governance in the financial sector to levels of public spending' (ibid, 72), while Thompson and Cook argue that across shifts in education policy, the figure of 'the unaccountable teacher' or 'teacher as the problem' is produced as a justification for neoliberal technologies of accountability (2014). All these authors suggest that Deleuze's conception of 'assemblage' offers a more productive way to understand the politics of 'neoliberalism'.

One feature of Deleuzian analyses is a resistance to an understanding of 'neoliberalism' as a temporal or spatial unity, or as a hegemonic structure with unitary or predictable subjectivating effects. Rather than seeking to identify coherence, an 'assemblage' anti-methodology suggests we map social formations as contingent but productive conjunctions of parts (Deleuze and Guattari 1984; McGimpsey 2017). For example, McGimpsey maps the conjunction of localism, austerity, and mechanisms for calculating the value of returns on social investments as the distinctive 'late neoliberal' public service assemblage that emerged in the UK after the financial crash (2017, 72). Walkerdine and Bansel (2010) compare communities in Sydney and in the South Wales valleys experiencing similar challenges of a globalized labor market that demands individualized 'entrepreneurial' worker identities. They argue that a recognizable vocabulary of entrepreneurial aspiration was evident in Sydney workers' narratives of solitary experiences of redundancy and restructuring. In contrast, the established presence of trade unions and sensitive interventions to support workers' planning post-redundancy in the South Wales community enabled ex-steel workers to experience creative new career possibilities 'less as aspiration than revelation' (503). They conclude: 'neo or advanced liberalism and globalisation are not monolithic forces that trample upon lives in such a way as to completely predict and specify the outcome' (506).

This use of 'assemblage' to explore re-orderings of partial elements of diverse contexts is consistent with policy enactment research (Ball et al. 2011; Braun et al. 2011; Bradbury 2014; Santori 2014), which uses ethnographic-type approaches to trace the way juxtapositions of these elements (of, for example, geography, knowledge or professional values, material infrastructure, external relations, see Braun et al. 2011, 588) produce diverse practices and subjects of education policy. So, for example, Bradbury observes the way the assessment profiles required in UK early years settings involve teachers' professional judgment, but then ask teachers to transform that judgment into a numerical record for purposes of accountability, simultaneously acknowledging and then undermining teachers' expert knowledge and status (2012; 2014). At the level of the teacher, Ball has described this as 'a kind of values schizophrenia' or 'splitting' (2003, 221; see also Rogers and Lapping 2012; Bernstein 2000), connoting the way that psychical processes are implicated in the formation of the policy subject. A Deleuzian perspective might describe this as a fusing of contradictory parts – partial elements of expert knowledge juxtaposed with partial elements of an accountability system – and a redirection of flows of affect within an early years' education assemblage.

A further space of articulation between Deleuzian assemblage theory and policy enactment research can be traced in the theorization of politics, agency, and the new. Deleuze's theorization of the assemblage is also a theorization of the possibility of the new, and a displacement of the 'self' as the subject of action. In this view, the possibility of the new requires a creative, political re-ordering of assemblage, difference as opposed to repetition (Thompson and Cook 2014, 712), and this creativity is associated with the affective capacities of desire (Bignall 2010). In contrast, some of the more traditionally Foucauldian aspects of policy enactment research can seem to view contemporary disciplinary technologies as uni-directional in their effects, squeezing the breath out of pockets of resistance. Ball's classic 2003 paper, 'The teacher's soul and the terrors of performativity', for example, concludes: 'The policy technologies of market, management and performativity leave no space of an autonomous or collective ethical self' (226). This recourse to a notion of autonomy or collectivity as a unified, though thwarted, subject of ethics appears to create a political impasse. Similarly, in recent work foregrounding the significance of micro-processes in the production of contingent 'versions of professionalism' (Perryman et al. 2017), the subject appears as politically inert, 'compliant in their domination' (ibid, 2). However, other research in the field has explicitly explored possibilities for teacher agency and theorized moments of resistance (Braun, Maguire, and Ball 2010; Ball et al. 2011; Bradbury 2012; 2014; Wright 2013). Bradbury's study of the early years' classroom, for example, develops Ball's notion of 'cynical compliance' as a painful mode of agency that appears in contexts that are tightly monitored by multiple technologies of accountability (2012). Her analysis points to the affective work this entails, arguing: 'we need to deromanticise the idea of teachers' resistance to dominant neo-liberal discourses and consider the emotional costs of their exercise of agency' (ibid, 183).

This body of work raises a series of questions. One set of questions relates to the way particular subjects take up positions of compliance/resistance: How might we better understand the appearance and dispersal of compliant/resistant subject positions within the field of education? What constitutes a subjectivity as a particular mode of agency/resistance?

There are also questions we might pose about the interpretation of psychical and affective processes in the production of these subjectivities: How might we better understand the 'emotional costs' associated with compliance/resistance? Is it possible to trace a relationship between affect, or desire, and the production of a subjectivity as a particular kind of compliant/resistant subject? Psychoanalytic understandings of both the unconscious and desire can help us explore these questions about subjectivity and affect.

Following from the insights into the significance of both affect and subjectivity developed in previous research, this paper explores these questions by tracing the movement of desire in teaching assistants' subjective relations to workplace practices of remuneration. Drawing on a Lacanian account of the way processes of identification channel affect, as desire, through signifying chains within a discursive field, we explore the associative chains of meaning that overdetermine the subjectivities produced within performative practices of remuneration. We suggest that the contradictory chains of signification embodied in the school environment constitute a space where fragile teaching assistant subjectivities reiterate relations to an ambiguous Other. This theorization of the movement of desire, foregrounding the role of unconscious, symbolic associations, provides insights into complex dynamics of stasis and change, and adds detail and nuance to existing accounts of agency and enactment in education policy research.

In addition we argue, speculatively and playfully, for an understanding of psychical objects and unconscious processes as a context for, or as partial objects within, a remuneration assemblage. Where, for example, Walkerdine and Bansel foreground contexts of time and place in their comparison across settings, the psyche might be seen as a displacement of historical and geographical contexts, condensing norms and principles across space–time. From the perspective of those who foreground the opposition between Lacanian and Deleuzian philosophies (e.g. O'Sullivan 2009), the juxtaposition of Lacanian and Deleuzian approaches might be considered problematic. However, Deleuze's acknowledgment of his debt to Lacan suggests that the juxtaposition of the two is not illegitimate, even though we are deploying some of the terms – 'signifier', 'symbolic', 'Oedipus' – that he explicitly renounced (Deleuze 1995, 13–4; Smith 2004, 642–3). We hope that it might perhaps be possible to mitigate the traditional psychoanalytic reification of Oedipal or familial relations within the psyche. We need to put this rider up front, as our analysis most certainly reiterates aspects of Oedipus. The question is whether we can avoid, in the words of Deleuze and Guattari: 'taking part in the work of bourgeois repression at its most far-reaching level [...] keeping European humanity harnessed to the yoke of daddy-mommy' (1984, 50). We hope that, rather than shouting 'daddy-mommy', although that is a risk, our analysis inflects the oedipal relation to a parental Other with Lacan's mobius strip, or even, though less directly, Deleuze and Guattari's mycelium-style rhizome metaphors, to disturb essentializing conceptions of inner and outer, or of the psychic and the social.

Before moving on to the project and analysis of the material, we briefly review the way psychoanalytic conceptions of repetition and resistance have been deployed in previous psychosocial analyses of relations to work.

Repetition and resistance in relations to work: a space for the unconscious?

In *Beyond the Pleasure Principle* (1920), Freud traced the relation between resistance and repetition. This forms the basis for the conceptualization of transference and also for Freud's understanding of the distinctive nature of the clinical space. Within psychoanalytic practice, it had initially been thought that a symptom might be overcome by explaining its meaning directly to the patient. Analysts discovered, however, that there was a resistance to this kind of direct interpretation. Freud then theorized this resistance as itself an aspect of the symptom: a clue that might shed light on repetitious patterns of behavior that impede satisfaction. The concept of the transference suggests that such patterns might be understood as repetitions of previous significant relationships within a new context, such as the clinical situation. Clinically, the transference is a distinctive situation in which the patient can both repeat previous patterns, and come to recognize and thus shift the unconscious desire that limited their relations in this way (ibid, 289). Psychosocial work that draws on psychoanalysis has used these ideas both to interpret repetitious patterns in interview narratives, and to interpret relations within the research process itself.

Moore's (2006) analysis of teachers' responses to policy directives uses the concept of repetition to trace conflicting position articulated in interview accounts. He distinguishes between more sociological interpretations, which focus on explicit statements of ideological affiliations, and psychoanalytic interpretations of reiterated desire. Where contradictions emerge in interview narratives, Moore suggests, it is productive to explore both these levels of analysis. He illustrates this with the case of one participant whose need to avoid conflict and to be seen as likable had won out over his political convictions when policy changes were introduced in his school: 'Bill seems to have been compelled to subordinate one set of feelings – to do with educational and political ideology – to another set, to do with not wanting to lose popularity'. Moore describes this as 'the triumph of desire over ideology' (2006, 497). Layton, a psychoanalyst, has traced similar dynamics in her analysis of class relations to the 'entrepreneurial' subjectivity demanded by neoliberal labor market. She identifies repetitious transferential patterns imbued with class-related expectations, and relates these both to her patients experiences at work, and to their relation with her in the clinic (2016). It is also worth noting that Thompson and Cook (2014) cite Moore's work on repetition and transference in their Deleuzian analysis of the failure of education policy-making to constitute difference. Their analysis posits the policy-making assemblage as needing to break out of the habit of 'teacher as problem' (712). Their argument is positioned within Deleuze's complex theorization of repetition as the imaginary product of contemplation (Deleuze 2004), which, while not directly psychoanalytic, has clear resonances with both Freudian and Lacanian ideas.

A number of researchers influenced by Lacanian ideas have been experimenting with what they describe as a psychoanalytically informed activist approach. These approaches have two defining objectives. Firstly, they aim to disrupt and/or re-signify dominant discourses of economic development and the way these discourses position disadvantaged communities as lacking independent discursive or political resources. Secondly, they aim to collaborate with, identify, name, and support existing and frequently unrecognized localized identities or groups (Özselçuk 2006, 232; Healy 2010, 498). In order to do this, they set up focus groups, interviews, conversations, and workshops that explicitly aim to introduce ideas about, for example, cooperative or worker takeovers as a response to the adoption of capitalist values in state organizations (Ozselcuk, ibid), or the recognition and development of alternative forms of economic value (Gibson-Graham 2002). These authors draw on psychoanalysis to analyze resistances that emerge in the encounters between researchers and participants: to understand, for example, Turkish workers' identifications with a position as 'state employee', despite the ambivalence of their relation to the term under 'state capitalism' (Ozselcuk, ibid). A psychoanalytic understanding of the significance of ambiguity is also explicitly deployed: collaborative workshops draw attention to the ambiguity or emptiness of naturalized terms such as 'the economy' (Healy and Graham 2008; Healy 2010); and researchers also reflect on the effects of their own position as an enigmatic other within the research process (Healy 2010, 499–500; see also Charalambous 2014).

The centrality and complexity of resistance and ambiguity in these projects are significant, as the level of direction in the activities the researchers initiate could be interpreted as impositions onto participants, from a position of authority. It is also noteworthy that while Healy and Graham, for example, report on their more productive encounters, in which they were able to trace developments in their own and participants' discourse (Healy 2010), they also record that this was not the norm. They explain that their interventions were more usually met with a variety of objections: arguments that alternatives to the existing 'economy' were exceptions, not reproducible, or liable to co-optation in support of capitalism (Healy and Graham 2008). In response to this, Healy argues: 'The psychoanalytic concept of fantasy allowed us to understand the expression of a passionate attachment to capitalo-centric conceptions of economic space, even when this attachment is painful or paralyzing' (2010, 504). While, as noted by Ozselcuk (ibid, 234), it is risky to explain away objections as irrational or unconscious attachments, a careful reading of emphases and contradictions within the data can support such interpretations.

The work of these researchers opens up a conceptual and a methodological space. Firstly, might it be possible to develop a more nuanced understanding of the unconscious structure of resistances identified in their analyses? And, following from this, might a more explicit use of free associative methodologies help us explore the nature of these unconscious processes in the constitution of relations between participants and the remunerative practices of the workplace? We elaborate on these questions in turn in the following sections. First, we set out the conceptualizations of overdetermination, identification, and desire that we will go on to use in the analysis of our project data; following that we explain the free associative approach we adopted in our interviews with teaching assistants.

Overdetermination, identification, and desire

In conceptualizing our data, we draw on the concept of overdetermination. In the *Interpretation of Dreams* (1958), Freud used this term to describe the multiple symbolic connections between the elements of a dream and the unconscious dream thoughts:

> Not only are the elements of a dream determined by the dream thoughts many times over, but the individual dream-thoughts are represented in the dream by several elements. (1958, 389)

Crucially, Freud argues, it is the fact that the manifest elements of a dream, like words, 'are predestined to ambiguity' (ibid: 456) that allows meanings to be disguised and expressed in this way, through processes of condensation. In addition, Freud suggests the concept of overdetermination can also explain the production of affect within a dream, so that elements or signifiers can be seen as a channel for the expression and transformation of affective intensities (ibid, 618). These fundamental insights about the articulation and disguise of meaning and affect through a linguistically structured process of signification provide the basis for our conceptualization of the interview material. However, whereas Freud's account suggests a complex network of dream thoughts that is the excessive material that determines the content of a dream, we draw on Laclau and Mouffe's (2001) conceptualization of a field of discursivity as the excessive material from which discourse is articulated. Our analysis traces elements of discourse that are temporarily fixed to constitute a space for subjectivity, and foregrounds open or ambiguous aspect of these elements. We do this by identifying relatively stable chains of meaning within the chaotic mass of signifying elements that constitute the interview data.

A Lacanian understanding of the relation between subject and other can help us trace the movement of desire in processes of overdetermination. In Lacanian theory, subjectivity comes into being when the infant identifies with a signifier that represents an Other who confers a sense of being on the subject (Fink 1995; Lacan 2010). For Lacan, as for Freud, this process is always simultaneously symbolic and affective. The infant hangs onto the (m) Other's words and actions in an effect to discern both her meaning and her desire and to dispel the intense precariousness associated with overwhelming experience of ambiguity. It is thus through the questioning of the desire of the (m)Other that the subject's affect is channeled, as desire, through the appropriation of meaningful signifiers. Throughout life, the subject continues to guess at the meaning and desire of an ambiguous Other, represented by a variety of signifiers embodied in/as individuals and institutions. The question: 'What does the Other desire of me?' and the identification with a signifier that might represent the desire of the Other are central to the ongoing production of subjectivity. It is thus possible to trace the movement of desire by asking the questions: Which Other constitutes the desire of the subject? To which Other do they address their being?

In Lacanian theory, a further refinement in the mapping of desire is constituted in the distinction between identification in the Symbolic and identification in the Imaginary (Lacan 2006 [1966]; Evans 1996). Symbolic identification is a relation to the Other, as represented by a signifier recognized as belonging to an open signifying system. The subject relates to the signifier as one element of a symbolically articulated set of norms or principles. These norms or principles constitute a position from which we can work out if we are good or bad, likeable or not likable. When we identify with a Symbolic Other, we are thus able to stabilize a sense of our identity in relation to an open but meaningful symbolic structure. Imaginary identification is a relation to the other, as represented by a signifier that is understood as if it is unified or whole, a self-evident value that does not require justification in relation to norms or principles. When we identify with an Imaginary other, it is as if our whole identity depends on similarity or difference with one ideal or signifier. Symbolic and Imaginary identifications are contrasting stances in relation to the same set of signifying elements; and any one signifying element can stand in for, or represent, a variety of o/Others. The different modes of identification are, however, associated with different affective investments: more intense feelings of rivalry or competition, for example, might be indicative of an Imaginary identification; in Symbolic identification, in contrast, affect is more dispersed, able to move across elements in the network of signifiers. These modes of identification thus differ, significantly, in the extent to which the signifying structure permits the movement of desire. The 'aim', in psychoanalytic terms, is identification in the Real: an overwhelming and unsustainable encounter with radical contingency and uncertainty, from which it might be possible for the subject to radically reformulate intransigent desire.

In relation to our project, the aim is to attempt to map desire, the channeling of affect, within relations to practices of remuneration at work. Our interest is in what sustains practices of remuneration (or what organizes the partial elements of a remuneration assemblage); and we speculate that desire has a part to play in the ongoing process of production of these practices. So, put another way, we are interested in the way the fragility of teaching assistants' unconscious – Symbolic, Imaginary, or Real – identifications might intersect with the fragility of practices of remuneration in the workplace. Politically, there is a question about how successfully subjective identifications within workplace practices can contain affect and articulate desire. Methodologically, there is a question about how it might be possible to interpret instances within our interview data as Symbolic or Imaginary identifications. Frequently, relations oscillate between the two modes. In the analysis section, we have decided to use 'o/Other', throughout, to foreground both the unpredictable movement of desire and the oscillation between identificatory modes.

A Lacanian inspired free associative methodology

Our project experimented with a range of techniques for producing and exploring free associative material with our interview participants. Bollas (1999) has described the contrasting modes of listening to or receiving a patient's speech in different schools of psychoanalysis. He contrasts Freud's technique, which uses the analyst's silence to allow the gradual emergence of material, with Kleinian technique, which recommends frequent intervention to interpret projections (188). Pure free association is impossible to achieve, so these approaches are not mutually exclusive or incompatible, they simply provoke or facilitate different trajectories in the associations (ibid, 63). Free associative approaches to interviews within psychosocial research have tended to recommend minimal intervention by the researcher, both to guard against potentially sensitive clinical-type interventions, and to avoid directing the material (Hollway and Jefferson 2000; Miller, Hoggett, and Mayo 2008). While paying attention to both these considerations, we developed a slightly different approach, inspired by the work of Lacan. In planning the interviews, our focus was explicitly on the use of signifiers, and on ways in which we might potentially draw our participants' attention to equivocation and ambiguities in their speech (see Fink 1997, 15). We also attempted to avoid responding to the material except at the level of language, or signifier, although, of course, we directed the narratives through our initial question, and additionally when we selected signifiers to use prompts for further associations within the interviews.

Our participants were four teaching assistants, working at different schools, but all in the final year of a part-time BA in Education Studies. They took part in series of group and individual interviews. In the first group interview, we invited participants to say anything that came to mind in relation to 'pay and remuneration'. We then interviewed each participant individually, using words and phrases we selected from the prior group interview (e.g. 'lucky girl', 'breadwinner', and/or 'behind closed doors') to prompt further associations. In the second group interview, we used three newspaper headlines as prompts for free associative writing and speaking ('Britain's bank bosses to get millions in share payments in bonus cap dodge'; 'Wayne Rooney signs up for Manchester United until June 2019 for £85 m'; 'Parents will struggle to understand teachers' strike action'). In the final individual interviews with two of the participants, we again used words and phrases from our prior meetings as prompts; with the other two participants, we borrowed from the Biographical Narrative Interpretive Method and began with the request: Please tell me the story of your life (Wengraf and Chamberlayne 2006). In the final interviews, we also invited participants to reflect on the experience of participating in the project. We met with participants jointly a few months after the final interviews to feedback initial findings, and this generated further material.

The ethics form stipulated that participants could withdraw at any time or ask us not to use any sensitive material, and there were instances where participants specified material in this way. In addition, at the beginning of the first group interview, and again in each subsequent interview, we explained the idea of free association: that this approach meant that they should not expect 'normal' conversational responses, and that this might make them anxious. Within the interviews, we invited them to let us know if it became too uncomfortable at any point. In this way, we gained consent for a certain level of anxiety in relation to participation in the project.

Mapping and layering the field of discursivity

We begin our analysis by mapping signifiers of remuneration within the data, tracing the way their more ambiguous aspects relate to the Symbolic order, or the field of the Other, in our case the field of primary education as embodied in the school environments experienced by our participants. We then explore contrasting chains of meanings attached to one signifier, 'sell yourself', an injunction offered to promote successful progression, but also a point of fissure within the group. In doing this, we trace clues that shed light on the o/Other to whom, we might say, participants were addressing their being. The o/Other appears frequently in our data in the concrete figure of the head teacher; but is also represented by professional ideals, political ideologies, and family-based moral values. As we saw earlier, such concrete figures or signifiers, like the elements of a dream, can serve as a portal through which any number of symbolic orders are transmitted, overdetermining the subject's relation to work-place norms. While our analysis reads these symbolic orders in terms of our participants' biographically inflected psychic investments, it is worth noting that biographical elements also transmit wider cultural and social norms. The same material might thus be interpreted to explore dimensions of, for example, gender, class, sexuality, or ethnicity, which resonate within the unconscious relations that are the focus of our discussion here.

Our initial analysis of the field of discursivity attempts to map signifiers both through frequency of appearance within the data and also in relation to level of fixity of meaning and relations to other signifiers. The frequency and discursive positioning of signifiers alone, however, do not fully capture their significance in relation to the production of subjectivity. Drawing inferences about whether signifying repetitions indicate interesting aspects of an identification process, a repetition compulsion, or mere coincidence requires further investigation. The final section of our analysis, therefore, traces in more detail repetitious patterns in the associative chains of signifiers of two of our participants, showing how they overdetermine contrasting identificatory positions. Through this we develop new insights into the apparent fissures and fixities in participants' constitution of a teaching assistant subjectivity.

Ambiguities: spaces of fissure or fixing of meaning

Our initial request, 'say anything that comes to mind about pay or remuneration', elicited a range of signifiers to represent mechanisms and objects of exchange in processes of remuneration. The first group interview began with a series of interventions about contracts, qualifications, courses, and pay scales (02:08–16:00 and on); 'money' (first at 05:28) was also mentioned, and relations to this signifier seemed particularly sensitive or affectively loaded; there were also references to hours, weeks, and years. In opposition to these relatively straightforward processes and objects of exchange, 'experience' (first at 05:28) was referred to, both as something to be gained through work, and something that work might look for in an employee. Other processes and objects of exchange that emerged as the interview progressed included: 'performance related pay' (first at 17:00), 'holidays' (first at 28:01), iPads (first at 28:10), and a range of other small gifts or bonuses. Later on in the interview, less concrete types of remuneration were discussed: 'being appreciated', 'being recognised', 'being valued', 'seeing children progress', 'making a difference' (70:38). So, while the iPads and other examples of one off gifts or bonuses had relatively fixed referents, other signifiers of objects of exchange were more ambiguous.

The ambiguous aspects it is possible to trace in signifiers of remuneration can be related to the position of an o/Other able to fix or destabilize meanings within a particular context. A contract, for example, might appear to specify clear and stable expectations with respect to employment and remuneration. However, this is not always how it is experienced. Aie reported that: 'Since September the headteacher changed my contract to unqualified teacher status, so my salary has gone up' (GI1, 2:08), suggesting that terms are dependent on the whim of authority. In a similar way, although with the opposite outcome, Bee said when she qualified as an HLTA, and expected her contract to change, she was told: 'sorry, I can't pay that' (GI1, 02:58). Ceé also reported difficulties in confirming her assignment to the appropriate pay grade. When new contracts came in and staff had to apply for a new grading, she said: 'I thought: they know what I can do, so I don't have to write all this down' (GI1, 14:41), and consequently was assigned to the lower grade. The indeterminate relation between 'contract', 'qualification', and role fulfilled, in this context, creates an ambiguity in each signifier. Although a range of possible meanings are in play, in most instances subjects turn to the head teacher – a stand in for the o/Other – as a way to resolve the ambiguity of the relation between 'contract' and 'qualification'.

The ambiguous connotations of the signifier 'money' seemed to evoke particularly strong feelings of ambivalence: simultaneous recognition of its existential significance and denial of its role as a motivating factor in relation to promotion at work. Bee said: 'although I need the money, desperately, I am really looking for experience of teaching [...] it's not really about the pay' (GI1, 05:28). When Aie challenged this claim, Bee reiterated: 'Do you know what? It's not the money, trust me' (06:00). At the same time, Aie said that she too would have accepted more responsibility 'even if [my headteacher] didn't give me any money' (05:54), and later emphasized: 'when [my headteacher] said to me [about a pay rise], I said 'really?' I was shocked. I said, 'look, I'm not doing this for the money'' (GI1, 08:21). Both participants thus distance themselves from suggestions that they might be working 'for the money'. So, while the literal referent of the signifier 'money' may be more stable than the relation between 'contract' and 'qualification', its ambiguous affective and moral connotations mean that it is unstable as a point of identification for participants in the group interview. There is no obvious position from which an o/Other might confer judgment on an appropriate relation between the subject and 'money'.

The momentary unity, in which both Bee and Aie articulated an identification with 'not doing it for the money', was undone in the individual interviews. In her first individual interview, Bee reiterated that, although undeniably important, 'money is not my aim' (BInt 1, 6). In contrast, associating to the prompt 'too much' in her second individual interview, Aie said 'I don't think you can ever have too much money' (AInt 2, 2). She elaborated a relation between money, salary, and worth: 'People associate the more money they earn the better worth they are'; 'I think it's a way of, your salary, the way you see yourself as well, how you're valued and it does something for your self-esteem as well, I think' (AInt 2, 3). It seems possible that the strong association between 'money' and 'self-esteem' constructed here put Aie in a position of relative vulnerability within the group interview, where other participants identified 'experience' and 'passion' as more important values in their relation to work.

In the first group interview, 'experience' appeared 29 times, but without any apparent fixing of a shared meaning. For example, at certain points, 'experience' was opposed to 'qualifications' and it was pointed out that sometimes teachers might have less relevant 'experience' than TAs (GI1, 67:36). However, in talking about differences between the nursery nurse qualification (NNEB) and the NVQ for teaching assistants, participant Ceé opposed 'experience' to 'theory', suggesting that the emphasis on placements in the NNEB was more valuable than the theory-based writing in the NVQ (GI1, 16:30). Here, experience was associated both with a specific qualification, and with activities directly related to work in the classroom. Ceé concluded:

> Ceé: I think, at the end of the day, there isn't anything that can compare with experience.
> [Group interview 1, 17:00]

The exchange that followed might be interpreted as a struggle over the meaning of 'experience'. Aie makes an association from 'experience' to the introduction of 'performance related pay' and to experiences outside education, 'banking' and 'being a mother'. She thus uses the openness of 'experience' as a signifier to expand the more limited definition that Ceé's intervention had implied:

> Aie: Of course. That's why they're bringing in this new structure -
>
> Ceé: And I still think –
>
> Aie: with the performance related pay, and then the Headteacher has got more power, you've got more . . . Because I've come from a banking background, I've only been in school for three years, but all the experiences that I bring in, of being a mother, from banking, doesn't mean that I'm going to be less capable because someone's got twenty years' experience and I've only got three years. [Ceé: that's true] I've still got life experiences that I can bring in to the job, it doesn't matter if you're in banking or teaching or whatever, that's what they're going to be able to take into consideration and give you your pay.
> [Group interview 1, 18:08]

The openness of the term 'experience' enables differences to be covered over, but at the same time leaves uncertainty about what might be recognized as deserving remuneration. The exchange immediately following Aie's intervention here re-exploded the discursive terrain of value in relation to the work of a teaching assistant. It opened up both discursive fissures and explicit oppositions within the group. Here, Aie asserts the need to 'sell yourself', and this seems to have significant affective valence within the group. Bee echoes Aie's words, while Ceé introduces a new vocabulary that stands in contradiction to the vocabulary of 'performance' and 'selling':

> Bee: Oh, so now I can see where I am.
>
> Aie: Yes.

Ceé: But not everyone will have it, not everyone that comes in from banking will have it

Aie: But it's down to you to sell yourself.

Ceé: Oh it's down to you yes

Bee: You have to sell yourself.

Aie: But everyone does. Even a teacher, you could be two teachers, if you go to an interview, you've still got to sell yourself, you're both qualified teachers, who are they going to take on? Whichever one promotes themselves better. That's how it works in any job you do. I've had a lot of ex…

Ceé: Well, I think teaching's a vocation.

        [Group interview 1, 18:38]

Ceé's use of 'it' here – 'not everyone will have it' – is open to interpretation. It initially seems to connote the 'experience' required to be a teaching assistant; however, her final intervention points to something more specific. It seems that while Aie is constructing an identification between teaching and work in commercial fields, Ceé's intervention creates a different point of identification via the signifier 'vocation'.

The question a Lacanian psychoanalytic framework directs us to explore is: To which o/ Other are these subjects addressing themselves as they construct these identifications? Or how is the subject interpreting the ambiguous desire of an o/Other in articulating identifications with these contrasting discursive positions?

Tracing associative chains of signification around the injunction to 'sell yourself'

Our initial account of ambiguities in the discursive terrain of the interviews indicates the way a series of associated signifying chains emerged that structured the space of teaching assistant subjectivity. It is possible to delineate two organizing chains: one included 'experience', 'passion', 'vocation', and 'care', resonating with analyses of professional identity (e.g. Bradbury 2014); the other included 'performance', 'targets', 'selling yourself', 'being vocal', and 'speaking up', and has clear continuities with other analyses of entrepreneurial and performative discourse within neoliberalism (Walkerdine and Bansel 2010; Ball et al. 2011; Layton 2016). In this section, we trace the complex way positions in these signifying chains were both articulated and resisted in the interviews.

The signifier 'sell yourself' appeared 12 times in the first group interview and, as already noted, seemed to carry a significant affective charge. Six times it appeared in interventions from Aie, who was most clearly identified with the 'selling yourself' position. It was also Aie who, in covering PPA time and being given an unqualified teacher's contract, appeared to have made most progress toward the aim of becoming a teacher. Aie also used the signifier 'vocal' seven times, four times in the imperative, as an explicit injunction to her peers: 'You've got to sell yourself and be vocal' (09:29); 'you should be more vocal' (36:18); 'you've got to be vocal' (60:00); 'you need to be vocal' (90:10). The injunction to 'sell yourself' and 'be vocal', articulated by Aie, seems to be associated with the need to assert yourself in order to make progress at work, and Aie refers to her own recent promotion as evidence of the 'truth' of this injunction.

Nevertheless, the evidence in the interviews suggests her advice meets hesitation and a degree of skepticism from the other participants, each of whom appeared to both acknowledge and resist recommendations to speak up and ask for what they wanted. Ceé appeared to gently tease Aie, saying that she was not very good at selling herself, but she could 'get some tips off Aie' (GI1, 23:39). Bee initially appeared more open to change, referring to Aie as 'inspiring' (BI1, 2) but seemed resigned to not acting: 'I'm actually reprimanding myself that I should be doing it, and I'm still doing the reprimanding but not doing anything' (BI1, 2). Participant Dee, in a similar way, acknowledged that there were possibilities for seeking more recognition for the additional roles she took on at work, but said she would never go and ask for an increment: 'because it's such a, you kind of, for what you are, and then you have to put a price on it' (DI1, 3). Her struggle for words here seems to mimic the problem she is describing: that of naming or 'putting a price' on 'who you are'.

In resisting the injunction to 'be more vocal', all three also described their work using terms that suggest an excess that can't be named or recompensed. Ceé used the terms 'it' and 'vocation', Bee talked about her 'passion', and Dee, 'satisfaction'. We might think of these signifiers, articulated as alternatives to 'speaking up' and 'selling yourself', as place holders for a more complex, as yet unspoken chain of signification. It is also worth noting the way that the contrasting signifying chains might be understood to sit somewhere between open Symbolic structure and more limited Imaginary points of identification: a level of movement of desire is possible within each chain, from 'experience' to 'vocation' or from 'performance' to 'selling yourself'; but movement across chains seems to be more restricted.

In the next section, we attempt to go further in exploring the overdetermination of these positions by examining the associative material that emerged across the interviews. We trace the more complex signifying chains that might contain the excess associated with articulations of 'passion', 'vocation', and 'satisfaction'. In doing this, we also explore the unconscious role of the o/Other and the o/Other's desire, as constitutive elements of the subject's address.

Responding to ambiguity via the desire of an other

How do workers resolve ambiguities about what may be demanded of them in the workplace, what is expected of them, and what they are remunerated for? They respond, perhaps, in patterns associated with another ambiguous demand, from an o/Other who is taken in some way as a guarantor of identity. Psychoanalysis suggests that these patterns of response are most frequently established in our earliest relationships, often with parents, within the family.

Two participants, Dee and Aie, talked about their fathers. To follow through our query about the way ambiguities about relations to practices of remuneration may resolved through unconscious relations to an o/Other, in the next section, we explore the chains of associations in material from Dee and Aie's interviews. In both these cases, there are references to strong affective responses associated with these chains of signification.

Participant Dee: 'you never ask for anything'

The repetition of the signifiers 'never … ask' at two moments in Dee's first interview creates a link that might also be understood as a symbolic or unconscious relation. First, talking about the possibility of progressing at work, Dee commented: 'I would never go and ask for an increment' (Int. 1, 11:07). The categorical nature of this claim might already suggest a distinctive affective investment. Then, in her associations to the prompt 'breadwinner', Dee said 'you know, it was my father, it was the man of the house who brings the money and has got more power and authority' (Int. 1, 17:34). She also commented, 'I'm trying to think about me but no, it's him' (19:25). CL asked: 'Any other thoughts that come to your mind around your father?' and Dee responded:

> Authoritative and you can't mess around and you can't ask for more [...] You never ask for anything [...] We never asked for anything. (Int 1, 21:06).

'Never asking' at work can thus be symbolically linked to 'never asking' her father, a provider who was also a figure of power and authority.

Another repetition that brought an element of her father into her relations to asking at work can be traced across Dee's first and second individual interviews. Describing how she'd felt when she'd gone to ask her head teacher about doing the degree course, Dee said: 'I found it a little bit uncomfortable'. She then seemed surprised by this feeling:

> I can't believe it's a bit uncomfortable [...] It's a bit funny, I haven't thought about it like this, because, I'm really digging in myself and this is what comes to mind [..] I don't think I'll ever be going in to ask because maybe it's against my principles or something. I don't have big principles, but I don't feel comfortable. (Int. 1, 13:22)

Here there is an association between feeling 'uncomfortable', 'asking', and 'principles', and the same association came up in Dee's second interview. In her associations to the prompt 'debt', Dee talked about an experience from her childhood:

> When you have to go and ask for money, everybody knows about it. It is like a shame and a feeling of, you know, disgrace [...] I have seen people in the past, not people actually, it was my dad, who is a person who has got lots of principles and everything. However, he always lent money, but at some point in his life he needed some money, he asked someone, and he was in debt and he couldn't pay back [...] Oh my Lord, I've seen that in front of my eyes, the way that people behaved. They keep repeating that, you know, you've taken my money and all these things, and it was really disgrace for my dad, and for myself. (Int. 2, 07:05)

So here we have 'never asking' for more, an increment, at work; and 'never asking' for more, or for anything, when she was a child. We also have an 'uncomfortable' feeling associated with asking, when, it is suggested, asking is against her principles; and a more painful feeling, 'shame' or 'disgrace', when her father, a principled man, had to ask for a loan.

Taking this nexus of associations together, we might ask: To whom does Dee address her strong sense that it is wrong to ask? Or, alternatively, we might ask, on behalf of whom does Dee experience shame in relation to money? Bearing in mind Dee's comment that: 'I'm trying to think about me but no, it's him', it may perhaps be plausible to suggest that when faced with ambiguity in the workplace, her response can be understood as an attempt to live up to her father's principles, to fulfill her father's desire. Dee's relation to articulated principles, as signifiers of the o/Other, might be interpreted as indicative of Symbolic rather than Imaginary identification. However, the merging suggested in 'I'm trying to think about me but no, it's him' might be interpreted as a more Imaginary feature. The powerful affective response suggests, perhaps, an opening into the Real.

Participant Aie: 'Is that a good thing? I don't know. But that's what we have to do'

It is also possible to trace a repeated associative pattern in participant Aie's account, which can similarly be associated with a parental relation. At several points, Aie's account evoked a moral reference point which was at odds with her actions, which were justified by reference to a sense of inevitability or of forces beyond her control, and an affective association to a negative or frightening experience.

One instance of this associative pattern came in her account of both recent strikes in school, in which Aie had not participated, and her memory of the miner's strike in the 1980s:

> So when they strike, when the unions went on strike at school, I didn't strike, I went to school. I know that's probably not seen as the right thing to do, but I just don't think it's going to achieve anything. [...] I was a kid, but I remember when all the people up North went on strike [...] all the miners went on strike. It was horrendous. We had cut electricity for a few days a week and it was just horrendous. (Int 2, 4)

Here Aie both acknowledges that her decision not to go on strike might be seen as 'not the right thing to do', but also justifies it, articulating a slightly fatalistic sense that nothing can be achieved through this type of action. At the same time, in the account of the miners' strike, there is an enigmatic reference, in the repetition of 'horrendous', to a strong affective experience.

A similar fatalistic pattern can be discerned in Aie's response to one of the words we selected from the group interview to use as a prompt for associations in the individual interviews. In her response to the term 'changing children', she referred to a course she had attended, Childhood Studies, in which they had discussed different ways of conceptualizing children and the implications these had for teaching. She contrasted some of the more idealistic curriculum principles they had discussed with current requirements and practices in school, and commented: 'Is it a good thing? I don't know. But that's what we have to do [...] Is it a good thing? I don't know. But this is the society we live in' (Int. 2, 7). Here, as in her comments about striking, Aie appears to point to a more moral or 'acceptable' position, but suggests that this ideal is in conflict with an externally imposed necessity. These might be understood as alternative sets of principles or symbolic chains in relation to which she might identify as 'good'.

It may be possible to associate this conflict with a reference to Aie's father in the second group interview. Participants were asked to respond first to the headline 'Britain's ban bosses to get millions in share payments in bonus cap dodge', and then to the word 'dodge'. There were associations to 'tricking', 'something false', 'avoiding', and 'something to do with tax'. Aie contributed:

> For example, I know people, my dad, years ago I know this is what he done. He had a business [...] and to avoid paying the tax he went bankrupt and changed the company name. The factory is still there, but he changed the name to avoid paying taxes. So things like that do go on. It's dodgy. But I think it was easier to get away with it back in the seventies.

Aie's memory of her father is presented as a neutral example – 'things like that do go on' – but within the story there are traces of the pattern identified in the previous two instances: i.e. sometimes the more 'acceptable' moral position has to be rejected. In the case of strikes and pedagogy, Aie cites external forces that appear impossible to counter, as a justification for not 'doing the right thing'. In this instance, the inevitability is more enigmatic, perhaps hinted at in her speculation: 'I think it was easier to get away with it back in the seventies'.

One possible, speculative, interpretation of this collection of instances is that Aie's stance in the workplace, and her conflicted positioning in relation to both strikes and pedagogy, reveals how her relation to workplace norms is constituted in an unconscious relation to her father. Her justifications of actions that don't conform to a recognized moral code might be interpreted as attempts to compensate in some way for her father's actions. Aie's more spontaneous occupation of a similar position to her father is suggestive of an Imaginary relation, while the articulation of a fatalistic principle of justification perhaps opens a space for a more Symbolic identification. These identifications might be understood as an unconscious glue that can help account for Aie's stance in the workplace.

Finally, it is important to note that our analysis has suggested the way identifications are constructed both within signifying chains associated with the workplace *and* via associations beyond the immediate workplace, but with a similar structure or symbolic resonance. These repetitious identifications, within and across discursive fields, are channels for the articulation of desire.

Conclusion: psychical contexts of practices of remuneration and the possibility of the new

We began with a question about what ties individual subjects into the remuneration regime of a particular sector of employment. We also wondered whether we might develop a more nuanced account of the repetitions and resistances identified in previous studies of subjects' relation to the workplace economy (Moore 2006; Özselçuk 2006; Healy 2010). Our analysis has explored the way such resistances can be traced through complex signifying chains and symbolic associations. They can thus be interpreted as responses to the ambiguous desire of an o/Other, suggesting the complex, powerfully affective, and potentially painful relations that are embedded within workplace relations.

Based on this analysis, it is possible to suggest, speculatively, that there may be two different points of potential fissure or fragility. In relation to the participants as subjects, we might point to moments of fragility in their identifications: moments where these identifications may fail to perform the function of resolving ambiguity and channeling potentially overwhelming affect. When we say identifications are fragile/fissured, we mean that this containing function of identification is at risk of breaking down. In relation to practices of remuneration, we understand fragility as a moment when the formation of the practice as such is put at risk. Various moments might constitute a shift in the formation of the practice: new regulatory policies, industrial action, or workforce attrition. We speculate that such moments might emerge when *existing* practices exert pressure on the possibility of subjects maintaining a containing relation to the presumed desire of the o/Other. In other words, there needs to be space within the discursive field for both the discourse that enables the subject to resolve ambiguity *and* the discourses that make sense of existing practices of remuneration. When these can't be either brought into alignment or maintained as separate, both are vulnerable. Perhaps, as Zizek and others have argued (Zizek 2005, 55; Straehler-Pohl and Pais 2014), it is precisely the space for *something else* that sustains the ideological landscape.

Alternatively, we might attempt to position our analysis in relation to the notion of assemblage, and the politics of the new. Deleuzian approaches foreground the contingent conjunction of parts within an assemblage, and the role of desire in the articulation of the new. We might, then, very loosely suggest that the signifying elements mapped in our analysis can be interpreted as parts within a workplace remuneration assemblage, and that Symbolic and Imaginary modes of identification can be understood as forms of conjunctions between parts. Very loosely, we might argue that these partial elements and contingent conjunctions might be thought of as one of the contexts, *a psychical context*, from which an assemblage is constituted. Additionally, from the perspective of politics, the idea of the new and its relation to desire can help us indicate the space of politics in our analysis. While desire is trapped in the old oppositional circuits – performativity versus vocational values – there can be no novelty (c.f. Thompson and Cook, 712–3). If desire is able to break free – call that a Lacanian traversal of the Real, or a Deleuzian event – we might then glimpse a politics of difference.

Disclosure statement

No potential conflict of interest was reported by the authors.

References

Ball, S. 2003. "The Teacher's Soul and the Terrors of Performativity." *Journal of Education Policy* 18 (2): 215–228.

Ball, S., M. Maguire, A. Braun, and K. Hoskins. 2011. "Policy Actors: Doing Policy Work in Schools." *Discourse: Studies in the Cultural Politics of Education* 32 (4): 625–639.

Bernstein, B. 2000. *Pedagogy, Symbolic Control and Identity*. 2nd ed. New York: Rowman and Littlefield.

Bignall, S. 2010. "Desire, Apathy and Activism." *Deleuze Studies* 4 (supplement): 7–27.

Bollas, C. 1999. *The Mystery of Things*. London: Routledge.

Bradbury, A. 2012. "'I Feel Absolutely Incompetent': Professionalism, Policy and Early Childhood Teachers." *Contemporary Issues in Early Childhood* 13 (3): 175–186.

Bradbury, A. 2014. "Early Childhood Assessment: Observation, Teacher 'Knowledge' and the Production of Attainment Data in Early Years Settings." *Comparative Education* 50 (3): 322–339.

Braun, A., S. Ball, M. Maguire, and K. Hoskins. 2011. "Taking Context Seriously: Towards Explaining Policy Enactments in the Secondary School." *Discourse: Studies in the Cultural Politics of Education* 32 (4): 585–596.

Braun, A., M. Maguire, and S. J. Ball. 2010. "Policy Enactments in the UK Secondary School: Examining Policy, Practice and School Positioning." *Journal of Education Policy* 25 (4): 547–560.

Charalambous, Z. (2014) *A Lacanian Study of the Effects of Creative Writing Exercises: Writing Fantasies and the Constitution of Writer Subjectivity*. PhD University of London Institute of Education.

Davies, W. 2014. *The Limits of Neoliberalism*. London: Sage.

Deleuze, G. 1995. *Negotiations*. New York: Columbia University Press.

Deleuze, G. 2004. *Difference and Repetition*. London: Continuum.

Deleuze, G., and F. Guattari. 1984. *Anti Oedipus: Capitalism and Schizophrenia*. London: Althone Press.

Evans, D. 1996. *An Introductory Dictionary of Lacanian Psychoanalysis*. London: Routledge.

Fink, B. 1995. *The Lacanian Subject: Between Language and Jouissance*. Princeton: Princeton University Press.

Fink, B. 1997. *A Clinical Introduction to Lacanian Psychoanalysis*. Harvard: Harvard University Press.

Freud, S. 1920. "Beyond the Pleasure Principle." In *On Metapsychology: The Theory of Psychoanalysis, The Pelican Freud Library Volume 11*, 1984, 275–338. London: Penguin Books.

Gibson-Graham, J. K. 2002. "Beyond Global Vs Local: Economic Politics outside the Binary Frame." In *Geographies of Power: Placing Scale*, edited by A. Herod, M. Wright, 25–60. Oxford: Blackwell.

Healy, S. 2010. "Traversing Fantasies, Activating Desires: Economic Geography, Activist Research, and Psychoanalytic Methodology." *The Professional Geographer* 62 (4): 496–506.

Healy, S., and J. Graham. 2008. "Building Community Economies: A Postcapitalist Project of Sustainable Development." In *Economic Representations: Academic and Everyday*, edited by D. Ruccio, 291–314. London: Routledge.

Hollway, W., and T. Jefferson. 2000. *Doing Qualitative Research Differently*. London: Sage.

Lacan, J. (2006[1966]) "The Subversion of the Subject and the Dialectic of Desire in the Freudian Unconscious." In *Ecrits*, translated by Bruce Fink, New York: WW Norton.

Lacan, J. 2010. *The Seminar of Jacques Lacan: Book Vi: 'Desire and Its Interpretation' 1958–59*. Translated by C. Gallagher. http://www.lacaninireland.com/web/wp-content/uploads/2010/06/THE-SEMINAR-OF-JACQUES-LACAN-VI.pdf.

Laclau, E., and C. Mouffe. 2001. *Hegemony and Socialist Strategy: Towards a Radical Democratic Politics*. 2nd ed. London: Verso.

Langley, P. 2008. *The Everyday Life of Global Finance*. Oxford: OUP.

Layton, L. 2016. "Yale or Jail: Class Struggles in Neoliberal times." In *The Ethical Turn: Otherness and Subjectivity in Contemporary Psychoanalysis*, edited by D. Goodman, and E. Severson, 75–100. London: Routledge.

McGimpsey, I. 2017. "Late Neoliberalism: Delineating a Policy Regime." *Critical Social Policy* 37 (1): 64–84.

Miller, C., P. Hoggett, and M. Mayo. 2008. "Psycho-social Perspectives in Policy and Professional Practice Research." In *Qualitative Research & Social Change – UK and Other European Contexts*, edited by P. Cox, T. Geisen and R. Green, 112–131. Basingstoke: Palgrave.

Moore, A. 2006. "Recognising Desire: A Psychosocial Approach to Understanding Education Policy Implementation and Effect." *Oxford Review of Education* 32 (4): 487–503.

National Union of Teachers. 2013. "Protecting School Teachers: NUT Briefing on School Teachers' Pay." Accessed online 2017.

O'Sullivan, S. 2009. "The Strange Temporality of the Subject: Badiou and Deleuze between the Finite and the Infintie." In *Subjectivity* Vol. 27, 155–171.

Özselçuk, C. 2006. "Mourning, Melancholy, and the Politics of Class Transformation." *Rethinking Marxism* 18 (2): 225–240.

Peck, J. 2009. *Constructions of Neoliberal Reason*. Oxford: OUP.

Perryman, Jane, Stephen J. Ball, Annette Braun, and Meg Maguire. 2017. "Translating Policy: Governmentality and the Reflective Teacher." *Journal of Education Policy*.

Resolution Foundation. 2013. *A Matter of Time: The Rise of Zero Hour Contracts*. London: Resolution Foundation.

Rogers, S., and Lapping, C. 2012. "Recontextualising 'Play' in Early Years Pedagogy: Competence, Performance and Excess in Policy and Practice." *British Journal of Educational Studies* 60 (3): 243–260.

Santori, D. 2014. *Intensified Market Environments in Education and the Development of Default Subjectivities: Chile as a Critical Case*. PhD University of London Institute of Education.

Smith, D. W. 2004. "The Inverse Side of the Structure: Zizek on Deleuze on Lacan." *Criticism* 45 (4): 635–650.

Straehler-Pohl, H., and A. Pais. 2014. "Learning to Fail and Learning from Failure – Ideology at Work in a Mathematics Classroom." *Pedagogy, Culture and Society* 22 (1): 79–96.

Thompson, G., and I. Cook. 2014. "Education Policy-Making and Time." *Journal of Education Policy* 29 (5): 700–715.

Times Education Supplement FAQ. 2005. *PPA*. Accessed 2016. http://www.tesfaq.co.uk/ppa

Walkerdine, V., P. Bansel. 2010. "Neoliberalism, Work and Subjectivity: Towards a More Complex Account." In *The Sage Handbook of Identities*, edited by M. Wetherell and C. T. Mohanty, 492–507.

Wengraf, T., P. Chamberlayne. 2006. Interviewing for Life Histories, Lived Situations and Personal Experience: The Biographical–Narrative–Interpretive Method (BNIM). *Short Guide to BNIM Interviewing and Interpretation*. Accessed tom@tomwengraf.com

Wright, A. 2013. "Contested Images of the School: A Post-marxist Analysis of Education Policy under the New Labour Government and the Divergent Approaches to Its Implementation in English Secondary Schools." PhD Thesis, University of Essex, Colchester.

Zizek, S. 2005. *The Metastases of Enjoyment Six Essays on Women and Causality*. London: Verso.

Talkin' 'bout a revolution: the social, political, and fantasmatic logics of education policy

Matthew Clarke

This paper provides a critical analysis of the Australian government's education revolution policy as promulgated in the media release document, *Quality Education: The Case for an Education Revolution in our Schools*. It seeks to problematize the government's claim to marry quality and equity, via an analysis of the discursive strategies of the Australian government's revolution talk. My analysis draws on the work of political theorists Jason Glynos and David Howarth and their synthesis of key ideas from Laclau and Mouffe's discourse theory and Lacanian psychoanalytic theory into a framework of explanatory 'logics.' This framework provides conceptual tools for conducting critical policy analysis, including: characterizing a discursive regime on a synchronic plane; accounting for its constitution, reproduction, and/or subversion on a diachronic plane; and explaining the ways in which it grips or seduces subjects at a nonrational level. Overall, the analysis of the education revolution in this paper demonstrates the value of this framework of explanatory logics for education policy analysis, in the process shedding some new light on the Australian government's education revolution policy agenda.

Introduction

According to the Federal government, contemporary Australia is in the midst of an 'education revolution' (Rudd and Gillard 2008), with social justice firmly back on the agenda alongside quality. My aim in this paper is to problematize this claim to marry quality and equity, via an analysis of the discursive strategies of the Australian government's revolution talk. Specifically, this paper provides a critical analysis of the government's education revolution policy rhetoric, as embodied in the media release document, *Quality Education: The Case for an Education Revolution in our Schools* (Rudd and Gillard 2008), in order to highlight, and at times question, the discursive strategies it employs. I focus on this document, since it is clearly a 'symbolic' (Rizvi and Lingard 2010, 9) or 'emblematic' policy document – flamboyantly designed, with the text set against a deep red background and further tapping into the social democratic tradition through its deployment of the term 'revolution,'[1] and with the mandatory 'signed' ministerial (and prime-ministerial in this case) foreword. The document,[2] and particular version of neoliberal policy discourse it inaugurated, is particularly significant in that it provided the means by which the new Australian labor government attempted to lay claim to a new and distinctive agenda for Australian school education, as politicians and policy-makers are wont to do (Rizvi and Lingard 2010, 9).

My analysis draws on recent poststructuralist theory, particularly the work of political theorists Glynos and Howarth (Glynos 2008; Glynos and Howarth 2007; Glynos and Stavrakakis 2008; Howarth 2009) and their synthesis of key ideas from Laclau and Mouffe (2001) and the psychoanalytic theory of Lacan (Fink 1995; Stavrakakis 1999) into a framework of explanatory 'logics.' Glynos and Howarth's work offers a framework for socio-political critique, providing conceptual tools for the analyst to characterize a discursive regime on a synchronic plane, account for its constitution and reproduction or subversion on a diachronic plane, and also explain the ways in which it grips or seduces subjects at a nonrational level. My understanding of critique here aligns with Simons, Olssen, and Peters (2009, 82), who characterize it as 'the attitude that involves an act of rereading resulting in an act of de-familiarization, and opening up a space for new thought or action in between past and future.' My purpose in this paper is to conduct such a rereading as an act of de-familiarization. But importantly, this is not a reading that harkens back to some imaginary golden era prior to the ascendency of neoliberalism; for not only was there no such era, but, as Harvey (2010, 255) reminds us in relation to the preneoliberal political landscape, 'it is clear now that it is insufficient to go back to such a political model with its social welfarism and Keynesian economics.' The demands of the future will always exceed what the past can supply.

In conducting this work using conceptual tools drawn from political theory, I am mindful of the mutual imbrications of policy and politics in education – of 'the politics of education policy and education policy as politics' (Lingard and Ozga 2007, 3). My main purpose is not so much to dispute the validity of the government's claim of inaugurating an education revolution, though I do this in places, or to argue for an alternative political position; rather I seek to illuminate and problematize the ideological and discursive strategies through which this claim is effected. Importantly, my analysis does not lay claim to a privileged purview outside discourse: rather it seeks to elucidate the workings of discourse from a position *within* discourse, thus constituting what Phillips and Jørgensen (2002, 203–11) describe as 'a positioned opening for discussion.' I begin by locating the Australian government's education revolution policy agenda within the global political discourse of neoliberalism and the concomitant globalization of education policy, given the central place of neoliberalism in the global social imaginary[3] in the late twentieth and early twenty-first centuries (Boltanski and Chiapello 2005; Couldry 2010; Olssen 2010; Rizvi and Lingard 2010; Steger 2008; Steger and Roy 2010).

Global neoliberalism and education policy

Despite – or perhaps due to – its being a global phenomenon that has become entwined with the social, political, and economic domains of experience in a range of spatial and temporal contexts, and at varying levels of complexity, neoliberalism defies easy definition; nonetheless, it typically carries particular 'traits' which enable us to recognize it when we see it (Saad Filho and Johnston 2005). These traits include preferences of governments for the monetary levers of interest rates, control of the money supply, and (typically lower) taxation, over fiscal policy as tools to influence the economy; the privatization of formerly state-owned organizations; financial deregulation; and the promotion of 'free trade.' Overall, as a reaction to the perceived failures of the Keynesian social contract, and reinforced by the fall of communism in Europe, neoliberalism – despite occasional lapses, such as the classic Keynesian stimulus adopted internationally in response to the 2008 global financial crisis – has embraced 'the market' as the master signifier governing and uniting all aspects of social, political, and economic life. As Dean (2009, 51) puts it, 'Redefining social and ethical life in accordance with economic criteria and expectations, neoliberalism holds that human freedom is best achieved through the operation of markets.'

In many ways, education, along with the healthcare sector, provides a classic example of the policy tendencies of neoliberal governments in recent decades (Fisher 2009; Youdell 2011). This has been the case across a range of international contexts, leading commentators to talk of a global policy space characterized by comparison and competition (Lingard and Rawolle 2011; Nóvoa and Yariv-Mashal 2003; Wiseman and Baker 2005). As Rizvi and Lingard (2010, 67), in their recent account of the globalizing of education policy put it,

> Just as a social imaginary of neoliberal globalization has been a central component in the creation of the global market, so it has been within the global field of education policy. A global field of education policy is now established … as a global commensurate space of measurement of educational performance.

This 'policy convergence' has important implications for policy analysis from any particular national perspective: 'Critical policy analysis in an era of globalization requires that we recognize the *relationality* and *interconnectivity* of policy developments' (Rizvi and Lingard 2010, 69, emphasis in original).

The manifestations of this globalized neoliberal policyscape in education include a number of key overarching policy themes – accountability, competition, and privatization (Rancière 2010, 19) – as well as key policy technologies – the market, managerialism, and peformativity (Ball 2003b). These themes and technologies overlap and are reflected in a number of intersecting policies typically pursued by neoliberal governments in the field of education, including: the imposition of performativity-oriented evaluation and accountability measures on schools and teachers, and a preference for the implementation of state/national testing regimes as a means of identifying 'incompetent' teachers and 'failing' schools; the legislation of mandatory ('teacher-proof') state/national curricula; the encouragement of more diverse forms of school provision (e.g. faith schools and selective schools), and the concomitant promotion of 'choice' for parents; and the devolution of budget and managerial responsibilities to principals (Ball 2008). Whilst, owing to differences in history or the salience of particular local, regional, or national issues, the particular mix of these policy trends has been different in particular global contexts – for example, while national testing has been tied to performance targets with funding consequences for schools in the UK and the US, this has not been the case in Australia to date – broadly speaking they reflect the central neoliberal technologies of accountability, competition, privatization, marketization, mangerial-ism, and performativity.

Global policy trends in Australia

These global neoliberal trends have been central policy tools in the Australian edu-cational context, notwithstanding the public critique of neoliberalism by the former prime minister (Rudd 2009). Indeed, despite some muted acknowledgment of the social and cultural purposes of education, the same unquestioned and unquestion-able shibboleths – that the central purposes and potential contributions of education are economic and that the organization and practices of the education sector should be more closely aligned with market principles – underpin most if not all of the Australian government's education rhetoric, policy, and practice (Connell, Fawcett, and Meagher 2009). Thus, under successive liberal and labor governments Austra-lian education has witnessed the promotion of selective and 'identity' (e.g. commu-nity/class/religion) specific schools under the globally deployed banner of 'choice,' facilitated by an increase in government funding for so-called 'independent' schools at the expense of the public school system (Bonnor and Caro 2008). It has seen a burgeoning of high-stakes national testing as a policy tool for enhancing 'account-ability' and raising 'standards,' despite increasing global evidence highlighting the detrimental effects of such policies (Alexander 2009; Au 2009; Hursh 2008). And it has been characterized by an emphasis on 'the basics' of literacy and numeracy (the focus of the nationwide National Assessment Project: Literacy and Numeracy [NAPLAN] tests), as well as on vocational education and training (Karmel 2007), both justified by rhetoric about increasing Australia's competitiveness in the global economy, despite evidence questioning the validity of the purported education–economy links (Chang 2010; Wolf 2002).

Overall, as has been the case in other international contexts, social mobility and social efficiency have been promoted at the expense of democratic equality (Cran-ston et al. 2010; Labaree 2003). As others have observed (e.g. Reid 2009), this has had the unfortunate effect of undermining the more social justice-oriented aspects of recent government policy in Australia. Such concerns are now addressed through add-on programs, such as the 'National Partnership' schemes, rather than being integral (Reid 2009). Thus, for example, the *National partnership scheme on low socioeconomic school communities* provides a range of initiatives aimed at stu-dents deemed to be at educational 'risk' due to their socieconomic status. Ran-cière's (2003, 223) point that 'equality is not a goal that governments or societies should succeed in reaching ... equality is a presupposition, an initial axiom – or it is nothing' is particularly pertinent here. But in its 'band aid' approach to issues of inequality, Australia is not unique. It merely reflects education agendas in a range of global contexts where economic efficiency has become the paramount concern and where the market has been adopted as the master template for addressing social issues (Ball 2008; Olssen, Codd, and O'neill 2004; Rizvi and Lingard 2010). The Australian government's economism – 'the passage from education to economy ...' which '... serves as a founding myth of national efficacy in a globalizing world' (Stronach 2010, 38) – is evident in the structure and organization of the education revolution policy document, the table of contents of which are presented in Figure 1.

Contents	
Foreword	5
Australia's Education and Skills Challenge	7
COAG's Agenda for Productivity Reform	11
Schools as a key element of the Education Revolution	15
High quality teaching in all schools	21
Ensuring all children benefit from schooling	25
Transparency and Accountability	31
We cannot afford to delay	35

Figure 1. Quality education: the case for an education revolution in our schools: table of contents (Rudd and Gillard 2008, 3).

The overarching line of argument implicit in these headings and explicit in the document's textual body runs something like this: Australia faces an education and skills challenge due to increasing global competition; this necessitates reform in terms of increased productivity; schools have a key role to play in meeting this challenge; meeting the productivity challenge will require raising the quality of education in schools as well as ensuring that all students benefit from schooling; this in turn requires a push for greater transparency and accountability; moreover, this needs to occur immediately and comprehensively if the challenges outlined in the early part of the document are to be met. Before commencing my analysis of this argument, examining some of the specific discursive moves through which it is constructed, I will outline the principles and strategies of my analytic approach.

Methodology: explanatory logics and policy critique

The framework of explanatory logics utilized in this paper offers a poststructuralist-informed approach to describing, analyzing, and explaining problematized social phenomena – education policy in this case – in terms of political processes of establishment, maintenance, and transformation (Glynos and Howarth 2007). Such an analysis thus instantiates the inextricable connections between education policy and politics (Lingard and Ozga 2007).

Key premises of this explanatory framework include: (1) the contingency of social events, practices, and regimes; (2) the inevitable slippage between our semiotic resources and any 'reality' they attempt to represent; and (3) the constitutive role of 'lack.' The first point, concerning contingency, involves the argument that, despite the sedimented and seemingly fixed, stable nature of many current discourses and practices, everything in principle could have been, and hence could become, different. This contingency is evident in the discontinuities in our histories and results from the complex interplay of myriad shifting social practices. The second point, concerning slippage, posits an unbridgeable gap between the symbolic and the 'real' dimensions of social reality, and in particular, the disruptive or dislocatory role of the latter dimension in relation to the former, entailing that our discursive practices can never fully capture or provide a complete account of social reality. The third point, concerning lack, provides the philosophical basis for the other two points and refers to the absence of any ultimate foundation to social reality. Yet lack, as conceived here, is not the opposite of a positive presence but is rather 'the name for an absence constitutive of and operative within presence ... [a] ... *productive negativity*' that deconstructs binaries such as absence–presence, positive–negative (Marchant 2005, 21, emphasis in original; see also Coole 2000). One way we can think of a discourse is as an articulatory practice, which attempts to organize and structure social reality and relations in the face of lack and the consequent impossibility of semiotic closure, but which can only ever do so in a partial manner, owing to the 'openness of the social, a result, in its turn, of the constant overflowing of every discourse by the infinitude of the field of discursivity' (Laclau and Mouffe 2001, 113). Viewed in this light, many political agendas can be read as attempts to overcome constitutive lack through fantasies of full-presence, completeness, and harmony.

The framework of logics utilized in this paper incorporates the key ideas outlined above as part of a set of conceptual tools for analyzing and critiquing political and policy agendas such as the Australian government's education revolution. Within this framework of explanatory logics, social logics provide a synoptic description or characterization of a particular regime or practice. We can think of social logics in terms of the rules structuring a particular aspect of social reality; however, it is important to bear in mind that such 'rules' are heuristic tools, enabling us to make sense of a practice, rather than existing externally to and controlling – or for that matter, being merely reducible to – social practices. As one example, social logics of the market could be used to describe the buying and selling activities of social actors, the ways in which they view each other as competitors, and the strategies they employ to try and gain an advantage over each other. Or, to take another example, 'enforced ethnic and racial segregation for the purposes of political domination and economic exploitation' is one way of characterizing the social logic of South African apartheid discourse (Howarth 2009, 325).

In contrast to social logics, which enable the researcher to delineate the contours of a regime or practice on a synchronic axis, political logics allow us to provide a diachronic explanation of the institution, reproduction, or contestation of a social practice or regime – how they are created or transformed. We can analyze the dynamics of social change further via Laclau and Mouffe's (2001) logics of equivalence and difference. The logic of equivalence involves the simplification of social space into two opposing, or antagonistic, camps – think of the anticolonial liberation struggle, which cancels out differences between local identities in the service of a new national identity whose meaning derives from its opposition to the occupying power; while the logic of difference involves the multiplication of difference as a strategy to prevent the establishment of a unified oppositional movement – the classic strategy of 'divide and rule' (Glynos and Howarth 2007, 144–45). A crucial point here, however, is that the ontological condition of radical contingency, and the inability of a particular discourse or set of discourses to fully capture and coincide with social reality, means that any given hegemonic fixation of meaning achieved through the operation of either of these political logics can only achieve its hegemonic status by concealing its incompleteness and partiality and will of necessity only be a temporary state of affairs. In this sense, an analysis of political logics seeks to expose the simplifications, reductions, exclusions, and omissions operating in the formation of any given discursive formation.

Fantasmatic logics, as the name suggests, involve a crucial element of fantasy, but the meaning of fantasy here, derived from Lacanian psychoanalytic theory, is not identical with common usage, i.e. something unrealistic that one nonetheless yearns for. In the current framework, fantasy subsumes, but is not identical with, this definition, designating an attempt at reestablishing an imaginary fullness and harmony, at attaining jouissance, a presymbolic, 'real' enjoyment that is lost when the subject enters the symbolic order (Marchant 2005, 21). Within this formulation, fantasies account for the way subjects are gripped by, and derive enjoyment from, discourses and practices in ways that lie beyond or outside the latter's rational or symbolic content. Fantasmatic narratives or logics can take a beatific form, involving promises of harmony and fullness once the obstacle to our full enjoyment is overcome, or a horrific form, in which the obstacle to our full enjoyment proves insurmountable (Glynos and Howarth 2007, 147). In either case, fantasy induces subjects to ignore, overlook, or forget the situated partiality and contingency of a particular discourse or practice, hence locating themselves in the realm of ideology:

> Ideology 'takes hold' of the subject at the point of the nugget of enjoyment outside the meaning or significance the ideological formation provides. This excess enjoyment marks the incompleteness of a formation, the limits of what it can explain, and the extra 'kick' it promises. Fantasies organize these remainders, accounting for societies' failures, ruptures, and inconsistencies in ways that promise and produce enjoyment. (Dean 2009, 50)

Fantasmatic logics are thus not so much about promoting illusions but more about backgrounding the contingent, fragmented, and incomplete nature of social reality in order to view the world as a well-structured, harmonious whole, thus blunting the latter's political dimension and reducing the likelihood of subjects engaging in resistant political practices (Glynos and Howarth 2007, 145–46). As we will see below, many neoliberal governance strategies can be read in this way. Before moving ahead to the analysis a summary of the explanatory logics – social, political, and fantasmatic – are presented below in Table 1.

Table 1. Definitions of the explanatory logics: social, political, and fantasmatic.

Explanatory logics	Definition	'Sublogics'
Social logics	Provide a *synoptic* or *synchronic* perspective on social practices and discourses	
Political logics	Provide a *dynamic* or *diachronic* perspective on social practices and discourses	*Logic of equivalence*: organizes discursive space into two opposing chains of equivalence *Logic of difference*: multiplies difference but resists the formation of dichotomies
Fantasmatic logics	Account for the *grip* of ideology beyond the limitations of pure rationalism, through the promise of beatific or horrific enjoyment	*Beatific*: offers promise of social salvation in the form of complete social harmony or efficiency *Horrific*: presents threat in form of specters of inexorable societal decline

Analysis of policy within this framework consists of articulating these three logics so as to render intelligible a problematized social phenomenon. In the following section I offer an analysis of the Australian labor government's notion of an education revolution through the lenses of social, political, and fantasmatic logics, in an effort to gain critical insights into this agenda.

The social logics of the education revolution

The education revolution policy document can be read as structured by a number of social logics. In particular, it can be read in terms of logics of competition, atomization, and instrumentalization. These three logics were among those identified by Glynos and Howarth (2007) in their analysis of recent developments in higher education in the UK, reflecting the global nature of policy discourses in education in the twenty-first century. I discuss each of these three interrelated logics in turn below.

The logic of competition is evident in the emphasis on rewards and sanctions for individual teachers and school leaders. Thus, for example, the document urges the 'removal of low performers' along with the reward of 'outstanding teaching performance' (ER[4] 22). The latter will be attracted to schools where they are most needed 'by providing the right incentives' (ER, 22), as part of an overall strategy to 'facilitate and reward reforms which improve the career pathways available to teachers and the performance culture in schools' (ER, 29). The armory of proposed performance data includes 'comparative information about schools' performance' (ER, 31) as part of the drive toward transparency and accountability that will help 'create a learning environment that encourages innovation and excellence from school leaders, teachers and students' and will ensure that 'students, parents and teachers have the evidence they need to make informed choices' (ER, 31). The apparent underlying assumption that educational decisions are made on the basis of technical, formal information, or 'cold knowledge' (Ball 2003a, 100), is indicative of neoliberalism's economistic vision, within which the education system is viewed as a competitive market, governed by performativity in the sense of 'a technology, a culture and a mode of regulation that employs judgments comparisons and displays as a means of incentive, control, attrition and change – based on rewards and sanctions' (Ball 2003b). As Ball goes on to note in the same paper, the key issue here is not so much one of the use of comparisons, displays, sanctions, and rewards, but one of who owns and controls the field of judgment. Within the world envisaged in the education revolution this is clearly the Australian Federal government, as teacher is pitted against teacher and schools vie with each other to attract those students deemed to be the high performers. For although some authority and legitimacy is accorded to parents and students at a rhetorical level, it is also the case that, as Apple notes, there has been a crucial but subtle shift from schools serving students and parents, to the latter serving schools (Apple 2001, 185). In this arena, technologies of performativity, underpinned by logics of competition, serve as techniques by which the Federal government engages in 'steering-at-a-distance' (Ball 2007, 27), for example, by installing sanctions and rewards that encourage schools and teachers to focus on national test results. Such a vision ignores the potentially corrosive effects on teachers – on the very professionalism it seeks to promote – of a logic that 'by ratcheting competition to unacceptable levels through over-assessment and auditing from the center, has done more to undermine the norms of self-management and autonomy that were traditionally central to their identity as professional groups' (Olssen 2010, 11).

Closely related to and supporting the logic of competition is a logic of atomization, by which students, teachers, and schools are positioned as individuated, each largely responsible for their own fate in the marketplaces of education, work, and life, and a concomitant downplaying of structural aspects of success and failure (Francis and Hey 2009). This can be seen in the emphasis 'on providing parents with clear, comparable and meaningful information' in order to facilitate 'being explicit about how schools perform against "like schools"' (ER, 32 emphasis added). In this vision, schools and teachers, parents and students, are positioned as individual entities seeking to maximize their market advantage, rather than representatives of a superordinate education 'system.' What is ignored or downplayed by government policy makers is that encouraging (more economically and socially mobile) parents to 'vote with their feet' is likely to residualize the abandoned school (Marginson 1997), an effect that is hardly consistent with the stated aim of the government's emphasis on transparency, i.e. 'building a system in which effort and resources are directed to the needs of every learner' (ER, 32). In a society and an education system built upon sedimented discourses of meritocratic individualism – a focus reinforced by the stress on standards and outcomes rather than on structures and inputs – the logic of atomization can be seen as tending toward 'the ongoing creation, not the mere reproduction, of educational inequalities and hierarchical categorization and ordering of students' (Youdell 2011, 14).

Finally, we can see the overall operation of a logic of instrumentalization, reflecting neoliberalism's signature theme of competitiveness in the global economy as the underlying rationale for education provision. As I noted in the previous section, this logic underpins overall structure of the document, but it is also reflected in specific comments, such as the opening statement after the foreword, 'The Australian economy is operating at the limits of its capacity and has been for a number of years' (7), which outlines a problem for which education is the solution: 'Schooling, along with early childhood development, is an important enabler of economic potential' (ER, 15) ... 'We know the difference that improved schooling can make. Sustaining the economy's growth rate in the future will depend on increasing our productive capacity, and in particular the productive capacity of Australian workers' (ER, 35). This logic, in which students are equivalent to workers and in which, pace human capital theory, the market is taken as the grand metaphor for all human activity, sees education's value as stemming primarily from its capacity to generate capital that can be traded for jobs and wealth in the marketplace of the global economy. Such exchange requires the creation of a common currency through which to measure and compare value, a role that is played at the national level by NAPLAN test data and internationally by Program for International Student Assessment (PISA) (see also Lingard 2010). As with competition, this emphasis on an instrumentality linked to economic growth has had negative consequences: 'Our preoccupation with education as an engine of growth has not only narrowed the way we think about education policy. It has also narrowed – dismally and progressively – our vision of education itself' (Wolf 2002, 254). Or as developmental economist, Chang (2010, 189), puts it, 'Education is valuable, but its main value is not in raising productivity. It lies in its ability to help us develop our potentials and live a more fulfilling and independent life.'

These three social logics of competition, atomization, and instrumentalization are interrelated and mutually reinforcing. Thus the instrumentalization of education underpinned by marketplace metaphors, lends itself to and suggests competition as a mode of operation, which in turn entails a view of schools, teachers, and students as rivals rather than collaborators. However, we can gain additional insights into how these social logics are instantiated and sustained – as well as potentially challenged – by examining the political logics through which these social logics are asserted and defended, which is the focus of the next section.

The political logics of the education revolution

As noted above, political logics account for the establishment, reproduction, and contestation of a particular regime or set of practices. Thus, whereas social logics provide a synchronic perspective on a regime, political logics offer a diachronic picture. Political logics can be characterized according to two contrasting discursive strategies, identified by Laclau and Mouffe (2001) as the logic of equivalence and the logic of difference. Whereas the logic of equivalence strives to simplify social and political space into two opposing camps, within each of which an array of differences are translated into an overarching equivalence, the logic of difference strives to prevent the formation of such a dichotomy, formed around two opposing chains of equivalence, by emphasizing and multiplying pure (in the sense of nonpoliticized; not linked to dichotomies like advantaged/disadvantaged) differences.

We can see the operation of the logic of equivalence in the connections asserted between, for example, disparate elements such as increased productivity, social inclusion, quality education, choice, transparency, and accountability. We can express this chain of equivalence formally as: increased productivity + social inclusion = quality education = quality teaching = flexibility and choice = transparency and accountability = publicly reported (high-stakes) testing. The order of the individual items is not the issue; the key point is their purported equivalence as part of a chain, which we might call (in reference to the title of the education revolution document) 'quality education,' and the opposition of this chain to an antagonistic chain of equivalence comprising an opposing set of values (i.e. declining productivity (and social exclusion) = nonquality education = nonquality teaching = rigidity = opacity and unaccountability = in-house (low-stakes) assessment). In the creation and assertion of such a chain of equivalence the slippages and tensions between the individual elements are glossed over for the purposes of unanimity. The important issue is to construct a united front against a posited opposing chain.

Thus, for example, the assertion in the document that 'there is good evidence, primarily from the United States and the OECD's PISA, that the publication of school-level test scores tends to improve the performance of all schools' (ER, 31) is questionable. Indeed, this view was directly contested by the conclusions of the Cambridge Primary Review in the UK:

> It is often claimed in defense of national tests that they raise standards. In fact, at best the impact of national tests on standards is oblique. The prospect of testing, especially high-stakes testing undertaken in the public arena, forces teachers, pupils and parents to concentrate their attention on those areas of learning to be tested, too often to the exclusion of other activities of considerable educational importance. It is this intensity of focus, and anxiety about the results and their consequences, which makes the initial difference to test scores. But it is essentially a halo effect and it does not last; for it is

not testing that raises standards but good teaching. (Alexander 2009, 497; see also Au 2009; Cuban 2008; Hursh 2008; Stobart 2008)

Seen in this light, the Australian government's fervor for testing can be seen as yet another example of policy-makers ignoring research evidence in pursuing particular policy agendas (Levin 2010). But the 'truth' of the assertion is not so much the issue as the role it plays as part of a web of signification, which gains legitimacy through repetition rather than substance. As Taubman (2009, 85) puts it,

> The regnant policy language of standards and accountability ... the incessant talk of measurement, numerical data, and quantification, the claims that teachers ... are responsible for the nation's economic, racial and political state, the contention that teaching is a science and that we know what works in classrooms, the calls for professionalization, all these are only a few of the linguistic nodal points in an elaborate discursive web of statements which find support mainly in their reiteration.

In contrast to the antagonistic discourse of standards and accountability which posits a world made up of success and failure, underperforming and performing, below and above average, the logic of difference can be seen in calls 'for all stakeholders in schooling in all jurisdictions and sectors to take action to ensure that every child gets an excellent education and that every school is a great school' (ER, 36). Here difference is subordinated to a vision of common purpose and community, with key work being effected by the terms 'all' and 'every.' As Popkewitz (2009, 534) observes in relation to education policy making, 'the phrase "all" implies this hope of future unity and harmony ... the "all" [and the "every"] erases differences as the proper application of procedures and planning produces sameness as there is only one "all children".' Such appeals are based on fantasmatic prototypes such as the unified nation or the happy family (Stavrakakis 1999, 77). I return to this vision of harmony in the discussion of fantasmatic logics below.

The logic of difference takes on a particular significance in comments making veiled reference to long-running debates over the funding of private and public schools and students in Australia, debates that have been described as 'the powder keg' of Australian school politics (Marginson 1994, 200). The idiosyncrasies of Australia's school funding arrangements[5] include nongovernment schools receiving over 40% of their income from government sources (Ministerial Committee on Education Early Childhood Development and Youth Affairs [MCEETYA] 2008) without being subject to the same accountability requirements as government schools. This has led to a situation where, rather than being one system with a variety of schools ownership types, Australia has two systems, with differing ownership, funding and accountability regimes (Stewart 2005).

The problem for the current Australian government is that these differences threaten to coalesce around two opposing chains of equivalence, with the policy landscape being read in terms of public = under-privileged vs. private = privileged. In order to preempt this, the document makes reference to:

> An education debate that, until now has overwhelmingly focused on inputs rather than student outcomes and has been run along sectoral lines. *All* governments acknowledge that we cannot hope to achieve the ambitious COAG[6] schooling outcomes and targets unless we put this stale debate behind us. (ER, 33 emphasis added)

An issue of significant social inequity in relation to the reproduction of social privileges and disadvantages is dismissed here as a 'stale debate' and its proponents disparaged as perpetrators of a divisive sectoralism, irresponsibly diverting attention away from 'outcomes and targets.' In this powerful rhetorical political gesture that simultaneously masks its own political nature via its claim to consensus among 'all governments,' the legitimacy of efforts to resist the formation and/or continuation of oppositional and antagonistic positions is undermined. The (political) message seems to be that social harmony, free from class struggle or other political disturbance, can be ours if we put aside our petty political positions and endorse the governments' policy stance. This message was reiterated in subsequent policy speeches on the education revolution by the then education minister, Julia Gillard. For instance, in a speech in the UK to the City of London Corporation, she asserted,

> The Rudd government supports the right of parents to choose a school for their children. We believe that diverse provision is needed to meet the needs of a diverse and growing population. But we reject the proposition that there is a conflict between diversity and universal excellence. (Gillard 2008b)

The following month she argued, 'The debate we need to having is not a sterile debate about public vs. private' (Gillard 2008a). Whitty's comment in relation to a similar attempt by the Blair government in the UK to depoliticize issues of unequal access seems equally pertinent to Australia here:

> In arguing that the key issue was 'standards not structures', the government tried to wish away a history in which the selection of children for unequal provision had been the dominant principle on which English secondary education had been organised. (2002, 128)

Meanwhile, Whitty's reference to 'wishing away' is suggestive of fantasy and the notion of fantasmatic logics, which are discussed in the following section.

The fantasmatic logics of the education revolution

Fantasmatic logics provide a vision of wholeness and harmoniousness, structuring reality in a way that serves to shield us from the inescapability of dissensus in social life. We can see the operation of fantasmatic logics in the assertion that 'we must simultaneously deliver equity and excellence in our schools' (ER, 35). The suggestion of the possible fulfillment of all needs and the satisfaction of all demands is another example of the document deploying the familiar neoliberal strategy of depoliticization for political ends. In reconciling the antagonism between excellence achieved via neoliberal performance regimes, and equity, the education revolution sustains at the level of fantasy what it strives to avoid at the level of material reality, namely, equal access to quality education for all. That is, it ignores the mounting evidence that its strategies for achieving excellence are at odds with its aspirations with regard to equity. As Savage (2011, 34) recently argued with reference to the Australian context,

> policy imaginations of schools as havens of excellence and equity are difficult to take seriously when infused into the architecture of an education system (and society) that

is deeply stratified and structured to discriminate between individuals in line with performance hierarchies.

This is not surprising, given that 'these imaginarizations of abundance and excess
remain the backbone of our fantasmatic life, the vehicle of our (personal, social and
political) desire' (Stavrakakis 2005, 187). We might describe this phenomenon as
the fantasy of 'illusory harmony.'

The fantasmatic element is evident in the slippage between the emphasis on
excellence, quality, and achievement and the simultaneous emphasis on competition,
which seems to ignore the uncomfortable fact that averages require under- as well
as over-achievement and that competition demands losers as well as winners
(Savage 2011). Similarly, and as noted above already, the message to parents to
move their children away from 'under-performing' schools contained in the emphasis on giving parents 'the evidence they need to make informed choices' (ER, 31),
maintains the illusion that choice is equally available to all – another version of the
fantasy of reconciling excellence and equity – and ignores the damaging effects of
middle-class flight from public schooling by imagining that individual choices do
not have systemic effects (Ball, Bowe, and Gewirtz 1996).[7]

Another fantasmatic element is the projection of a machine-like feedback loop
between testing, performance data, and educational improvement, reflecting what
we might describe as the fantasy of 'illusory efficiency.' The arguments that 'clear
accountability helps create a learning environment that encourages innovation and
excellence from school leaders, teachers and students' and that 'the publication of
test scores tends to improve the performance of all schools' (ER, 31) ignore the
points made above in the quote from the Cambridge Primary Review (Alexander
2009), and reflected in the work of a number of other researchers (e.g. Au 2009;
Cuban 2008; Hursh 2008; Stobart 2008), which underscore the negative and nar-
rowing consequences of the publication of data from high-stakes testing. However,
the impression of the testing-performance loop as a smoothly functioning machine
is not only inaccurate; it also serves an ideological function installing 'a performa-
tivist metanarrative ... where everything is measured against the criteria of effectiveness and efficiency of outcomes ... [which] ... because of its technicist nature
performativity projects itself deceptively as being non-ideological' (Wain 2008,
105). Thus the economistic fantasy of efficiency performs the ideological double
trick of squeezing out any discursive space that might allow for consideration of
complex and messy issues involving ethics and politics, whilst simultaneously deny-
ing its own ideological nature.

Finally, it is important to note that fantasmatic logics typically involve a beatific
narrative, a utopian vision of a state of affairs yet to come but achievable once an
implied obstacle is overcome, alongside a 'horrific' vision of disaster that will threaten if the purported obstacle prevails and the desired state of affairs is not achieved,
i.e. if schools fail to meet 'Australia's education and skills challenge' (ER, 7). Such
disaster is implicit in the statement in the final page of the document that, 'As other
countries continue to advance, we cannot afford to delay' (ER, 36). We might
describe this phenomenon as the fantasy of 'horrific enjoyment.' As noted above, the
demand to achieve both excellence and equity asserts the beatific fantasy of social
harmony and universal participation in the benefits accruing from education, reflecting 'the dream of a state without disturbances and dislocations, a state in which we
are supposed to get back the enjoyment (jouissance) sacrificed upon entering the

symbolic order' (Stavrakakis 2005, 189); lurking within this utopian vision is the horrific fantasy of social division and economic decline that will descend unless we succeed in keeping the demons of unaccountable, opaque, and hence poor quality education and teaching at bay. Such fantasizing ignores the scapegoating that inevitably accompanies utopian thinking. As Stavrakakis (1999, 100) notes, we need to be mindful of, 'the deeply problematic nature of utopian politics ... Every utopian fantasy produces its reverse and calls for its elimination.' This may sound melodramatic until we note threats from the former education minister and current prime minister, Julia Gillard, to sack the principals of 'underperforming' schools (Chilcott 2009), and recall the policies of her education mentor, New York Schools Chancellor Joel Klein, who has implemented a punitive but discredited system of report cards for schools (Caldwell 2010). Such instances should alert us to the naivety and potential danger inhering in utopian discourses (Stavrakakis 1999, 100).

Conclusion

My analysis of Australian federal government's education revolution policy document – conducted through a framework of explanatory logics drawn from political theory – substantiates the inextricable links between politics and policy. In particular, in addition to describing the prevalent discourses operating in a particular policy via the notion of social logics, the framework has allowed me to foreground the active construction, promotion, reproduction, and contestation of particular social meanings in terms of the political logics of equivalence and difference, whilst also highlighting the operation of fantasy and desire in policy-making in terms of fantasmatic logics. Thus, in addition to identifying the social logics of competition, atomization, and instrumentalization in the education revolution, I have argued that these social logics are established, reproduced, and maintained through a set of political logics, involving, *on the one hand*, the assertion of *equivalences* between economic productivity and global competitiveness, 'quality' teaching, and accountability and transparency mechanisms and, *on the other hand*, the assertion of pure (i.e. nondichotomized) *difference* in relation to the issue of school sector funding. I have also argued that the education revolution policy agenda is further sustained by fantasmatic logics involving beatific fantasies centered on the illusory harmonization of equality with excellence (the latter achieved through markets, managerialism, and performativity), along with horrific fantasies of inexorable economic decline if the government's policy preferences are not followed. If my analysis of the education revolution has demonstrated the value of these conceptual tools whilst also shedding some new light on the Australian government's policy agenda in relation to education, it has served its purpose.

It is important to stress, however, that the education revolution is not a unique policy instance, but rather a 'vernacular' expression of the global neoliberal 'policyscape' (Rizvi and Lingard 2010) with its penchant for markets, managerialism, and performativity, as technologies for promoting the development of self-entrepreneurial individuals and institutions. Commensurate with these values, as societies around the world have backed away from explicit policies of redistribution, responsibility for the social policy functions of providing equality of access to social and economic goods has devolved to education and schools; and in this light, the Blair government's mantra of 'Education, Education, Education,' the Bush government's 'No Child Left Behind' policy, and the Rudd/Gillard government's education revolution can be seen as cut from the same neoliberal rhetorical cloth. The dilemma here for governments, particularly those espousing third-way politics that seeks to reconcile advanced capitalist and social democratic values, is that on the one hand they need to be seen to be addressing significant issues like social inequality and mobility, whilst on the other, they want to avoid class-based diagnoses, in the name of consensual politics. Market-based language comprising terms like 'choice,' 'inclusion,' and 'exclusion' proves useful here:

> By redefining the structural inequalities produced by the market in terms of 'exclusion', one can dispense with the structural analyses of their causes, thereby avoiding the fundamental issue of which changes in power relations are required in order to tackle them. (Mouffe 2005, 62)

The result of this consensual approach is that 'Instead of being the terrain where agonistic debate takes place between left and right policies, politics is reduced to "spinning"' (Mouffe 2005, 63; see also Gewirtz, Dickson, and Power, 2004), as governments and political parties rely on marketing and sound bites to sell their policies (Lingard and Rawolle 2004). In this context, the irony of the use of the term 'revolution' by the Australian government is evident.

In all of these policy agendas, education is envisaged as the key to social and particularly socioeconomic salvation. Such fantasizing ignores the 'double gestures' of inclusion and exclusion in which 'strategies of remediation and rescue' are also 'processes of abjection' and whereby the populations and individuals targeted for salvation are concomitantly defined as problematic (Popkewitz 2009, 546). These salvation narratives can also be read as the beatific fantasies whose horrific counterpart is the ongoing demonization and derision of education, teachers, and schools in the mainstream media.

It is also important to note that, despite the almost universal subordination of education to economic ends and the questionable assumption of a direct correlation between increased educational spending and economic benefit, this valorization of education has been beneficial in a number of ways, not least in raising educational expenditure. But it has also been part of a regressive depoliticization of education that has undermined the interests of the very groups it has claimed to champion. Specifically, it has been detrimental to socially and economically disadvantaged students and communities, in that it has enabled governments to individualize responsibility for persistent social inequalities, thereby 'holding these very groups, as groups and individuals, accountable for their failure to meet specified standards' (Taubman, 2009, 107). It has also been detrimental to teachers, in that the technicist emphasis on effectiveness in the classroom evident in discourses of teacher effectiveness and teacher centrality in contemporary political and media debates, serve to disconnect teachers from broader questions regarding the social contexts of education, thereby depoliticizing teachers and teaching (Larsen 2010; Taubman 2009) and deflecting attention from pressing political issues, such as the socioeconomically reproductive nature of current school funding arrangements.

This ideological concealment is evident in the Rudd/Gillard government document, *Quality Education: The Case for an Education Revolution in our Schools*, which naturalizes its social logics of competition, atomization, and instrumentalization and which glosses over the tensions between its aspirations for inclusiveness and its preference for audit and accountability mechanisms, whilst circumventing any discussion of school funding arrangements via a fantasmatic vision of social harmony and unity. The education revolution rhetoric is not unique in deploying these strategies, which are symptomatic of much education policy in today's textualized, mediatized, and globalized world. This is a world where policies strive to present a simplified version of social reality, aligned with shared desires and unquestionably in the public interest, and where the latter is presented as an unproblematic, uncontested, and unified entity (Rizvi and Lingard 2010, 5–6). It is a world that is deeply political in its depoliticization and ideologically saturated in its disavowal of ideology.

Indeed, a major contribution of this paper and its analysis of the Australian government's education revolution policy in terms of its social, political, and fantasmatic logics has been to foreground how, despite its attempts to escape politics, education policy remains inescapably political in a number of ways. It remains political in its assertion, reproduction, or resistance of a particular, situated, and contingent version of a social reality that can always be interpreted and constructed in other ways. And it remains political in its deployment of fantasy, whereby the contradictions, tensions, and other uncomfortable aspects of social reality are glossed over and obscured, in exchange for a fantasmatic vision of harmony and wholeness. The alternative to such fantasizing is to accept difference, antagonism, and contestation as essential constituents of democratic politics. Such acceptance could potentially be the starting point of a genuine education revolution.

Acknowledgements

Thanks are extended to my colleagues, Kalervo Gulson and Michael Michell, as well as four anonymous reviewers, for their insightful comments on earlier drafts of this paper.

Notes

1. Though as Dean (2009) notes, revolution is a term that the left has largely abandoned, while the right has embraced it to name their triumphs, pace the Thatcher and Reagan 'revolutions.'
2. The document was published in 2008 under the co-authorship of education minister and deputy prime minister (now prime minister) Julia Gillard and the then prime minister, Kevin Rudd, who led the Australian Labor party to victory in 2007 after 11 years of the conservative, liberal–national coalition government of John Howard. The document can be found at http://www.deewr.gov.au/Schooling/Programs/Documents/QualityEducation-EducationRevolutionWEB.pdf.
3. By social imaginary I mean 'that common understanding which makes possible common practices, and a widely shared sense of legitimacy' (Taylor 2007, 172). The point made by authors such as Arjun Appadurai, Manfred Steger, and others is that, rather than restricting this notion to the nation-state, it now makes sense to think in terms of a global social imaginary.
4. References to specific pages of the document, *Quality Education: The Case for an Education Revolution in Our Schools*, are forthwith denoted 'ER, xx.'
5. The complexities of this aspect of Australian education policy are beyond the scope of this paper; but for a detailed account see Dowling (2008).
6. COAG, the Council of Australian Governments, is the peak intergovernmental forum in Australia, comprising the Prime Minister, State Premiers, Territory Chief Ministers, and the President of the Australian Local Government Association.
7. See Bonnor and Caro (2008), for a discussion of the discourse of 'choice' in the context of Australian education; see O'Neill (2011), for another antipodean-based discussion of privatization in education.

References

Alexander, R., ed. 2009. *Children, their world, their education: Final report and recommendations of the Cambridge primary review.* London: Routledge.

Apple, M. 2001. Markets, standards, teaching, and teacher education. *Journal of Teacher Education* 52, no. 2: 182–96.

Au, W. 2009. *Unequal by design: High stakes testing and the standardization of inequality.* New York, NY: Routledge.

Ball, S. 2003a. *Class strategies and the education market: The middle classes and social advantage.* London: Routledge.

Ball, S. 2003b. The teacher's soul and the terrors of performativity. *Journal of Education Policy* 18, no. 2: 215–28.

Ball, S. 2007. *Education plc: Understanding private sector participation in public education.* Abingdon: Routledge.

Ball, S. 2008. *The education debate.* Bristol: The Policy Press.

Ball, S., R. Bowe, and S. Gewirtz. 1996. School choice, social class and distinction: The realization of social advantage in education. *Journal of Education Policy* 11, no. 1: 89–112.

Boltanski, L., and E. Chiapello. 2005. *The new spirit of capitalism.* London: Verso.

Bonnor, C., and J. Caro. 2008. *The stupid country: How Australia is dismantling public education.* Sydney: UNSW Press.

Caldwell, B. 2010. Why the education revolution is not transforming our schools. *Public forum on education.* Hamilton, Victoria.

Chang, H.-J. 2010. *23 Things they don't tell you about capitalism.* London: Allen Lane.

Chilcott, T. 2009. *Julia Gillard warns of sack threat to school principals.* The Courier-Mail, August 20.

Connell, R., B. Fawcett, and G. Meagher. 2009. Neoliberalism, new public management and the human service professions: Introduction to the special issue. *Journal of Sociology* 45, no. 4: 331–8.

Coole, D. 2000. *Negativity and politics: Dionysus and dialectics from Kant to poststructuralism.* London: Routledge.

Couldry, N. 2010. *Why voice matters: Culture and politics after neoliberalism.* London: Sage.

Cranston, N., M. Kimber, B. Mulford, A. Reid, and J. Keating. 2010. Politics and school education in Australia: A case of shifting purposes. *Journal of Educational Administration* 48, no. 2: 182–95.

Cuban, L. 2008. *Hugging the middle: How teachers teach in an era of testing and accountability.* Columbia, NY: Teachers College Press.

Dean, J. 2009. *Democracy and other neoliberal fantasies.* Durham, NC: Duke University Press.

Dowling, A. 2008. Unhelpfully complex and exceedingly opaque: Australia's school funding system. *Australian Journal of Education* 52, no. 2: 129–50.

Fink, B. 1995. *The Lacanian subject: Between language and jouissance.* Princeton, NJ: Princeton University Press.

Fisher, M. 2009. *Capitalist realism: Is there no alternative?* London: Zero Books.

Francis, B., and V. Hey. 2009. Talking back to power: Snowballs in hell and the imperative of insisting on structural explanations. *Gender and Education* 21, no. 2: 225–32.

Gewirtz, S., M. Dickson, and S. Power. 2004. Unravelling a 'spun' policy: A case study of the constitutive role of 'spin' in the education policy process. *Journal of Education Policy* 19, no. 3: 321–42.

Gillard, J. 2008a. *Pollitics and integrity: Delivering an education revolution*. Melbourne: John Button Memorial Lecture.

Gillard, J. 2008b. *Reforming education and skills: Challenges of the twenty first century*. London, UK: Speech to the City of London Corporation.

Glynos, J. 2008. Ideological fantasy at work. *Journal of Political Ideologies* 13, no. 3: 275–96.

Glynos, J., and D. Howarth. 2007. *Logics of critical explanation in social and political theory*. London: Routledge.

Glynos, J., and Y. Stavrakakis. 2008. Lacan and political subjectivity: Fantasy and enjoyment in psychoanalysis and political theory. *Subjectivity* 24, no. 1: 256–74.

Harvey, D. 2010. *The enigma of capital and the crises of capitalism*. London: Profile Books.

Howarth, D. 2009. Power, discourse, and policy: Articulating a hegemony approach to critical policy studies. *Critical Policy Studies* 3, no. 3: 309–35.

Hursh, D. 2008. *High-stakes testing and the decline of teaching and learning: The real crisis in education*. Lanham, MD: Rowman & Littlefield.

Karmel, T. 2007. Vocational education and training in Australian schools. *Australian Educational Researcher* 34, no. 3: 101–17.

Labaree, D. 2003. The peculiar problems of preparing educational researchers. *Educational Researcher* 32, no. 4: 13–22.

Laclau, E., and C. Mouffe. 2001. *Hegemony and socialist strategy: Towards a radical democratic politics*. 2nd ed. London: Verso.

Larsen, M. 2010. Troubling the discourse of teacher centrality: A comparative perspective. *Journal of Education Policy* 25, no. 2: 207–31.

Levin, B. 2010. Governments and education reform: Some lessons from the last 50 years. *Journal of Education Policy* 25, no. 6: 739–47.

Lingard, B. 2010. Policy borrowing, policy learning: Testing times in Australian schooling. *Critical Studies in Education* 51, no. 2: 129–47.

Lingard, B., and J. Ozga. 2007. Introduction: Reading education policy and politics. In *The Routledgefalmer reader in education policy and politics*, ed. B. Lingard and J. Ozga, 1–8. London: Routledge.

Lingard, B., and S. Rawolle. 2004. Mediatizing educational policy: The journalistic field, science policy, and cross-field effects. *Journal of Education Policy* 19, no. 3: 361–80.

Lingard, B., and S. Rawolle. 2011. *New scalar politics: Implications for education policy. Comparative Education*, 1–14. Published online June 09, 2011 (iFirst).

Marchant, O. 2005. The absence at the heart of presence: Radical democracy and the 'ontology of lack'. In *Radical democracy: Politics between abundance and lack*, ed. L. Tønder and L. Thomassen, 17–31. Manchester: Manchester University Press.

Marginson, S. 1994. *Education and public policy in Australia*. Cambridge: Cambridge University Press.

Marginson, S. 1997. *Markets in education*. St Leonards, NSW: Allen and Unwin.

Ministerial Committee on Education Early Childhood Development and Youth Affairs (MCEETYA). 2008. *National report on schooling in Australia 2008*. Canberra: Commonwealth Government.

Mouffe, C. 2005. *On the political*. Abingdon: Routledge.

Nóvoa, A., and T. Yariv-Mashal. 2003. Comparative research in education: A mode of governance or a historical journey? *Comparative Education* 39, no. 4: 423–38.

Olssen, M. 2010. *Liberalism, neoliberalism, social democracy: Thin communitarian perspectives on political philosophy*. New York, NY: Routledge.

Olssen, M., J. Codd, and A.-M. O'Neill. 2004. *Education policy: Globalization, citizenship and democracy*. London: Sage.

O'Neill, J. 2011. The privatisation of public schooling in New Zealand. *Journal of Education Policy* 26, no. 1: 17–31.

Phillips, L., and M. Jørgensen. 2002. *Discourse analysis as theory and method*. Thousand Oaks, CA: Sage.

Popkewitz, T. 2009. Inclusion and exclusion as double gestures in policy and education sciences. In *Re-reading education policies: A handbook studying the policy agenda of the twenty-first century*, ed. M. Simons, M. Olssen, and M. Peters, 531–48. Rotterdam: Sense Publishers.

Rancière, J. 2003. *The philosopher and his poor*. Durham, NC: Duke University Press.

Rancière, J. 2010. On ignorant schoolmasters. In *Jacques rancière: Education, truth, emancipation*, ed. C. Bingham and G. Biesta, 1–24. London: Continuum.

Reid, A. 2009. Is this a revolution? A critical analysis of the Rudd governmentís national education agenda. *Curriculum Perspectives* 29, no. 3: 1–13.

Rizvi, F., and B. Lingard. 2010. *Globalizing education policy*. New York, NY: Routledge.

Rudd, K. 2009. The global financial crisis. *The Monthly*, no. 42, February: 20–9.

Rudd, K., and J. Gillard. 2008. *Quality education: The case for an education revolution in our schools*. Address to the National Press Club, Canberra.

Saad Filho, A., and D. Johnston. 2005. Introduction. In *Neoliberalism: A critical reader*, ed. A. Saad Filho and D. Johnston, 1–6. London: Pluto Press.

Savage, G. 2011. When worlds collide: Excellent and equitable learning communities? Australia's 'social capitalist' paradox? *Journal of Education Policy* 26, no. 1: 33–59.

Simons, M., M. Olssen, and M. Peters. 2009. Re-reading education policies: Part 2: Challenges, horizons, approaches, tools and styles. In *Re-reading education policies: A handbook studying the policy agenda of the twenty-first century*, ed. M. Simons, M. Olssen, and M. Peters, 1–35. Rotterdam: Sense Publishers.

Stavrakakis, Y. 1999. *Lacan and the political*. London: Routledge.

Stavrakakis, Y. 2005. Negativity and radical democracy. In *Radical democracy: Politics between abundance and lack*, ed. L. Tønder and L. Thomassen, 185–202. Manchester: Manchester University Press.

Steger, M. 2008. *The rise of the global imaginary: Political ideologies from the French revolution to the global war on terror*. Oxford: Oxford University Press.

Steger, M., and V. Roy. 2010. *Neoliberalism: A very short introduction*. Oxford: Oxford University Press.

Stewart, J. 2005. Educational policy: Politics, markets and the decline of 'publicness'. *Policy and Politics* 33, no. 3: 475–87.

Stobart, G. 2008. *Testing times: The uses and abuses of assessment*. New York, NY: Routledge.

Stronach, I. 2010. *Globalizing education, educating the local: How method made us mad*. Abingdon: Routledge.

Taubman, P. 2009. *Teaching by numbers: Deconstructing the discourse of standards and accountability in education*. New York, NY: Routledge.

Taylor, C. 2007. *A secular age*. Cambridge, MA: Belknap Press.

Wain, K. 2008. The future of education … And its philosophy. *Studies in Philosophy and Education* 27, no. 2: 103–14.

Whitty, G. 2002. *Making sense of education policy*. London: Paul Chapman.

Wiseman, A., and D. Baker. 2005. The worldwide explosion of internationalized education policy. In *Global trends in education policy*, ed. A. Wiseman and D. Baker, 1–21. Oxford: Elsevier.

Wolf, A. 2002. *Does education matter? Myths about education and economic growth*. London: Penguin.

Youdell, D. 2011. *School trouble: Identity, power and politics in education*. London: Routledge.

The sublime objects of education policy: quality, equity and ideology

Matthew Clarke

Quality and equity are touchstones of education policy in the twenty-first century in a range of global contexts. On the surface, this seems fitting: after all, who could object to more quality and greater equity in education? Yet what do we mean by quality and equity, and how are they related? This paper draws on Lacanian psychoanalytic theory to argue that not only are quality and equity far more complex than education policy formulations typically imply, but also that despite their elevated place in policy debates they remain elusive, serving as sublime objects that function as sites for the investment of desire, while simultaneously covering over and compensating for the ultimate impossibility of a complete and harmonious society. The paper argues that it is a result of their occupying this empty place, and through their holding out the (illusive) promise of enjoyment, rather than as a consequence of their specific or intrinsic content, that sublime objects such as equity and quality exert their particular ideological force.

The key to improving outcomes … lies in redressing disadvantage and hence reducing the underperforming 'tail', and improving the quality of teaching to raise the performance of all. In other words, we must simultaneously deliver equity and excellence in our schools. (Rudd & Gillard, 2008, p. 35)

Our education system – our country – is still held back by two weaknesses. We have – for generations – failed to stretch every child to the limit of their ability. And we have – for all our lifetimes – failed the poorest most of all. (Gove, 2012)

The Sublime is an object in which we can experience this very impossibility, this permanent failure of representation to reach after the Thing. (Žižek, 1989, p. 203)

Introduction

If policy is viewed as the authoritative allocation of values (Easton, 1953; Rizvi & Lingard, 2010), it is clear that governments of various political labels and persuasions strive to identify themselves and their education policies with the twin values of quality – or excellence in US parlance – and equity. Indeed, quality and equity – as exemplified in the Rudd and Gillard quote above (Australia's Labor Government), the Gove quote (from the UK's conservative/liberal–democratic coalition government), as well as in the title of a recent OECD, *Equity and quality in education* (2012) – might be described as interdependent touchstones of contemporary education systems. Linda Darling-Hammond captures this spirit when she writes, 'now more than ever, high-quality education for all is a public good that is essential for the good of the public. Smart, equitable investments will, in the long run, save far more than they cost' (2010, p. 328).

Taken at face value, this seems quite right and proper. After all, who could possibly be against more quality or greater equity? But, as always, the devil is at least partially in the detail. More specifically, it lies in the question as to what we mean or understand by quality and equity? And of course, like all values in education and education policy, quality and equity are contested notions (Stout, Tallerico, & Scribner, 1994) with debate centring, in the case of equity, around questions of *what* is to be distributed (e.g. outcomes? opportunities?), *who* it is to be distributed to, and *how* it is to be distributed (Stein, 2004). Or, in the case of quality, it concerns questions of whether the focus should be on *process or product*, on *universal or particular values*.

This conceptual complexity is redoubled when we take *context* seriously (Ball, Maguire, & Braun, 2012), and recall that policy is not just about government policy-makers and the policy texts that they generate. Policy is also an ongoing and unending process, embodied in everyday practices and artefacts, shaped and enacted by multiple actors – including other policies – in a range of interrelated contexts from the local to the global, the exalted to the mundane (Ball, 2012; Ball et al., 2012).

In one sense, the contestability of policy is merely a reflection of the more general contingency of all discourse, which Laclau captures elegantly and incisively in his preface to Žižek's, *The sublime object of ideology*:

> ... if the unity of the object is the retroactive effect of naming itself, then naming is not just the pure nominalistic game of attributing an empty name to a preconstituted subject. (1989, p. xiv)

Laclau goes on to make the political implications of this contingency explicit:

> ... if the process of naming the objects amounts to the very act of their constitution, then the descriptive features will be fundamentally unstable and open to all kinds of hegemonic rearticulations. (1989, p. xiv)

In a later piece, co-authored with Judith Butler, in which he explicitly comments on his earlier writing, he links this instability to the iterativity of language, with particular salience for the current paper, as becomes clear if we replace the term 'names' with 'policy' in the following:

> ... names [policies] are natural places for hegemonic rearticulations because their contents are constantly being negotiated. If the emptiness of names [policies] is partially limited by transient stabilizations, any stabilization, in time, is threatened by the emptiness inherent in the structure of naming [doing policy]. (Butler & Laclau, 2004, p. 344)

This paper argues that the 'transient stabilizations' resulting from policy's iterative nature – the ways in which it is articulated and rearticulated across spatially and temporally varied political contexts without ever being definitively tied down – provide the operative conditions within which quality and equity function as what I am describing as sublime objects of contemporary education policy. Thus, the paper argues that not only are the values of quality and equity complex and contested, but also that they function as forms of the Lacanian 'sublime', as things that are at once elevated and elusive, as untouchable objects of inestimable value that serve as ultimate horizons, fascinating and capturing us as 'policy subjects' (Ball et al., 2012; Stein, 2004), whilst at the same time being perceived as constantly under threat (Sharpe & Boucher, 2010, p. 56) and hence in need of constant re-inscription. In what follows, I begin by outlining the context of the discussion in terms of the economic reconstitution of education as a facet of neoliberal globalization of education policy. I then discuss the notion of sublime objects and its links to a Lacanian theorization of ideology. This is followed by discussions of quality and of equity, which unpack some of their complexities before going on to consider the ways in which they operate as sublime objects of education policy.

The economic reconstitution of education policy

A key factor explaining the hegemony of contemporary neoliberal policy lies in its capacity to connect and merge, or suture, disparate domains, aims and values. This is evident, for instance, in the 'joining up' of policy (Ball, 2008, p. 3), including the ways that education policy is developed in relation to other areas of policy such as parenting, childcare, health and the economy. It is also reflected in the ways that local and national policy patterns across these fields 'join up' with – both reflecting and shaping – global policy trends (Ball, 2012; Rizvi & Lingard, 2010).

Another aspect of this joining up is the capture by instrumental purposes of policy of what we might call, after Castoriadis (1997), the imaginary dimensions of policy, i.e. the ways that policy envisages certain models of society and seeks to bring into being particular types of individuals ideally suited to populating this imagined world. Thus, reflecting on curriculum reform in the context of the globalization of education policy, Rizvi and Lingard note that such reform 'has been linked to the reconstitution of education as a central arm of national economic policy, as well as being central to the imagined community the nation wishes to construct through schooling' (2010, p. 96).

This reconstitution of education reflects the convergence of, on the one hand, *economic* concerns with productivity in the face of global competition (reflected in education policy's focus on 'quality') with, on the other hand, *political* concerns about sustaining democratic ideals of access, inclusion and participation in the context of increasingly multi-ethnic nature of the nation in an era of rapid social change and global migration (reflected in education policy's focus on 'equity'). This reconstitution of education can be read as 'indicative of the strange merging of democracy and capitalism in which contemporary subjects are produced and trapped' (Dean, 2009, p. 22). For just as the economic fact that capitalism creates winners and losers is occluded by the uncritical celebration of democracy within a politics which sees capitalism as an intrinsic element, so the 'collateral damage' (Nichols & Berliner, 2007) from competitively oriented approaches to quality is obscured by an ostensible commitment to equity in education policy. But not only is the antagonism between these values occluded; when we interrogate the aura surrounding these twin values in contemporary education policy, we see that, despite the resigned sense of their being 'no alternative', as a result of the recurrent re-inscription of neoliberal policy across disparate fields and at multiple scales described above – a phenomenon aptly characterised by Stronach as a global 'hegemonic "hypernarrative"' (2010, p. 10) – these values are, in one sense at least, hollow or empty. The distinctiveness of my argument, particularly in relation to critical policy studies with a sociological emphasis (Ball, 2006; Ozga, 2000), lies in its use of concepts of desire, enjoyment and fantasy, in addition to the notion of the sublime, from Lacanian psychoanalytic theory and the work of theorists like Žižek (e.g. 1989, 1997) and Dean (2006, 2009, 2010), as a means of gaining further insights into this emptiness, as well as into the suturing of domains, aims and values in education policy that serves to cover-up and compensate for such aporia.

Sublime objects and ideology

Sublimation and the sublime are usually conceived in Freudian terms as referring to the re-channelling of base sexual desire into higher and more acceptable forms such as literature or art. Lacanian theory develops this idea in another direction, 'suggesting that desire sublimates the object ... the inestimable value of an object is invented precisely through the restlessness/insatiability of desire' (Hurst, 2008, p. 341). Thus, in this Lacanian theorization, the sublime nature of otherwise everyday objects or concepts derives from desire and specifically the inability of such sublime objects to satiate that desire. As a result, sublime objects are invested with an excessive nature constituted by the object's nature or identity plus the supplement of my desire. As Hurst notes, there are links to be made here to Derrida's notion of iterability:

> 'Iterability' is Derrida's name for this paradoxical logic of excess, whereby I repeat the object as just what it is but always with the inestimable difference made by the 'supplement' of my love/interest. (Hurst, 2008, p. 342)

That is to say, in a non-foundational world, with all its insecurities and uncertainties, the self and its desire are the source of the missing elements of authority and legitimation. However, 'because that authority is itself in some sense "magical", that is, unsubstantiated, without ultimate foundation in a final ground qua substantive reason', it is, 'in the final analysis, a citation of lack, and so never settled once and for all' (Santner, 2001, p. 50). In other words, as Santner continues:

> ... every call to order addressed to a human subject – and a symbolic investiture is such a call – secretes a 'surplus value' of psychic excitation that, as it were, bears the burden, holds the place, of the missing foundation of the institutional authority that issued the call. (2001, pp. 50–51)

This surplus value of psychic excitation that secures symbolic investment is one of the characteristics of sublime objects.

Sublime objects are also linked to ideology, which, for Lacanians like Žižek, is sustained by enjoyment. Specifically, Žižek describes a nonrational kernel, remainder or supplement that is the condition of ideological subscription, 'which – in so far as it escapes ideological sense – sustains what we might call the ideological *jouis-sense*, enjoyment-in-the-sense (enjoy-meant), proper to ideology' (Žižek, 1989, pp. 43–44). Such enjoyment derives in part from the sense of fullness and harmony, associated with notions of fantasy that are also key to understanding Lacanian theorizations of ideology, as distinct from Marxist versions. As Žižek puts it:

> ... in the predominant Marxist perspective the ideological gaze is a *partial* gaze overlooking the *totality* of the social relations, whereas in the Lacanian perspective ideology designates *a totality set on effacing the traces of its own impossibility.* (1989, p. 49, emphasis in original)

The epigrammatic quote from Rudd and Gillard, arguing that Australian education needs to simultaneously achieve both equity and quality, exemplifies this point in the way that it posits a 'fantasmatically' complete and harmonious world – a totality, in Žižek's terms – in which the tensions between equity and a quality agenda premised on notions of choice and accountability are occluded. The way in which such sublime objects of policy – quality and equity in this case – embody fantasmatic desires to construct an ideologically acceptable social reality that grips us through its links to enjoyment is a key theme of this paper.

This theorization helps to explain the special aura accruing to concepts such as quality and equity in policy discourse. But the sublimation of values has at least three potential risks. First, as a result of their elevation as irrefutably desirable entities associated with fantasmatic visions of harmony and totality, sublime objects are prone to assume 'a transcendent status over dynamic phenomenal reality' (Hurst, 2008, p. 81). Second, by believing that her/his decisions actualize or realize the sublime object, a political agent may assume a similarly transcendent and unquestionable status. Third, by being perceived as actualized in and through present policy decisions, a sublime object may lose its status as an aspirational horizon indexing a future, yet-to-come state of affairs that needs to be continually worked towards (Hurst, 2008, pp. 81–82). Each of these risks is serious in itself, but taken collectively they combine to undermine the very values they purport to serve, bringing us perilously close to proto-fascism (Giroux, 2004a, 2004b; Webb & Gulson, 2011), as certainty and inevitability replace contingency and contestation.

Quality as a sublime object: matrices of flexible envelopment

Quality is one of the touchstones of modern education systems, as evidenced by the title of the policy document heralding Australia's 'education revolution', *Quality education: The case for an education revolution in our schools* (Rudd & Gillard, 2008). Like '*No Child Left Behind*' in the USA, this title is calculated to preempt opposition – who is going to stand up and oppose 'quality education'? But as Kipnis (2011) notes – in the specific context of education reform in China but with wider global relevance –

> … the education for quality policy and the discourse surrounding it have been quite stable, in part because the term 'quality' is extremely vague and a wide variety of specific policies can be justified in education for quality rhetoric. (2011, p. 291)

Furthermore, as Biesta (2010) points out, quality, like effectiveness, is not a self-sufficient concept but rather, begs the question of quality for what ends, and according to what criteria? The elusiveness of any satisfactory answer to this question suggests that we are possibly dealing with a sublime object.

Thus, for example, contemporary neoliberal education systems operate within a somewhat circular model, where quality is typically assumed to equate to improving test scores in high-stakes tests (Au, 2009; Hursh, 2008; Ravitch, 2009) and hence notions of quality are limited to what can be measured by those scores:

> … increasingly, educationally worthwhile 'knowledge' is being defined in terms of what standardized tests can measure. If tests cannot measure something, then it is not regarded as an essential part of the curriculum. (Burbules, 2004, p. 5)

Yet this begs the question of what these tests are capturing that *is* deemed as being of value?

In thinking about this question, it is useful to stand back and consider the conceptual underpinnings of various notions of quality. One way of conceptualizing education is as a teleological practice that identifies and pursues particular goals or endpoints. Such teleologies can take 'stronger' forms, identifying particular content or knowledge as valued, or 'weaker' forms, focusing more on processes and skills. Strong teleologies can be further divided, with some positing universal or transcendent knowledge, whilst others view knowledge as culturally or situationally specific; weak teleologies vary between perspectives linking educationally valued skills to capacities required beyond education and those in which the purpose of education or learning is more education and learning (Burbules, 2004).

Linking this to contemporary global education policy, strong teleological perspectives are dominant in the promulgation of national curricula that specify, often in exhaustive detail, the knowledge that must be transmitted to students, while weak teleological views are reflected in the economic instrumentalism that emphasizes the need to prepare students with the skills and capacities valued in the global economy. The current 'testing mania' (Orfield & Wald, 2000) can be seen as a perverse version of the weak teleological variant in which the purpose of education is more education and learning, except here test scores supplant education, so that quality education is reduced to improving test scores. As Ravitch (2009) comments in the context of Bush's *No Child Left Behind* policy, 'test-based accountability – not standards – became our national education policy. There was no underlying vision of what education should be or how one might improve schools' (p. 21). This example illustrates the role of desire – in this instance a desire for complete and incontrovertible means for the measurement and comparison of quality in education – in the constitution of quality as a sublime object of policy.

In one sense, this perverse teleological circularity parallels the hollow, self-contained nature of freedom – surely neoliberalism's master virtue (Žižek, 1999) – in neoliberal politics. Within this vision, as Mirowski (2009) notes:

> ... freedom is not the realization of any political, human, or cultural *telos*, but rather is the positing of autonomous self-governed individuals, all coming naturally equipped with a neoclassical version of rationality and motives of ineffable self-interest, striving to improve their lot in life by engaging in market exchange. (2009, p. 437)

As a consequence, education is seen in largely utilitarian ways, becoming, as Mirowski goes on to argue, 'a consumer good, not a life-transforming experience' (p. 437), while knowledge is restricted to that which is useful within the system rather than that which questions the very nature and status of the system per se. To echo Ravitch again, there ceases to be any deep 'underlying vision' regarding the individual or societal purpose of education. In Lacanian terms, quality becomes a sublime object, as the constitutive uncertainties and ambiguities in knowledge and education are sacrificed to the desire for certainty and self-contained totality.

In another sense, it is impossible to think about education in non-teleological ways. As Biesta (2010) puts it, 'education, be it in the form of schooling, workplace learning, vocational training or learning through life, is by its very nature a process with direction and purpose' (p. 2). However, we need to be mindful of a number of issues Burbules (2004, pp. 7–9) identifies as inherent to teleological thinking in education.

The first of these issues involves the relationship between means and ends. Of particular relevance in today's testing culture is the tendency to assume that ends and means can be clearly separated and to ignore the mutually constitutive relationship existing between them, 'as if we merely identify our aims and then, separately, identify the most effective and efficient means of attaining them' (Burbules, 2004, p. 7). The co-implication of means and ends poses both a threat – the familiar practice of teaching to the test, whereby the end unduly influences the means – but is also potentially productive – in so far as changing or (re)affirming practice may undermine the validity of an unduly limiting end. Thus, for example, a decision by a school to emphasize extended inquiry and interdisciplinary project work may assist in promoting a more sceptical attitude in teachers, parents and students towards the outcomes of high-stakes testing in discrete curricular areas.

The second issue, related to the first, concerns the danger of blindness to the exclusions, aporia and unintended consequences flowing from the articulation of particular goals and purposes in education. As Willinsky (1998) reminds us, education is very much about 'learning to divide the world', about becoming 'schooled in differences great and small' (p. 1). All curricular choices entail other possibilities that are not chosen; and these choices reflect explicit or implicit hierarchies of significance. More specifically, again in the context of neoliberal education policies, it is now evident how the reduction of understandings of quality in education to improved test scores in literacy and numeracy has had the collateral effect of diminishing the time and resources devoted to learning in other, non-tested, curriculum areas such as social studies and science. This is something that education regime in New York city discovered in 2007 when its students were among the weakest in these areas, despite the laurels they had gained for purportedly raising literacy and numeracy scores (Ravitch, 2009, pp. 88–90). Such events remind us of the need to recall the contingent and potentially contested nature of any educational goals, which demand ongoing vigilance with respect to their unintended meanings, effects and consequences.

The third issue, and the one most significant for the purposes of this paper, is that the identification of any particular educational value is at the same time the identification of a population that lacks that value; in education as in all human social affairs value derives from scarcity. In this sense, quality education is predicated on inequality. As Rancière (1991) puts it, 'public instruction is the secular arm of progress, the way to equalize inequality progressively, that is to say, to unequalize equality indefinitely' (p. 131). Education in this sense is inseparably linked to notions of hierarchy and practices of stratification. Burbules links this insight to today's high-stakes tests:

> ... *tests are made to be failed*. If a test were designed on which the vast majority of people could score highly, then it would be judged insufficiently difficult, and would be made harder, until only a relative few could do well at it. (2004, p. 8, emphasis in original)

Viewed in this light, calls for improved quality of education, particularly those centred on high-stakes testing programmes, are in effect technologies for 'devising inequality' (Au, 2009), blind to the tensions, inconsistencies and contradictions inhering in their own rhetorical claims to be simultaneously increasing quality and equity though punitive accountability regimes (Clarke, 2012b; Savage, 2011). As Barker (2010) puts it:

> ... school reform has thus become circular and self-defeating. Each advance highlights those who have not advanced enough, so that the illusion of perpetual success generates the reality of endless failure. (p. 82)

What this points us towards is the insight that discourses of quality in educational policy are always premised on a purported *lack*, on a perceived need to redress a situation of insufficient educational quality, as exemplified in the title of the policy document heralding the Australian government's 'education revolution' agenda: *Quality education: The case for a revolution in our schools* (Rudd & Gillard, 2008; see Clarke, 2012b for a critique).

This insight helps to explain contemporary policy's fixation on testing and accountability, its desire to establish, consolidate and reproduce a hegemonic numeric 'politic': if educational quality is to be enhanced it needs to be measurable; hence the need for a world within which the qualitative – i.e. *quality* – can only be made intelligible through the quantitative. Education thus becomes amenable to, and colonized by, a 'policy as numbers' approach (Lingard, 2011). Within this approach, education and educational quality are each conceptualized as a thing or commodity that people have less more of, thereby affording convenient alignment with the predominant quantitative modes of thinking and talking about the economy (MacEwan, 1999) and providing a justification for the appointing of those with expertise in the worlds of business and finance as educational leaders and managers. This trend towards quantification in education policy can be read as a continuation of the historical development, depicted by Ian Hacking (1990, 2006; see also Rose, 1999, pp. 197–232), in which the explanatory capacities of statistical patterns, combined with notions of human normalcy (and deviance), served to 'enumerate' people and their habits, and to hold out the prospect of taming chance, thereby bringing order out of chaos, constraining ambiguity, and offering certainty and control in an increasingly uncertain world. That is, quality as a sublime object becomes amenable to technologies of calculation, measurement, prediction and government.

Moreover, in recent decades, facilitated by modern computing power, this drive for control has moved beyond mere calculation to enter a new 'qualculative' (Thrift, 2008, p. 90) stage, marked by the exponentially increasing speed, volume, range, penetration, ubiquity, synchronicity and connectedness of numerical calculation. In this stage 'there are no longer calculations with definite beginnings and ends. Rather, there is an endless plane of calculation and recalculation, across which intensities continually build and fade' (Thrift, 2008, p. 97). The advantage this brings, from the perspective of political power, is an increased ability to shift narrative in the name of flexibility. As Thrift argues:

> ... it is no longer possible to think of calculation as being necessarily precise. Rather, because of massive increases in computing power, it has become a means of making qualitative judgments and working with ambiguity ... [it] ... can cope with uncertainty in ways previously unknown. (2008, p. 90)

Qualculation's flexible envelopment, its 'endless plane of calculation and recalculation', thus further enables the pervasive vagueness accompanying discourses of quality in education noted above, while facilitating the ever-shifting deluge of education policy initiatives. The notion of qualculation also complements emphases on markets as 'evolving computational entities' (Mirowski & Somefun, 1998), comprising 'constantly evolving preferences and fluctuating prices' (Davies & McGoey, 2012, p. 70), on contemporary social and organizational life as permeated by uncertainty, ignorance, risk and ambiguity and on neoliberal capitalism's adaptive capacities and its ability to integrate seemingly oppositional discourses, to become the 'real' determining what we understand by 'social reality' (Žižek, 1999, p. 276). When viewed in this light, it becomes clear that the flexible vagueness attending to discourses of quality, combined with their underlying assumptions about deficiency and lack, has provided these discourses with considerable integrative power in ways that resonate more broadly with 'the shift neoliberalism heralds from relatively differentiated moral, economic and political rationalities and venues in liberal democratic orders to their discursive and practical integration' (Brown, 2005, p. 45).

In this way, discourses of quality in contemporary education embody the risks associated with sublime objects of policy: elevated, they thus take precedence over dynamic, emergent phenomenal reality, even as they nonetheless remain elusive; anointed with a transcendent status, they, along with their policy promulgators, assume a degree of unquestionability; and presumed to be realized in present policy decisions, they occlude the aspirational value of their futural status. One significant dimension of this sublimation is the masking of any tensions between quality and equity, to which the discussion now turns.

Equity as a sublime object: accountability with a conscience

In conceptual terms, equity, like quality, is a complex notion that admits of no single accepted definition (Espinoza, 2007). It is commonly associated with ideas of justice or fairness but that only begs further questions as to what we mean by *these* terms. In short, 'the concept of equity is, of course, riddled with ambiguities and nuances and weighed down with emotional, conceptual and political baggage' (Paquette, 1998/2007, p. 335). To confuse matters further, equity is frequently used interchangeably with equality, a term with which it shares etymological roots and common conceptual terrain, but from which it, nonetheless, maintains a degree of conceptual distinctness, in so far as equality is 'basically objective', involving quantitative judgments regarding sameness of treatment, while equity is 'basically subjective', requiring quantitative *and* ethical adjudication regarding fairness (Bronfenbrenner, 1973, p. 9; Espinoza, 2007, p. 346). The combination of emotional investment, ethical baggage and potential amenability to quantification makes equity ripe as a candidate for elevation to sublime status.

In policy terms, according to the definition in a recent OECD report, *Quality and equity in education*, equity comprises two dimensions: equity as inclusion, which 'means ensuring that all students reach at least a basic minimum level of skills'; and equity as fairness, which 'implies that personal or socio-economic circumstances, such as gender, ethnic origin or family background are not obstacles to educational success' (OECD, 2012, p. 15). Equity as fairness aligns with the position adopted in the recent review of school funding in Australia, which defined 'equity in schooling as ensuring that differences in educational outcomes are not the result of differences in wealth, income, power or possessions' (Gonski et al., 2011, p. 105). The OECD report takes this a step further, suggesting a more active notion of equity by arguing that 'an equitable education system can redress the effect of broader social and economic inequalities' (2012, p. 15).

The implicit connections to quality in these policy definitions of equity have been made explicit in dramatic fashion in recent years in the USA, where legal requirements for schools to meet particular standards for all students in literacy and numeracy have raised questions as to whether schools and school systems are providing adequate opportunities for students to meet these standards. This has resulted in a flurry of equity litigation, in which the case has been argued that some states have not provided all schools and districts with the requisite resources to meet mandated standards. However, the course of such legal action has been painful and slow, not only due to wrangling over the connections between educational resources and educational achievement, but also 'because of differing interpretations regarding what courts should take on and because our nation's comfort level with inequality often makes the current situation seem tolerable – even appropriate' (Darling-Hammond, 2010, p. 100). This episode provides a stark reminder – if one were needed – of the inextricably political nature of equity. It also highlights how equity functions as a sublime object of desire, in this case a desire on the part of policy-makers for all to succeed, as part of a fantasmatic vision of an inclusive society.

The above discussion also highlights a significant element of the common conceptual terrain occupied by equity and equality, pertaining to their shared concern with questions of (re)distribution, where the allocation of social and economic goods intersects with the allocation of values, i.e. with policy. As Deborah Stone (2012) reminds us, 'distributions – whether of goods and services, wealth and income, health and illness, or opportunity and disadvantage – are at the heart of policy controversies' (p. 39). Here I would add, 'and of politics', in so far as the hegemony achieved by a given set of distributive arrangements needs to be established, defended, reproduced, challenged or resisted (Glynos & Howarth, 2007). This link is particularly clear when we recall that distribution decisions regarding who gets what also entail decisions as to who misses out: distribution involves inclusions *and* exclusions. Indeed, as Ernesto Laclau notes, in a dialogue with Judith Butler, 'politics is, to a large extent, a series of negotiations around the principle of exclusion which is always there as the ineradicable terrain of the social' (Butler & Laclau, 2004, p. 332). What this means is that any political decision logically entails options that are foreclosed by that act of decision. At a societal level, these foreclosures will involve the preferences of particular groups who are thereby to some degree excluded: decision is thus at the same time denial. Yet what we see in contemporary political rhetoric is a disavowal of the exclusive and antagonistic nature of politics (see Clarke, 2012a) in relation to equity, in favour of sublime visions of total inclusion, as in the Australian Prime Minister's recent comments in the context of debates about school funding, advocating 'a model that strips away all the old debates about private versus public and puts children at the centre of the funding system' as part of a wider call for 'a national crusade, a chance for change, education transforming the life of every child' (Gillard, 2012).

Such disavowals notwithstanding, given that equity seeks to engage with issues of inclusion and fairness – however we understand these terms – in relation to decisions about *who* gets *what* and *how*, equity dilemmas are never far from centre stage in social and political life. As noted above, an implication of this location in political debate is that particular visions of equity are subject to political logics, involving assertion, instantiation, reproduction and/or resistance (Glynos & Howarth, 2007). A further implication is that, as we saw with quality, policy discourses around equity are premised on *lack*, on the assumption that current equity arrangements are inadequate or iniquitous (or, in the case of reproductive equity discourses, that alterative visions are inadequate in contrast to present arrangements). Yet, just as we saw with quality, the presumption of inadequacy in relation to equity lends itself to demands for calculability.

Thus, in recent decades, as the welfare state has become, as it were, status non grata, and as the neoliberal shibboleths of markets and choice have increasingly come to govern educational policy, equity policies have been rethought within the calculative frames of competitive individualism. In this context, the paradox identified over a decade ago by Paquette (1998/2007) is even more relevant today, in so far as whilst equity talk is alive and well, its meaning, in a political context increasingly mistrustful of 'public' solutions to societal issues and demanding ever more 'evidence' of achievement in 'core' curriculum areas, has been reconfigured to the point that it has been effectively drained of any radical potential. The effect has been to, at least partially, undermine equity, as it becomes equated with access and thus amenable to the 'policy as numbers' approach noted above, whereby rising test scores and growing participation and retention rates are deemed to be evidence of inclusion and fairness, and where broader issues of social and educational politics are rendered invisible and irrelevant (Rizvi & Lingard, 2010, pp. 158–159). In this sense, equity has been colonized by, and subordinated to, discourses of quality in education, becoming, in a sense, another form of accountability, if one with a conscience.

Thus, as we saw with quality, contemporary education policy discourses around equity reflect the risks associated with sublime objects of policy, if in somewhat different ways. Equity's elevated status in rhetorical terms deflects attention from its elusive character in practice, while its mystical status as a site for investment of desire and hence for the promise of (universal) enjoyment – note the inclusive echoes of *No Child Left Behind* in Gillard's picture, cited above, of 'education transforming the life of every child' – endows the fantasmatic visions of its policy-makers with a degree of inviolability.

Quality and equity as sublime objects of ideology

> There is nothing intrinsically sublime in a sublime object … it is its structural place – the fact that it occupies the sacred/forbidden place of *jouissance* [enjoyment] – and not its intrinsic qualities that confers on it its sublime qualities. (Žižek, 1989, p. 194, emphasis in original)

A number of points can be drawn from the preceding discussion. Clearly, both quality and equity are problematic notions: conceptually complex, rather than obvious, and politically contested, rather than innocent. Yet both concepts are often deployed in educational policy as if their meaning was transparent and their implementation merely technical. As we have also seen, they are clearly terms with a strong degree of mutual implication, a point embodied in the *No child left behind* policy, even if the latter's effect of unravelling and undermining both quality and equity in US schooling (Sadovnik, O'Day, Bohrnstedt, & Borman, 2008) raises questions regarding the relative influence of naïveté and cynicism in the policy development process.

In addition, we have seen that both discourses of quality and of equity are premised on a fundamental lack, on the inadequate provision of each entity in contemporary education. This can be read on two distinct but related levels. In the everyday sense, the discourses of quality and equity in educational policy posit a deficiency in past and present education – this is clearly evident in the epigraphs at the beginning of this paper from Rudd and Gillard, and Gove, which both lament a simultaneous insufficiency of quality and equity in their respective education systems. Addressing this purported insufficiency, grounded in irrefutable 'evidence' from national and international test data, provides a political strategy by which these governments strive to differentiate themselves from their predecessors, whilst also offering a relentless mode of governance and a powerful source of legitimacy (Ozga, 2009). But lack here can also be read in the Lacanian sense of a constitutive lack, or more specifically, 'lack in the symbolic Other', which Laclau captures in his notion of the 'impossibility of society' (Laclau, 1991). This impossibility is a consequence of the discursive construction of the social, the differential nature of all meaning and identity, and the impossibility of permanently arresting the play of signifiers; for these axiomatic assumptions entail that 'we will never be in a situation where society has found its ultimate ground or achieved totality, where antagonism disappears and politics ends' (Critchley & Marchart, 2004, p. 4). One way to think about this is in terms of the unbridgeable gap between our symbolic resources and the 'real', where the latter refers to 'what cannot be included within any of our symbolic systems, but whose very absence skews them out of shape, as a kind of vortex around which they are bent out of true' (Eagleton, 2001, p. 41). Because of the impossibility of any sign adequately rendering or capturing the complex and dislocated nature of social reality, 'any signifier that claims to close off this field will never be adequate to the task, and will play the role of an impostor' (Glynos, 2001, p. 198). Sublime objects perform precisely this role, promising to overcome the constitutively incomplete and fractured nature of social reality. Within the field of education, quality and equity can each be read as sublime objects, promising fullness and harmony through the resolution of social conflicts and antagonisms afflicting the educational field and its subjects. Such sublime objects sustain their emptiness, while simultaneously promising fullness, by being linked to more concrete[1] signifiers (Glynos, 2001, p. 198), like 'tests', 'results', 'scores', 'achievement' or 'evidence'. However, precisely because, like an empty signifier, a sublime object is *empty*, the relationship between it and any specific, concrete signifier will be contingent rather than necessary; ideology can be seen as residing in the invisibility of this contingency to social subjects (Glynos, 2001, pp. 198–199).

However, if all that was required was to highlight the contingency of the specific content associated with a sublime object, then challenging the grip of ideology would be a much more straightforward affair. Perhaps the most compelling insight of Lacanian ideology theory, as propounded by theorists like Žižek and Dean, is the role of enjoyment as a crucial category of sociopolitical analysis and in particular,

> ... the way that fantasy keeps open the possibility of enjoyment by telling us why we are not really enjoying ... fantasy prevents me from confronting the lack in the symbolic (its inconsistency and rupture) and instead organizes this lack to promise and deliver enjoyment. (Dean, 2006, pp. 12, 36)

This economy of enjoyment, structured around the promise of fullness and harmony – in the words of the Australian government's education revolution, to 'simultaneously deliver equity and excellence in our schools' – is key to the enduring yet elusive, everyday yet elevated, nature of sublime objects. At the same time, because such sublime policy objects occupy an empty place, in the sense of compensating for and covering over a fundamental lack, they rely on the symbolic authority provided by their establishment in official policy discourses, as well as on fantasmatic desires for harmony and totality, in order to fulfil their role as quilting points for a range of concrete signifiers. The key insight here is how in neoliberal education policies, regulative reason is both enlisted to support totalizing discourses of *quality*, with their aspirations to provide comprehensive maps of knowledge through national curricula and to obtain an omniscient gaze on the achievements of students, teachers and schools through accountability and testing regimes, whilst simultaneously being suspended, in so far as critical insights into the wider historical, social and economic framing of inequalities are rendered illegitimate and invisible, thus preventing them from despoiling fantasmatic policy attachments to *equity*. In these contrasting but complementary ways, quality and equity mutually sustain their existence as education policy's sublime objects.

Acknowledgements

Thanks are extended to my colleagues, Kalervo Gulson and Stephen Marshall, as well as two anonymous reviewers, for their comments on earlier drafts of this paper.

Note

1. Concreteness here is a matter of degree: each of the terms listed here is contingent and susceptible to deconstructive analysis.

References

Au, W. (2009). *Unequal by design: High stakes testing and the standardization of inequality.* New York, NY: Routledge.

Ball, S. (2006). *Education policy and social class: The selected works of Stephen J. Ball.* London: Routledge.

Ball, S. (2008). *The education debate.* Bristol: The Policy Press.

Ball, S. (2012). *Global education inc: New policy networks and the neo-liberal imaginary.* London: Routledge.

Ball, S., Maguire, M., & Braun, A. (2012). *How schools do policy: Policy enactments in secondary schools.* London: Routledge.

Barker, B. (2010). *The pendulum swings: Transforming school reform.* Stoke-on-Trent: Trentham Books.

Biesta, G. (2010). *Good education in age of measurement: Ethics, politics, democracy.* Boulder, CO: Paradigm.

Bronfenbrenner, M. (1973). Equality and equity. *The ANNALS of the American Academy of Political and Social Science, 409*(1), 9–23. doi:10.1177/000271627340900103

Brown, W. (2005). *Edgework: Critical essays in knowledge and politics.* Princeton, NJ: Princeton University Press.

Burbules, N. C. (2004). Ways of thinking about educational quality. *Educational Researcher, 33*(6), 4–10. doi:10.3102/0013189X033006004

Butler, J., & Laclau, E. (2004). Appendix 1: The uses of equality. In S. Critchley & O. Marchart (Eds.), *Laclau: A critical reader* (pp. 329–244). London: Routledge.

Castoriadis, C. (1997). *The imaginary institution of society.* Cambridge: Polity Press.

Clarke, M. (2012a). The (absent) politics of neo-liberal education policy. *Critical Studies in Education, 53,* 297–310. doi:10.1080/17508487.2012.703139

Clarke, M. (2012b). Talkin' 'bout a revolution: The social, political and fantasmatic logics of education policy. *Journal of Education Policy, 27,* 173–191. doi:10.1080/02680939.2011.623244

Critchley, S., & Marchart, O. (2004). Introduction. In S. Critchley & O. Marchart (Eds.), *Laclau: A critical reader* (pp. 1–13). London: Routledge.

Darling-Hammond, L. (2010). *The flat world and education: How America's commitment to equity will determine our future.* Columbia: Teachers College Press.

Davies, W., & McGoey, L. (2012). Rationalities of ignorance: On financial crisis and the ambivalence of neo-liberal epistemology. *Economy and Society, 41*(1), 64–83. doi:10.1080/03085147.2011.637331

Dean, J. (2006). *Žižek's politics.* New York, NY: Routledge.

Dean, J. (2009). *Democracy and other neoliberal fantasies.* Durham, NC: Duke University Press.

Dean, J. (2010). *Blog theory: Feedback and capture in the circuits of drive.* Cambridge: Polity Press.

Eagleton, T. (2001). Enjoy! *Paragraph, 24*(2), 40–52. doi:10.3366/jsp.2001.24.2.40

Easton, D. (1953). *The political system.* New York, NY: Knopf.

Espinoza, O. (2007). Solving the equity-equality conceptual dilemma: A new model for analysis of the educational process. *Educational Research, 49,* 343–363. doi:10.1080/00131880701717198

Gillard, J. (2012). '*A national plan for school improvement', Speech to the National Press Club, 03 September, 2012.* Canberra: Press Office. Retrieved November 2, 2012 from http://www.pm.gov.au/press-office/%E2%80%9C-national-plan-school-improvement%E2%80%9D-speech-national-press-club-canberra.

Giroux, H. (2004a). *Proto-fascism in America: Neo-liberalism and the demise of democracy.* Bloomington: Phi Delta Kappa Educational Foundation.

Giroux, H. (2004b). *The terror of neoliberalism: Authoritarianism and the eclipse of democracy.* Boulder, CO: Paradigm.

Glynos, J. (2001). The grip of ideology: A Lacanian approach to the theory of ideology. *Journal of Political Ideologies, 6,* 191–214. doi:10.1080/13569310120053858

Glynos, J., & Howarth, D. (2007). *Logics of critical explanation in social and political theory.* London: Routledge.

Gonski, D., Boston, K., Greiner, K., Lawrence, C., Scales, B., & Tannock, P. (2011). *Review of funding for schooling.* Canberra: Department of Education, Employment and Workplace Relations.

Gove, M. (2012). *Education Secretary's speech to the association for school and college leaders.* Retrieved November 2, 2012 from http://www.education.gov.uk/inthenews/speeches/a00205750/asc2012

Hacking, I. (1990). *The taming of chance.* Cambridge: Cambridge University Press.

Hacking, I. (2006). *The emergence of probability: A philosophical study of early ideas about probability, induction and statistical inference* (2nd ed.). Cambridge: Cambridge University Press.

Hursh, D. (2008). *High-stakes testing and the decline of teaching and learning: The real crisis in education.* Lanham, MD: Rowman & Littlefield.

Hurst, A. (2008). *Derrida vis-à-vis Lacan: Interweaving deconstruction and psychoanalysis.* New York, NY: Fordham University Press.

Kipnis, A. B. (2011). Subjectification and education for quality in China. *Economy and Society, 40,* 289–306. doi:10.1080/03085147.2011.548950

Laclau, E. (1989). Preface. In S. Žižek (Ed.), *The sublime object of ideology* (pp. ix–xv). London: Verso.

Laclau, E. (1991). The impossibility of society. *Canadian Journal of Political and Social Theory, 15*(1/3), 24–27.

Lingard, B. (2011). Policy as numbers: Ac/counting for educational research. *The Australian Educational Researcher, 38,* 355–382. doi:10.1007/s13384-011-0041-9

MacEwan, A. (1999). *Neo-liberalism or democracy: Economic strategy, markets, and alternatives for the 21st century.* London: Zed.

Mirowski, P. (2009). Postface: Defining neoliberalism. In P. Mirowski & D. Plehwe (Eds.), *The road to Mont Pelerin: The making of the neoliberal thought collective* (pp. 417–455). Cambridge, MA: Harvard University Press.

Mirowski, P., & Somefun, K. (1998). Markets as evolving computational entities. *Journal of Evolutionary Economics, 8,* 329–356. doi:10.1007/s001910050067

Nichols, S., & Berliner, D. (2007). *Collateral damage: How high-stakes testing corrupts America's schools.* Cambridge, MA: Harvard University Press.

Orfield, G., & Wald, J. (2000). Testing, testing: The high-stakes testing mania hurts poor and minority students the most. *The Nation, 270*(22), 38–40.

Organization for Economic Co-Operation and Development (OECD). (2012). *Equity and quality in education: Supporting disadvantaged students and schools.* Paris: OECD.

Ozga, J. (2000). *Policy research in educational settings.* Maidenhead: Open University Press.

Ozga, J. (2009). Governing education through data in England: From regulation to self-evaluation. *Journal of Education Policy, 24*(2), 149–162. doi:10.1080/02680930902733121

Paquette, J. (1998/2007). Equity in educational policy: A priority in transformation or in trouble? In S. Ball, I. Goodson, & M. Maguire (Eds.), *Education, globalisation and new times* (pp. 335–359). London: Routledge.

Rancière, J. (1991). *The ignorant schoolmaster: Five lessons in intellectual emancipation* (K. Ross, Trans.). Stanford, CA: Stanford University Press.

Ravitch, D. (2009). *The death and life of great American school system: How testing and choice are undermining education.* New York, NY: Basic Books.

Rizvi, F., & Lingard, B. (2010). *Globalizing education policy.* New York, NY: Routledge.

Rose, N. (1999). *Powers of freedom: Reframing political thought.* Cambridge: Cambridge University Press.

Rudd, K., & Gillard, J. (2008). *Quality education: The case for an education revolution in our schools.* Retrieved August 15, 2010 from http://www.deewr.gov.au/Schooling/Programs/Pages/QualityEducation-ThecaseforanEducationRevolutioninourSchools.aspx

Sadovnik, A., O'Day, J., Bohrnstedt, G., & Borman, K. M. (Eds.). (2008). *No child left behind and the reduction of the achievement gap: Sociological perspectives on federal educational policy.* New York, NY: Routledge.

Santner, E. (2001). *On the psychotheology of everyday life.* Chicago: Chicago University Press.

Savage, G. C. (2011). When worlds collide: Excellent and equitable learning communities? Australia's 'social capitalist' paradox? *Journal of Education Policy, 26*(1), 33–59. doi:10.1080/02680939.2010.493229

Sharpe, M., & Boucher, G. (2010). *Žižek and politics: A critical introduction.* Edinburgh: Edinburgh University Press.

Stein, S. (2004). *The culture of education policy.* Columbia: Teachers College Press.

Stone, D. (2012). *Policy paradox: The art of political decision making* (3rd ed.). New York, NY: Norton.

Stout, R. T., Tallerico, M., & Scribner, K. P. (1994). Values: The 'what?' of the politics of education. *Journal of Education Policy, 9*(5), 5–20. doi:10.1080/0268093940090505

Stronach, I. (2010). *Globalizing education, educating the local: How method made us mad.* Abingdon: Routledge.

Thrift, N. (2008). *Non-representational theory: Space, politics, affect.* London: Routledge.

Webb, P. T., & Gulson, K. N. (2011). Education policy as proto-fascism: The aesthetics of racial neo-liberalism. *Journal of Pedagogy/Pedagogický casopis, 2*, 173–194. doi:10.2478/v10159-011-0009-x

Willinsky, J. (1998). *Learning to divide the world: Education at empire's end.* Minneapolis: University of Minnesota Press.

Žižek, S. (1989). *The sublime object of ideology.* London: Verso.

Žižek, S. (1997). *The plague of fantasies.* London: Verso.

Žižek, S. (1999). *The ticklish subject: The absent centre of political ontology.* London: Verso.

The explosion of real time and the structural conditions of temporality in a society of control: durations and urgencies of academic research

Claudia Lapping

ABSTRACT

In the context of ongoing debates about the distinctive temporalities associated with contemporary regulative regimes, this paper explores the interpretive trajectories initiated in contrasting conceptualisations of the politics of time. This exploration is developed through analysis of interview data from a study of unconscious relations in academic practice. Section one uses one moment of data to contrast phenomenological, Deleuzian and Lacanian theorisations of the relation between time and subjectivity. Section two is an exegesis of Lacan's paper on Logical Time. This outlines the way temporality is structured in relation to the subject's guess about the expectations of the Other. Section three uses this to develop an interpretation of three temporalities that constitute the space of contemporary academic subjectivities. The final section considers the intensification of the juxtaposition of these incongruent temporalities, contrasting Lacanian and Deleuzian theorisations of time in the Real/virtual and their implications for both methodological and political strategy.

Introduction: the politics of time and the subject

In the context of ongoing debates about the distinctive temporalities associated with contemporary regulative regimes, this paper explores the interpretive trajectories initiated in contrasting conceptualisations of the politics of time. The discussion is situated in relation to Deleuze's (1995) theorisation of the contrast between the disciplinary mechanisms of the modern state and contemporary societies of control, and Bernstein's (2000) analysis of the contrast between competence and performance pedagogies. Both these analyses foreground the way practices of surveillance and observation within contemporary regulative processes reconstitute temporal relations in professional practice.

In his brief, rhetorical and influential essay 'Postscript on Control Societies', Deleuze (1995) argues that the disciplinary processes associated with the modern state are being overwritten with mechanisms associated with a society of control. A key feature of this shift is the displacement of hierarchically positioned professional subjects by digital and administrative systems: processes that used to be constituted in relation to substantive objectives of bounded institutions are now more frequently unbounded, emptied out, lacking clearly defined goals or end points (Deleuze, 1995, pp. 179–181). This coincides with a decrease in the grip of disciplinary modes of observation or surveillance that have been conceptualised as central to the mechanisms of production of the modern subject. Disciplinary surveillance emerges within delimited spatial relations through the application of professional knowledge to define the interiority of the subject (Foucault, 1977; Lazzarato, 2006; Savat, 2009). In contrast the administrative mechanisms of surveillance within a society of control are exercised at a distance, compiling large scale quantitative data. Savat (2009) foregrounds digital technologies as an exemplary mode of synchronous observation and recording in which 'one always already writes or constitutes oneself as code' (p. 50). This mode of surveillance also shifts temporal relations: whereas disciplinary modes of observation are focused on the application of professional knowledge within a present relation, surveillance within mechanisms of control works at a distance to produce a predictive relation to a projected future subjectivity. Furthermore, these predictions are not stable; they constantly shift as new data is incorporated into the recorded observation.

Bernstein's model of contrasting pedagogies resonates with this Deleuzian analysis. In *Class and Pedagogies: visible and invisible*, Bernstein (1975) argued that modern child-centred pedagogies are enacted through teachers' covert surveillance of children's activity, which they interpret through the lens of pedagogical theories of development and learning. Child-centred pedagogies thus constitute the present interiority of the child through the teacher's professional interpretation of meanings within the child's activities. Bernstein's later analysis contrasted 'professional' with 'neoliberal'/'performance' pedagogic identities, describing the former as 'driven by inner dedication' and the latter as 'an outwardly responsive identity' (2000, p. 69). The 'performance' model of pedagogy associated with 'neoliberal' identities no longer focuses on the child's activity and inner development. Instead, pedagogy is articulated in relation to externally defined criteria, which constitute absences to be diagnosed and repaired in the child's performance of tasks, so the texts that they produce are required to progress in quality in line with these external expectations. Thus Bernstein suggests: 'in the case of performance models, the future is made visible, but that which has constructed this future is a past invisible to the acquirer' (2000, p. 48). The data used to construct national and individual targets or 'expected levels' in contemporary classrooms are an exemplary production of the new modes of surveillance described by Savat, and also of their predictive relation to future identities.

These accounts of shifting mechanisms of production of practices and identities, and the displacement of professional objectives by administrative processes of 'endless postponement' (Deleuze, 1995, p. 179), have implications for our understanding of services across the public sector (McGimpsey, 2012; Thompson & Cook, 2014). They also provide the context for my exploration of the temporalities of academic research practice and subjectivities. The paper develops two main arguments. A more empirical argument interprets three contrasting temporalities in academics' accounts of their practice; it suggests an intensification of juxtapositions of bizarrely incongruent temporalities, as we are increasingly caught up in processes associated with a society of control. A more methodological argument plays with the contrasting interpretive trajectories opened up by different theorisations of 'time'. The paper attempts to maintain an in-between position, avoiding reification of any one epistemological frame. My overall aim is to avoid any sense of a finalized conception of 'time'; but at the same time to use philosophical accounts that conceptualise duration as an animating force in static materiality (Grosz, 2000, p. 230) to open up ways of seeing academic practice as an instance of more generalised political formations.

The politics of time and subjectivity: three interpretive trajectories

The analysis in this paper was initiated by a sense of contrasting temporalities in participants' accounts in an interview-based project exploring psychical or unconscious relations in academic methodologies. The project was explicitly designed to explore the recontextualisation of psychoanalytic approaches in research interviews. This informed the construction of both temporal and interactional aspects of the interviews.

Participants, eight academics working in the humanities and social sciences, were initially selected to represent disciplines with contrasting objects, methodologies and fields of applications. Six of the eight were based in selective, research intensive institutions. All were research active and had experience of the most recent national research assessment process. They were interviewed eight times each, over a period of up to two years. For each interview they were asked to provide a text that in some way related to their field of research, which became the initial prompt for the interview: 'Say something about the text that you have chosen'. The aim was to produce free associative material, but also to avoid the traditional psychoanalytic focus on biography, instead attending to the relation between the subject and their research practice. During the interviews I attempted to maintain something like 'evenly hovering attentiveness' (see, e.g. Bollas, 1999). My interventions were intended to elicit additional associations, or to offer my initial interpretations. As far as possible these interpretations were presented as provisional and playful, rather than authoritative; intended to draw participants' attention to connections and associations in their narration of their practice, and to provide opportunities for them to elaborate or refine these very provisional interpretations.

My analysis of this data has drawn on psychoanalytic and psychoanalytically informed social theory, from a predominantly Lacanian perspective (Lapping, 2013a, 2013b). The analysis offered here also engages primarily with Lacanian ideas. However, my aim is to keep other theorisations of time in play, to maintain a sense of contingency in relation to the different interpretive and political trajectories that they open up. This is important as a strategy for keeping in mind the provisional, complementary and incommensurable status of all epistemologies (Lapping, 2015; Plotnitsky, 1994).

The most pertinent line of differentiation in marking out these theories is the possibilities they construct for conceptualising a subject that is distinct from temporality. Are time and conscious temporal experience in some way external to the subject of consciousness and temporality? Or are prolongation and duration inherent to the very possibility of the subject? In parallel to these questions there are different positions on whether continuous duration, with its stabilising effect on identities, is given or constructed. More realist phenomenological approaches conceptualise the continuous duration of time as a given that is subjectively mediated through a consciousness that structures the subject's experience of temporality. Approaches that question the unity of the subject can also be associated with a critique of continuity, seeing continuity as a construction that supports the fantasy of unified identity. Both Deleuze and Lacan can be associated with this position.

The interpretive trajectories suggested by these contrasting theorisations can be explored by looking at a moment from one interview. This moment suggests a preliminary delineation of contrasting temporalities in the participant's research practice. B, an early career researcher who was in the middle of her first major funded research project, explained how this new position affected her relation to writing and publication:

> Because this is a funded research, I mean, it has to have an output, because of its connection to the public funding that it receives. And I think I will say, for this particular project I'm more aware of, like, having a publication plan, than I would have for just my own – I mean, there is lots of stuff that I'm thinking I'd like to work on, but I have no clear agenda of when and how I will write those papers. Whereas, with this one, I'm actually feeling a little bit more responsible of having a plan. So it's not how I usually work. I think the way I would usually work would be a bit more organic and things sort of unfold. (B, Interview 2)

Her account invokes temporality as she contrasts the 'publication plan' associated with her current project with the 'no clear agenda' of her usual practice. From a realist, phenomenological perspective, this kind of account might be interpreted to explore the structuring of consciousness, and to trace, for example, B's conscious awareness of different aspects of what might perhaps be thought of as objective 'time'. It would be possible, for example, to interpret a foregrounding in consciousness of a linear, progressive temporality, in the formulation of a 'publication plan'. This might be contrasted with the B's usual absorption in a more 'organic' or recursive temporal dimension, in which 'things sort of unfold'. It would also be possible to trace B's relation to these contrasting temporalities. She articulated, for example, a sense of alienation from her own project: 'I'm treating something that I actually have created – I just completely came up with this research – as if it was something that was there and I'm kind of working for it' (B, Interview 2). Through this kind of analysis we might gradually begin to map a subjective experience of temporality within the structures of consciousness; and explore way these structures produce distinct subjective identities with shifting relations to both 'time' and research.

Politically, this kind of approach can help to foreground a 'desynchronization' of the temporalities of diverse social, cultural and psychical spheres (Clancy, 2014; Rosa, 2013; Vostal, 2014). In B's account this might refer to a break between the temporalities of funded and unfunded research. From a Heideggerian perspective, Clancy suggests, both these temporalities might be understood as removed from originary temporality, and thus associated with reduced opportunities for authentic engagement, in a way that is associated with psychological harm (Clancy, 2014, p. 34). Political or therapeutic interventions might be conducted at either an individual or a collective level, and work to unsettle taken for granted, conscious relations to time (p. 39). The aim, however, is to produce 'temporal coherence' (p. 42) through a more authentic relation to originary temporality that also, in Vostal's (2014) formulation in the context of academic work in higher education, recognises subjects' differentiated experience of time in relation to complex sociological variables (p. 19). The danger is that this collapses into an individualised demand that fails to engage with the specific conditions of the observed 'desynchronization'.

A more Deleuzian framing would direct attention to the relational construction of an appearance of unity and temporal continuity. This appearance is produced through processes of contemplation and contraction, through which habitual relations between organic elements become established as an 'assemblage'. Using the Deleuzian language of 'assemblage', in B's account we might interpret one 'researcher-assemblage' constituted in a habituated contemplation/contraction between B's 'stuff that I'm thinking I'd like to work on' and her yet-to-be written 'papers'; and another 'researcher-assemblage' in habituated contemplation/contraction between a publication plan, funding, and, B's account also suggested, a new relation of responsibility for a researcher on her funded project (Interview 2).

The temporality of these assemblages might be understood in terms of Deleuze's (2004) first, passive synthesis of time. This, he says, 'constitutes time as a living present' (p. 97). His conception of a present temporality as the product of synthesis can be understood as a critique of continuity as given. It is informed by Bergson's and Dedekind's philosophical and mathematical critiques of the conflation of extensive, quantifiable space with intensive movement or continuity (Olma, 2006; Voss, 2013). The key point is that time is not a succession of instants, and that the intensive quality of continuity is not given, but contingently produced through the organic process of contemplation, habit and contraction. The apparently unified and continuous entity of researcher identity/ assemblage is the outcome of habitual contractions between body parts, funding, publication plans, papers, co-researchers. Through a process of organic contemplation actions contract into habituated repetitions: 'When we say that habit is a contraction we are speaking … of the fusion of that repetition in the contemplating mind' (Deleuze, 2004, p. 95; see also Bignall, 2010, pp. 14–15). The repetition itself is an imaginary product of contemplation, which contracts its objects so that they appear as repeated instances of the same element (Deleuze, 2004, p. 97).

The concept of duration here relates to the continuity resulting from habit, and Deleuze says, 'The duration of an organism's present … will vary according to the natural contractile range of its contemplative souls' (p. 98). That is: the present endures just as long as the contracted relations between the contemplated elements brought together in the assemblage. This duration, though, appears in a variety of forms: 'All our rhythms, our reserves, our reaction times, the thousand intertwinings, the presents and fatigues of which we are composed, are defined on the basis of our contemplations' (p. 98). So contemplation, habit and duration might be understood as the unconscious conditions of multiple temporal forms. Or, rather than interpreting contrasting 'temporalities' in B's account, we might instead talk about one 'rhythm' constituted in linear and recursive relations. The naturalisation of these relations is politically important: the passive synthesis is trapped in the habitual repetition of the 'natural' signs and rhythms that constitute the living present. Politics requires the artificial construction of new signs or rhythms: materialities produced through desirous, active syntheses of time (see Bignall, 2010).

Deleuze's conception of the organic processes of contemplation and contraction as unconscious conditions of the living present offers one perspective on the unconscious conditions of duration. Lacan offers a contrasting conceptualisation of the unconscious conditions of temporality. He maps the relation between subjectively experienced duration and the dispersed signifying elements that constitute subjectivity by channelling the forces of desire and 'time'. This Lacanian framework draws attention to the network of signifiers, the big Other (see Hook, 2008), in relation to which the shifting temporalities of B's research emerge. B's more explicit publication plan relates both to the ambiguous demand of the funder of her project and to her new position of responsibility in relation to the project researcher. Importantly, though, there is no suggestion that either the funder or the researcher specified the necessity to work with the kind of awareness of a publication plan that is suggested in B's account. Lacan draws attention to the way we constantly make guesses about the desire of the Other ('What does the Other want from me?'); and to the way these guesses are also constituted as a channel for our own recurring and idiosyncratic patterns of desire. For example, in B's interviews there was a recurring motif of a pleasurable oscillation between mess and order. Her response to the gaze of the funder and of her researcher as signifiers of big Other, imposing the linear temporality of a publication plan, might thus be interpreted as a repetition of this familiar oscillation. From a Lacanian perspective we might read this repetition as indicative of an-other, unconscious and a-temporal desire.

For Lacan, then, the phenomenological subject or consciousness is not the primary condition for a subjective temporal experience of an authentic or objective time. Instead we can see the naturalised phenomenological experience of the subject as constituted in a web of unconscious relations to the network of signifiers, the big Other, and to desire. The unconscious conditions of temporality, theorised by Deleuze (from the perspective of the organism) and Lacan (from the perspective of the subject) disintegrate any sense of a unified ego or phenomenological subject as a primary condition of temporality; and disaggregate the dispersed elements bound together as the naturalized continuity and durational temporal experience of the subject. The next section develops an exegesis of Lacan's paper on Logical Time. More than anything else I have read, this paper makes visible the workings of the exceedingly peculiar experience that is temporality.

Lacan's story of logical time

In 'Logical Time and the Assertion of Anticipated Certainty', Lacan (2006) uses a prisoner's dilemma to explore the function of symbolic structures and the gaze of the other in the production of temporality and subjectivity. A logical puzzle is presented to three inmates: they are shown five discs, two black, three white. The warden will fasten one disc to each prisoner's back; they will be left in a room to consider, but forbidden from communicating amongst each other. The first to leave the room able to tell the warden the colour of her disc 'founded upon logical and not simply probabilistic grounds' (p. 198), will be freed. Having explained the task, the warden fixes a white disc to each inmate's back.

Lacan's discussion of this scenario develops a thesis about the relation between time, subjectivity and the o/Other: an imaginary, unified other or reciprocal subjectivity; or the big Other of institutionalized structures or language. The key point I want to foreground, initially, is the dialectical moves Lacan depicts between the subjective experience of duration/hesitation and the objectification of this experience in what he calls Logical Time. Objectified time here is not, of course, clock time, or time unmediated by social interference. Logical Time is represented by a *structural* hesitation without a delimited duration. Subjective time, in contrast, is the subject's experience of duration. The points I want to explain, then, are:

- The role of hesitation in interrupting, or 'scanding' (Lacan's term, see Fink, 1997), the prisoners' movement to the exit.
- The subject's speculation on the thought process of the o/Other.
- The shifts between subjective experience of hesitation as temporal duration and objectified understanding of hesitation as Logical Time.
- The meaning of, and relation between, 'subjective' and 'objective' time in Lacan's account.

Lacan's (2006) account is an expansion/explosion of what he describes as the 'sophistic' solution to the logical puzzle. This solution suggests that, after contemplating for 'a certain time' (and the simultaneous specificity and ambiguity of 'a certain time' is pertinent) each of the three prisoners moves towards the door, at the same moment, and each offers the same explanation:

> I am a white, and here is how I know it. Since my companions were whites, I thought that, had I been a black, each of them would have been able to infer the following: 'If I too were a black, the other would necessarily have realized straight away that he was a white and would have left immediately; therefore I am not a black'. And both would have left together, convinced they were whites. As they did nothing of the kind, I must be a white like them. At that I made for the door to make my conclusion known. (p. 162)

Lacan's expansion/explosion of this solution – in which he claims 'the philosopher's garb', associated with 'the comedian's banter' and the 'politician's secretive action' (p. 163) – draws attention to three moments: modes of duration that interrupt or modulate the unity or meaning of 'a certain time'.

In the first moment, *the moment of the glance*, the subject, seeing two whites, excludes the only scenario offering certainty about her identity: that is, it is immediately apparent that it is *not* the case that 'I must be white because I see two blacks'. The prisoner does not need to consider the thought processes of her peers in order to make this first logical exclusion. The instantaneous logical inference of this first moment, Lacan points out, is constituted in imaginary identification with an generalized 'other', a noetic, reasoning or intellectual subject: '*one who knows that*' (p. 170).

In the second moment, the subject develops a hypothesis, based on the first logical exclusion, which she now imaginatively inserts into the thinking process of the two other inmates to produce the solution outlined above: the result of which being that the hesitation of the two others convinces the subject that she is white. This is the moment of *comprehending*, which presupposes a duration, the time taken for each to meditate on the possibilities: that is, the subject attributes a certain duration as appropriate for this meditation in her interpretation of the hesitation of her peers. Where the experience of temporality in the *moment of the glance* is constituted in identification with a generalized speculating subject; in the *moment of comprehending*, the experience of temporality – that is, the duration of the hesitation – is constituted in imaginary identification with a specific other – her fellow prisoners. Of this second stage of the hypothesizing process, Lacan comments:

> The objectivity of this time thus vacillates with its limits. Its meaning alone subsists, along with the form it engenders of subjects who are *undefined except by their reciprocity* ... (p. 168, emphasis in original)

The *meaning* of the hesitation Lacan suggests, is fixed, within the logical scenario, that is, the hesitation leads the subject to comprehend that she must be white; but the *duration* of the hesitation vacillates, or is not yet fixed at this point of the scenario. This vacillation has its effect, and produces a third temporal moment.

In the third moment, the subject reflects that if she is in fact a black, then her two peers will conclude their speculations a moment before her, since they have one less stage in their hypothesizing. This produces an urgency for the subject to move from the *moment of comprehending* to the *moment of concluding*, to ensure that the others do not conclude ahead of her – which would throw into doubt her conclusion that she is white. The *moment of concluding* thus involves a certain urgency and a move to action. The urgency, though, Lacan clarifies, is not, as some have suggested (Johnston, 2005, p. 28) to do with the opportunity for release, but rather is dependent on the logical meaning of movement in this concluding temporality:

> It is thus not because of some dramatic contingency, the seriousness of the stakes, or the competitiveness of the game, that time presses; it is owing to [sous] the urgency of the logical movement that the subject precipitates both his judgment and his departure .... (Lacan, 2006, p. 169)

The urgency relates to the imminent possibility that the time of comprehending might 'lose its meaning' (p. 169). It is thus more existential than the specifics of the prison scenario, it relates to the possibility of a name, an identity, or a fixed relation to a signifier. The urgency is an urgency, and a temporality, common to *all* subjectivity.

It is important to recognise the combination of frivolity and seriousness in Lacan's account. He is deliberately exploding the sophistry of the logical puzzle, demonstrating how it relies on a ridiculous assumption of reciprocity between subjects. However, his demonstration of the way we experience temporality in relation to a guess about the expectations of an unknowable o/Other, and to the existential urgency of finding and fixing a name, is quite serious. So it is important to note that whereas in the *moment of the glance* and in the *moment of comprehending* there was reciprocity between subject and other, in the *moment of concluding* the subject has to make a final subjective assertion on their own behalf: '*I* am white'. This replicates the psychological move from Imaginary identification with a reciprocal other to Symbolic identification with language or structural authority. Making this point, Lacan notes how the subjective assertion of the moment of concluding is analogous to the initial psychological formation of the subject in language:

> The 'I' subject of the conclusive assertion, is isolated from the other – that is, from the relation of reciprocity – by a logical beat. This movement of the logical genesis of the 'I' through a process of decanting of its own logical time largely parallels its psychological birth. (p. 170)

Lacan's Logical Time helps us to notice the role of the o/Other in the construction of temporal experience. It distinguishes between a generalised imaginary other, a specific imaginary other, and the symbolic Other or structure of signifiers that captures or fixes the subject in language. It also illustrates the way that punctuations – here in the form of interruption or hesitation in 'a certain time' – bring about a shift in meaning ('scansion' in Lacan's terms). The temporal experiences of duration or urgency are (a) produced in relation to an o/Other, and (b) inherent to the process of identification or capture as a subject of a signifying system with a diachronic structuring of meaning.

The additional distinction between 'time' and 'temporality' is also worth noting. In part, Lacan's aim in the paper is to subvert or avoid the phenomenological distinction between objective 'time' and subjective 'temporality'. He aims to do this by disrupting the assumed synchronicity of logic, by demonstrating the necessity of the diachronic durational hesitations to the logical scenario (Johnston, 2005, pp. 32–33; Lacan, 2006, p. 10). However, Johnston suggests that Lacan's aim is not fulfilled, because the durational instances are constituted and recuperated by the overarching logical form of the puzzle:

> Lacan's temporal logic is a false temporality, a staged time in which the diachronic unfolding of crucial moments is immanent to the synchronic script of the *grand Autre*. (2005, p. 33)

He argues that the 'Logical Time' paper on its own does not present a psychoanalytic theory of 'time' as such. The exploration of temporality within the structure of the logical puzzle might rather be seen as a parodic or hyperbolic illustration of the fantasmatic status of temporal/durational experience, and of the impossibility of a direct engagement with anything we might inappropriately name as Real Time.

I would want to add a rider to this reading of Lacan's argument as wholly re-absorbed into the synchronic structure of the puzzle. The very metaphor of the prison, with its seductive narrative drama, alongside Lacan's other contextualising allusions, undercut the presumed universality of structure, offering glimpses of its more paradoxical aspect (cf. Butler, Laclau, & Zizek, 2000; Dolar, 2015). Nevertheless, the structural aspects of Lacan's theory are productive for an understanding of temporality in a society of control.

The structural conditions of temporality

My analysis of participants' accounts of their research practice suggests how the relation to an o/Other can be understood as productive of contrasting subjective experiences of duration in contemporary higher education institutions. These might be distinguished as chronological, teleological and narcissistic modes of temporality.

The production of chronological temporality in identification with signifiers of perpetual process

The constitution of duration in relation to the UK research evaluation exercise provides an obvious example of the way temporality can be implicated in the loosening of institutional boundaries and emptying out of substantive objectives associated with Deleuze's 'mechanisms of control'. Under the previous block grant system, the formula used by the UK University Grants Committee (UGC) to distribute funds was deliberately not published, in order that universities would continue to base the internal distribution of resources on their own principles, rather than those of the external body (Brown, 2013). Despite the *invisible* (cf. Bernstein, 1975) control exercised by the UGC, this can be understood as a reiteration of an institutional identity, the university, with substantive values beyond the criteria articulated by the funding body. The models of funding that replaced this system allocate resources via regular assessment exercises and in relation to explicit, published criteria of research quality (Brown, 2013, p. 53). This projection of externally defined deadlines into the university also has implications for temporality, punctuating research practice with a-synchronous criteria that reconstitute duration as an explicit linear chronology of ambiguous expectations.

The explicit chronology of research evaluation was directly referenced in interview accounts. The replacement of institutional criteria of value with external indicators of quality was also referenced, interpreted as a restriction on both scholarly and pedagogic production. F's account, for example, constituted a fantasy of a previous era of uninterrupted duration for research:

> There are two professors who were my heads of department when I was an undergraduate and in their whole lifetimes they published one massive book each, one really important book in their field, and some small articles, maybe kind of three or four. (Interview 1)

This contrasted with her account of the way the assessment exercises punctuated her research with deadlines and targets. Asked if she was happy with her own writing, she responded:

> No, God, you know, in the next four years I've got to produce two books and two big articles, and in the four years after that I've probably got to produce two more and two more. I'm 46 now, and if I work for another 20 years, that's five more sets, that's ten more books that I've got to produce. And there's no way I've got more than ten times more to say than my old professors have. (Interview 1)

In addition to the explicit chronology, F's account interprets the meaning of temporal punctuations in terms of significance of research output. Participant C's account similarly referenced the chronological frame of the accountability exercise, 'RAE', that punctuated his practice, but interpreted its meaning in terms of restrictions on genre:

> Colleagues have said to me 'don't waste your time with textbooks because it doesn't work, RAE-wise' ... This is a book written during that period, but it didn't go in as one of my four publications, because it was a text book. (Interview 1)

Participant E's account suggested an alternative interpretation of the meaning of chronological interruptions. Here the punctuation of the external evaluation process appeared to intensify an existing institutional demand for disciplinary identification. She explained how her research fell between two fields, and described this as 'high maintenance', especially in relation to the RAE:

> This kind of came during the Research Assessment Exercise, you know, there were concerns about whether some of the stuff we should put with law and some of the stuff with politics ... there were doubts, not about whether it was good or not, but maybe it feeds into that as well. (Interview 1)

The Other here is represented by the extra-institutional timetable of the Research Assessment Exercise, and the subjectively experienced temporality of research is constituted in relation to each participant's guess about what this Other desires of them. There is an apparent clarity in the chronological punctuations that reconstitute the linear temporality of research. However, the object of this chronological demand is ambiguous: since the exercise aims at selective attribution of prestige, it is not desirable for everyone to conform. The message is further confused by the empty criteria of perpetual process, interpreted variously as 'dumb down!', 'smarten up!', 'fit in!'. We might say that within this dimension of temporality, *chronology* is foregrounded, while substantive *teleology* is relatively obscure.

The production of teleological temporality in identification with signifiers of substantive value

In the face of uncertainty, C's account vacillated in a way that, following Lacan's logic, we might read as indicative of the urgency of a loss of subjectivity. His account references points of reassurance in relations to media and to political consultancy: 'A non-academic … invited me for lunch, and it became clear that he thought my paper was the best thing that had been written in the area' (Interview 4). However, as well as reassurance, these relations constituted an additional layer of temporally inflected linear demand: 'I just have to keep up … and, you know, that's a constant, it's two hours a day you'd have to spend reading the papers … the media phone you up, you've got to know everything' (Interview 2). The financial incentive associated with consultancy – 'I need the money, the bottom line is of course that one has to earn a living' (Interview 2) – connotes another level of existential urgency in the temporality invoked in C's account. It is possible to interpret the fields of media and consultancy as offering a more substantive, if transitory, point of recognition, with a clear teleology beyond perpetual process.

For most participants, more obvious substantive points of identification were within strongly institutionalized methodological or academic systems of value. They referred to methodological frameworks, theoretical affiliations, and canonical texts and authors; as well as connections with journals, conferences, or established groups of researchers within their field. Participants F and M, both in literary studies, referenced 'historicism' as a major point of identification for their work. They named key authors or terms as signifiers of sources and controversial positions within contemporary debates. Their accounts also described relations to co-authors and to colleagues with shared interests who they met regularly at conferences. Similarly, participant G, a historian, positioned his research in an account that juxtaposed the influence of his PhD supervisor, alternative theories, and a contrast between generalizing versus particularistic methodologies. Like F and M, he also described specific interactions at recent scholarly events. These instances indicate chains of signifiers of methodological and academic position that constitute both substantive objectives and points of identification for researcher subjectivities.

In terms of duration and urgency, relations to signifiers within these chains constitute a variety of temporalities. The sense of duration produced in imaginary relation to ideas and colleagues frequently appears as one of continuity and stability. In addition, punctuations to this duration are constituted in relation to a certain level of reciprocity of expectations about regularity of meetings, timing of feedback, and submission of writing. There is, however, still uncertainty associated with the meaning of durational limits. G had recently sent a draft paper to some colleagues and noted: 'They've had the piece about a week now, and I'll be less nervous when they write back' (Interview 3). The uncertain subjective temporality of colleagues as reciprocal others, we might say, temporarily casts them in the role of big Other of disciplinary judgment. Relations to methodological signifiers of the disciplinary big Other could also produce vacillations in durational limits. M, for example, reflected that her identification with historicism was sometimes too categorical (Interview 6) and this produced an existential temporal tension, as the next diachronic move in her narrative of her methodological position was cast into uncertainty (Lapping, 2011, pp. 129–130). There is a substantive teleology to these temporalities, which relates to security of position within a combination of methodological and intellectual fields.

To return to the sociological productivity of this analysis: my suggestion is that signifiers of methodological and academic practice constitute more substantive, enduring conditions of temporality than the empty, ambiguous processes associated with societies of control. While they carve out different trajectories of duration and intensity, both sets of conditions constitute a largely linear subjective experience. This linearity is differentiated by a foregrounding of chronological (perpetual process) or teleological (discipline) aspects. However, within both sets of conditions, a sense of futurity is constituted via points of identification, signifiers, whose meanings are fixed within discourses that precede and subsist in relative independence of the individualised subject (cf. Bernstein, 2000; Savat, 2009). This is not the case with the more narcissistic temporality of embedded research practice.

The production of narcissistic temporality in identification with signifiers produced in the practice of research

My exploration of temporality was initiated by sections of my participants' accounts that suggested an intense build-up of relations to specific texts or practices related to the projects they were working on, resulting in a tacit presence of amassed potential connections. These extracts suggested a cumulative, continuous duration, constituted within this intense set of relations. These relations appeared recursive, with connections emerging within present activity, rather than in relation to a prior chronology or objective. As opposed to a linear drive forward, these accounts depicted a more suspended, back and forth temporality, without an explicit sense of futurity. Several narratives of this temporality included associations to a sense of retreat, nurture or insulation from other aspects of their practice (Lapping, 2013b). The question suggested by the Lacanian logic of temporality is: in relation to which 'other' is this sense of recursive, nurturing, or narcissistic temporality constituted?

Participant B's account of carrying out the interviews for her project exemplifies the construction of a sense of a continuous and cumulative duration:

> The interviews are quite, it has a very cumulative effect in terms of understanding them … now it is almost over a hundred interviews … and it has happened through time and I participated in almost all of them. So I was there doing the interviews, which is great, because in another interview you constantly sort of add them back to back, you know, I rephrased questions with the next person and the next person. And I constantly think through the data, even during the interview process, and you make connections one to the other. (Interview 2)

The account describes a 'cumulative effect' that has 'happened through time'. The phraseology of 'the next person and the next person', might be said to replicate or reiterate a sense of cumulative and similar instances; repetitions of 'constantly' and 'I' add to the fantasmatic, symbolically structured, sense of continuous duration.

There are similar features in F's account of her sense of loss in relation to the project she had been working on at the time of our previous interview but had not been able to continue:

> It rather upsets me to think about the reading I did on that project, because I'd have to do it again, because it would be so long after the fact that although the structures of understanding are there, the cobwebby stuff that research is like, you know, just those delicate threads that are kind of hanging in your mind when you're in it, are what go very quickly … Because you,

it's all that stuff you don't even know that you're thinking when you're working on something else, and then that thing, I don't know, lights up or the connection comes, and then it becomes, you realise you were thinking it. ... (Interview 4)

This foregrounds the effect of an intense period of reading that results in a spatialized image of amassed 'cobwebby' understanding: 'those delicate threads that are just kind of hanging in your mind when you're in it'. F's account of her reading is similar to B's presence in her 'almost over a hundred' interviews: both suggest an intense period of activity leading to an almost ghostly familiarity with the material, which haunts the continuing activity, constituting multiple hanging or suspended possibilities for 'connection' or interpretation.

In thinking about the 'other' of these temporalities, it is worth bearing in mind B's own account of her project as 'something that I actually have created – I just completely came up with this research' (Interview 2). Respectively, B creates her interviews and F reconfigures texts as the objects of their research. As signifiers, then, these objects have a narcissistic relation to the subject, reflecting a self-created world or discourse. Other participants cited similarly self-referencing pleasures of the process of research: 'spending a long time writing a sentence' (Participant A); 'wasting time' following up entries in the Oxford English Dictionary 'even if they're not going to make it into the final paper' (Participant A); spending time in library archives (Participant G); or, in M's case, identifying with the medieval subjects of the text she was working on: 'sometimes on winter afternoons when you've been closeted away working, you do feel quite Anchoritic' (Participant M). The 'cobwebby' temporality constructed in relation to these self-created or self-referential signifying systems has a suspended duration, and an as yet unspecified objective or teleology.

Is there a political potentiality in this suspended or narcissistic temporality? Or, put another way, what force might enable self-created or self-referential signifiers to find a place in discourse? There are resonances between this state of narcissistic retreat and Guattari's (2011) account of the potential political productivity of 'chaosmosis', which he associates with psychosis, but also with childhood and aesthetic production (p. 17). He describes this as a state of 'ontological petrification' or 'existential freezing' located in the delirium 'of the dream and of passion' (p. 20). This 'extreme degree of intensification' (p. 20) can produce 'an emergent alterification freed from the mimetic barriers of the ego' (p. 22). Guattari suggests that the interpretation of moments of productive escape involves a sensibility to the multiplicity of 'real complexions' that 'do not have the same ontological colouring as each other' (p. 18). Where the Deleuzian/Guattarian ontological orientation foregrounds politics as a sensibility to new materialities, the Lacanian (anti)epistemological orientation foregrounds an ethical commitment to ignorance, sensitive to the dangers of imposing the interpretations of the analyst onto the other (Lacan, 1991; Lapping, 2011, 2013a). This contrasting orientation plays out in the contrasting conceptualisations of 'time', as virtuality, or as a traumatic and unknowable Real.

Theorising real or virtual 'time': methodological and political implications

Each of the three temporalities marked out in this analysis is constituted in relation to the O/others of a signifying system. These are fantasmatic temporalities: they are not 'time' as such, but rather timeless, an apparently temporal unfolding that is in Adrian Johnston's words: 'an epiphenomenal effect dictated by structures that are out of joint with time' (2005, p. 37). Whether conceptualised as structurally conditioned temporalities or, in more Deleuzian terms, as elements of a rhythm assemblage, this analysis suggests how the regulatory processes associated with societies of control produce an intensified juxta-position of incongruent subjective perceptions of temporality or duration.

What does this analysis tell us about our current position and about possibilities for the future? To conclude, it is worth reflecting on the theorisation of 'time' as either Deleuzian virtual potentiality or as Lacanian traumatic Real, and on the implications of these specu-lations for a politics of destabilisation or change. Central to this problematic is the way in which we understand the (im)possibility of a relation to that which is beyond actualised discourse.

For Deleuze and Guattari, the materiality of infinitude, the virtual, is the basis for diverse actualisations (Guattari, 2011, p. 18). The paradoxical status of the virtual as the un-actua-lised basis of material actualisations can be traced in Deleuze's account of the living present:

> The synthesis of time constitutes the present in time. It is not that the present is a dimension of time: the present alone exists. Rather, synthesis constitutes time as a living present ... (2004, p. 97)

This suggests an ontology in which 'time' is both constitutive of that which exists but without existence ('the present alone exists'). The ontological distinction between that which is constitutive and that which exists is the distinction between the Deleuzian 'virtual' and 'actual'. Time is virtual, while the temporalities of the living present are actualisations of the hovering potentiality of the virtual. Within this ontology, the 'new' might be brought into being by varying the habitual rhythmic interplay between existing temporalities of academic practice. To do this the animating but also stultifying effects of duration must be replaced by the affective capacities of desire; a shift frequently associated with aesthetic modes of intervention, but also with the organism's incomplete but developing awareness of its complex and multifa-ceted relations to elements of other bodies (Bignall, 2010). It is a politics of fragmentary but affectively pleasurable engagement. The virtual is not horrific or overwhelming, and the process of actualisation is one of joy (Bignall, 2010). In the context of academic research, this process might involve the creation of spaces where signifiers produced within narcissistically suspended rhythms could be shared, away from either teleologi-cal or chronological linear rhythms; or, alternatively, a more integrated rhythmic relation between disciplinary and processual technologies (Thompson & Cook, 2014, p. 712).

In contrast, a Lacanian foregrounding of structure, an apparent apolitical immanence, can be (mis)understood as a limitation on conceptualisation of a politics of time. Lacan's story of temporality reasserts the way duration and urgency are bounded by unconscious, structural relations to signifiers, foreclosing a direct relation to 'time'. 'Time' is beyond language, beyond signifiers, overwhelming both in its finitude (circum-scribed by birth and death) and its infinitude (amorphous, unstructured, never-ending). Time in this Lacanian Real has no possibility of symbolic articulation.

However, Johnston (2005) draws on Lacan's discussion of topological objects to develop a speculative theorisation of a relation between 'time' in the Real and symbolically structured temporalities. He proposes that the bends, the points of shift in surface or per-spective in these impossible topological objects, can be used as an analogy for a kind of registration of the Real:

> In terms of temporality, these turning points are none other than the registration of the *tuche* of traumatic Real time. (p. 55)

From this it is possible to extrapolate that it is precisely the bizarre turns and shifts in our taken for granted experience of 'time', of duration and of urgency, that reveal not only the fantasmatic status of temporality, but also *the shift itself* as a point of impact of something else. It is the simultaneous co-existence and incommensurability of the three temporalities of academic practice traced in my analysis, the points at which they are hinged together, that indicate something radically beyond. This something else, Real Time, registers without ever coming within the realm of the knowable.

Here, Johnston (2005) draws attention to the important distinction between Real as regulative or as constitutive principle. The first, which he suggests is the correct reading of the Lacanian Real, sets a limit to legitimate interpretation. The second ontologises, and thus might be associated with the Deleuzo-Guattarian conception of the virtual. The contrasting politics of regulative ignorance and constitutive alterification suggest different stances in relation to irruptions of the Real/virtual. Lacanian anti-epistemology requires a rigorous reassertion of the ignorance of the analyst; while the more ontological language of Deleuze and Guattari argues for a sensibility to alternative materialisations of the virtual.

Finally, the Lacanian position might also suggest that the juxtaposition of bizarrely incongruent temporalities, intensified under processes of control, will produce ever more traumatic registrations of horrific, overwhelming and unknowable Real Time. The effects of these traumatic encounters with absolute and shattering ignorance are unpre-dictable: it seems, however, that the obedient position of research, or legitimised knowl-edge, within institutions of higher education is ever more likely to explode. A Lacanian position warns against optimism; but alerts us to the need to prepare for the evaporation of that which we think we once knew.

Acknowledgements

Zain Davis sent me Lacan's paper and Johnston's book. Colleagues at UCT, the BSA conference 2015, and the Goldsmith's 'Austerity Futures' conference, 2015, as well as Natasha Whiteman, Jenny Parkes, Russell Dudley Smith, Alex Moore, Caroline Pelletier and Emily F Henderson gave feedback on early versions. The Time and the Subject reading group read Lacan's paper with me. Dawn Butler and the referees of the paper provided incredibly helpful support and feedback.

Disclosure statement

No potential conflict of interest was reported by the author.

Funding

This work was supported by Economic and Social Research Council [grant number RES-061-25-0379].

References

Bernstein, B. (1975). *Class and pedagogies: Visible and invisible*. Paris: OECD.

Bernstein, B. (2000). *Pedagogy, symbolic control and identity* (2nd ed.). New York, NY: Rowman and Littlefield.

Bignall, S. (2010). Desire, apathy and activism. *Deleuze Studies, 4*(4), 7–27.

Bollas, C. (1999). *The mystery of things*. London: Routledge.

Brown, R., with Carasso, H. (2013). *Everything for sale? The marketisation of UK higher education*. London: Routledge and the Society for Research into Higher Education.

Butler, J., Laclau, E., & Zizek, S. (2000). *Contingency, hegemony, universality: Contemporary dialogues on the left*. London: Verso.

Clancy, C. A. (2014). The politics of temporality: Autonomy, temporal spaces and resoluteness. *Time and Society, 23*(1), 28–48.

Deleuze, G. (1995). *Negotiations*. New York, NY: Columbia University Press.

Deleuze, G. (2004). *Difference and repetition*. London: Continuum.

Dolar, M. (2015, December 2–4). *Cutting Off the King's Head*. Presentation at Lacan Contra Foucault: Subjectivity, universalism, politics. Video available at: http://mariborchan.si/video/lacan-contra-foucault-subjectivity-universalism-politics/

Fink, B. (1997). *A clinical introduction to Lacanian psychoanalysis: Theory and technique*. Cambridge: Harvard University Press.

Foucault, M. (1977). *Discipline and punish: The birth of the prison*. London: Penguin Books.

Grosz, E. (2000). Deleuze's Bergson: Duration, the virtual and a politics of the future. In I. Buchanan & C. Colebrook (Eds.), *Deleuze and feminist theory* (pp. 214–234). Edinburgh: Edinburgh University Press.

Guattari, F. (2011). Schizo chaosmosis. In E. Alliez & A. Goffey (Eds.), *The Guattari effect* (pp. 17–24). London: Continuum.

Hook, D. (2008). Absolute other: Lacan's 'big Other' as adjunct to critical social psychological analysis? *Social and Personality Psychology Compass, 2*(1), 51–73.

Johnston, A. (2005). *Time driven: Metapsychology and the splitting of the drive*. Evanston, IL: Northwestern University Press.

Lacan, J. (1991). *The seminar of Jacques Lacan Book II: The ego in Freud's theory and in the technique of psychoanalysis, 1954–1955*. London: W. W. Norton and Company.

Lacan, J. (2006). Logical time and the assertion of anticipated certainty. In B. Fink (Tr), *Jacques Lacan Ecrits: The first complete edition in English* (pp. 161–175). London: W. W. Norton and Company.

Lapping, C. (2011). *Psychoanalysis in social research: Shifting theories and reframing concepts*. London: Routledge.

Lapping, C. (2013a). Which subject, whose desire? The constitution of subjectivity and the articulation of desire in the practice of research. *Journal of Psychoanalysis, Culture and Society, 18*(4), 368–385.

Lapping, C. (2013b). Institutional accountability and intellectual authority: Unconscious fantasies and fragile identifications in contemporary academic practice. In C. Maxwell & P. Aggleton (Eds.), *Privilege, agency and affect* (pp. 88–105). Basingstoke: Palgrave Macmillan.

Lapping, C. (2015). Writing and the articulation of disciplinary identifications: A psychoanalytic exploration of epistemological and interpretive aspects of methodological practice. In M. Griffiths, P. Smeyers, D. Bridges, & N. Burbules (Eds.), *International handbook on interpretation in educational research* (pp. 1551–1570). Dordrecht: Springer.

Lazzarato, M. (2006). The concepts of life and the living in the societies of control. In M. Fuglsang & B. Meier Sorensen (Eds.), *Deleuze and the social* (pp. 171–190). Edinburgh: Edinburgh University Press.

McGimpsey, I. (2012). *Youth service assemblage: Youth work subjectivity and practice in the context of changing youth service policy* (Unpublished PhD thesis). Institute of Education, University of London.

Olma, S. (2006). Social time. *Theory, Culture and Society, 23*(2–3), 127–129.

Plotnitsky, A. (1994). *Complementarity: Anti-epistemology after Bohr and Derrida*. Durham, NC: Duke University Press.

Rosa, H. (2013). *Social acceleration: A new theory of modernity*. New York, NY: Columbia University Press.

Savat, D. (2009). Deleuze's objectile: From discipline to modulation. In M. Poster & D. Savat (Eds.), *Deleuze and new technology* (pp. 45–62). Edinburgh: Edinburgh University Press.

Thompson, G., & Cook, I. (2014). Education policy-making and time. *Journal of Education Policy, 29*(5), 700–715.

Voss, D. (2013). Deleuze's third synthesis of time. *Deleuze Studies, 7*(2), 194–216.

Vostal, F. (2014). Academic life in the fast lane: The experience of time and speed in British academia. *Time and Society, 24*(1), 71–95.

Index

For Product Safety Concerns and Information please contact our EU
representative GPSR@taylorandfrancis.com
Taylor & Francis Verlag GmbH, Kaufingerstraße 24, 80331 München, Germany

www.ingramcontent.com/pod-product-compliance
Ingram Content Group UK Ltd.
Pitfield, Milton Keynes, MK11 3LW, UK
UKHW051831180425
457613UK00022B/1205